Advance Praise for *Megatrends 2010:*

"In *Megatrends 2010*, Patricia Aburdene reveals with clarity seven new trends that compel business to recognize the financial power of integrity, measure the economic impact of trust, and learn the behaviors of high trust leaders. That's why I tell everyone to read Patricia's insightful book."

—Stephen R. Covey, author of *The Speed of Trust*

"Patricia Aburdene, who honed her vision of the future co-writing the Megatrends books, now addresses the transformation of business. What she sees will excite and inspire you. The Age of Information is indeed drawing to a close and an exciting new era is taking its place. *Megatrends 2010* is passionate and prescient."

—Dan Pink, author of *A Whole New Mind*

"A new ethic is arising in the business world, a perspective based on consciousness, spirit and responsibility to the earth and all its creatures. If we are to survive and flourish, this approach is not optional but mandatory. *Megatrends 2010: The Rise of Conscious Capitalism* is an inspiring blueprint for this transformation. Whether you run a corporation or a household, this book should be required reading."

—Larry Dossey, M.D., author, *The Extraordinary Healing Power of Ordinary Things, Reinventing Medicine,* and *Healing Words*

"We've come a long way since Adam Smith spoke of the amoral 'invisible hand' in the late eighteenth century. In this fast-paced book, Patricia Aburdene describes the new, sophisticated and morally rich influences that shape successful businesses over 230 years later. It's a great read!"

—Joan Bavaria, CEO, Trillium Asset Management

"In *Megatrends 2010*, Patricia Aburdene puts a mirror to the heart of business and concludes that the spirit of the people will drive performance and shareholder value. We've experienced this reality in creativity, dedication and double-digit annual results. At REDKEN 5th Avenue NYC, we continue to develop a high-performing team through every person performing every job function. *Megatrends 2010* is a must-read."

—Patrick T. Parenty, Senior Vice President, L'Oréal USA, General Manager, REDKEN 5th Avenue NYC

"Today's best companies succeed by balancing the needs of all their stakeholders—not just shareholders. This book effectively highlights that trend and offers compelling evidence for the business case for corporate responsibility and conscious capitalism through integrity, transparency and good corporate governance."

—Michael Mitchell, Director Corporate Communications and Investor Relations, Chiquita Brands International, Inc.

"Right on the mark. Patricia Aburdene weaves together seemingly disparate themes and builds the case that they are all part of a whole, all ingredients in the rise of conscious capitalism. And she's right. A sea-change is underway in how the world works, and this is good news for all of us. Read it, enjoy it and feel uplifted by it."

—Amy Domini, Founder, CEO, Domini Social Investments

"The way we work together can change business and, even more importantly, the world. This book is inspiring because it communicates the powerful connection between our spirit and the work we do."

—Eileen Fisher, Founder and CEO, Eileen Fisher Inc.

"When IBM's Watson spoke the words 'Put your heart in your business and your business in your heart,' little did he know that Patricia Aburdene would seek out and spotlight those companies that live the creed and profit from it. In *Megatrends 2010* she proves the unmistakable connection between the collective heart of a high-performing team and the individual heart of the employee who feels important, informed and included. Read this fascinating book for yourself; read it for your business."

—Ann J. Mincey, Vice President Global Communications, REDKEN 5th Avenue NYC—a division of L'Oréal USA

"*Megatrends 2010* filled me with insights about how we conduct business today and inspired me to rethink my own brand of leadership. From meditating CEOs to the financial benefits of 'doing the right thing,' Patricia Aburdene serves up the trends transforming business—and shows you how to capitalize on them! This book is a winner."

—Deborah Wahl Meyer, Vice President, Lexus Marketing, Toyota Motor Corporation

"*Megatrends 2010* confirms the idea of a paradigm shift from matter-based science to a consciousness-based science, and also the idea of a subtle evolution of consciousness that is underway. Believe it! In the meantime, God bless you Patricia Aburdene for your work. This is a must-read for all optimists."

—Amit Goswami, author, *The Self-Aware Universe,*
Physics of the Soul and *The Quantum Doctor*

"In the concept of 'conscious capitalism,' the author elegantly frames the argument that we are no longer in the one-dimensional corporate world where shareholder concerns always reign supreme. Success is not only measured through a shareholder's lens, but also on behalf of a wider stakeholder constituency where, increasingly, 'values' play a role. If you care about a more sensitive capitalism, this book is a must-read."

—Robert Glassman, Cofounder, Wainwright Bank

"*Megatrends 2010: The Rise of Conscious Capitalism* brilliantly articulates something I've always felt but couldn't prove: spiritual values such as integrity and trust translate into healthy profits. *Megatrends 2010* provides incontrovertible proof that doing good and giving back pays off for everyone. This book is thrilling."

—Christiane Northrup, M.D., author, *Mother-Daughter Wisdom*

"I've long believed corporate responsibility is simply good business. *Megatrends 2010* explains why that's true and hits on key trends like the importance of individuals in corporate transformation and the growing power of socially responsible investing. If you want the 'Big Picture' on the changes rocking business, this book is for you."

—Dave Stangis, Director, Corporate Responsibility, Intel Corporation

Books by Patricia Aburdene and John Naisbitt

Megatrends for Women

Megatrends 2000

Re-Inventing the Corporation

Megatrends (collaboration)

Patricia Aburdene

Megatrends 2010

THE RISE OF
CONSCIOUS CAPITALISM

HAMPTON ROADS
PUBLISHING COMPANY, INC.

Cover design by Frame25 Productions

Hampton Roads Publishing Company, Inc.
1125 Stoney Ridge Road
Charlottesville, VA 22902

434-296-2772
fax: 434-296-5096
e-mail: hrpc@hrpub.com
www.hrpub.com

If you are unable to order this book from your local
bookseller, you may order directly from the publisher.
Call 1-800-766-8009, toll-free.

The Library of Congress has catalogued the hardcover edition as follows:

Aburdene, Patricia.
   Megatrends 2010 : the rise of conscious capitalism / Patricia Aburdene.
      p. cm.
   Summary: "The rise of conscious capitalism. Co-author of best-selling *Megatrends 2000*
investigates corporate social responsibility; finds that significant numbers of companies are
placing social, spiritual, and environmental values ahead of the bottom line; and reports
data showing that socially responsible practices actually help boost profits. Identifies eight
new trends that will redefine how we work, live, shop, and invest"--Provided by publisher.
   Includes bibliographical references and index.
   ISBN 1-57174-456-8 (6x9 tc : alk. paper)
   1. Business--United States--Religious aspects. 2. Social responsibility
of business--United States. 3. Business ethics--United States. 4.
Capitalism--United States--Religious aspects. I. Title: Megatrends two
thousand and ten. II. Title: Megatrends two thousand ten. III. Title:
Megatrends twenty ten. IV. Title.
   HF5388.A28 2005
   658.4'08--dc22
                                    2005015913

ISBN 978-1-57174-539-2
10 9 8 7 6 5 4 3 2 1
Printed on acid-free recycled paper in Canada

This book is dedicated with great love and enormous pride to three beautiful and courageous young women who make my heart sing: my niece Jennifer Jones, my granddaughter Lily Sullivan and my grandniece Hunter Jones.

Contents

Acknowledgments

In January 2003 I addressed the Business & Consciousness conference in Santa Fe, New Mexico. Later, my new friend Barbara Waugh, whom you'll meet in chapter three, told me, "You won't like this, but here goes: The best part of your speech was the megatrends part. You should recast the whole thing as a megatrends talk."

I don't think so, I thought. But I could not get Barbara's message out of my mind. Two months later I received clear guidance to write a new megatrends book. Thank you Barb for speaking the truth, even though you knew I'd resist the heck out of it!

Speaking of guidance, I could never have kept the faith, let go of past projects and completed this book, let alone known the peace and joy that now fill my life, without five incredible years of loving, support-filled sessions with Kathleen Loughery and Guidance Energy (innersight online.com). From the bottom of my heart, you have my profound and eternal gratitude.

Thank you John Naisbitt, co-author, former husband and gracious mentor, for your kindness, generosity and unfailing support.

Thank you to Anamika, my spiritual teacher and dear friend.

I am deeply grateful to the friends, friends of friends and business leaders (some of whom became new friends) who shared their stories in interviews and/or endured my tedious fact checking. The big breakthrough for me came when I realized the megatrends I am writing about are being lived by people day by day.

Thank you Judi Neal, Cindy Wigglesworth, Richard Whiteley, Ann Mincey, Cliff Feigenbaum, Shelley Alpern, Alisa Gravitz, Barbara Waugh, Bill George, Greg Merten, Jeff Swartz, Robin Giampa, Tevis Trower, Joel Smernoff,

Eric Biskamp, Marcy Ward, Elsie Maio, Christiane Perrin, Terry Mollner, Amber Chand, Joe O'Keefe, Frank Dixon, Joyce Orecchia, Marjorie Kelly, Dave Stangis, Gil Press, Fred Luskin, Deborah Thayer, Sarah Q. Hargrave, Debra Mugnani Monroe, Rona Fried and Ruby Yeh.

Thank you Spirituality in Business for sponsoring the 2003 San Francisco conference where I met several of the people cited above as well as Jared Rosen to whom I owe much. Jared read my manuscript, offered numerous suggestions and renamed it *Megatrends 2010*. He also insisted I talk to his agent.

I am deeply grateful to Bill Gladstone of Waterside Productions, Jared's agent—and now mine. From day one, Bill "got," loved and was devoted to this book. Bill's enthusiasm, integrity and, especially, his good humor are a joy to know. Bill referred me to Gary Brozek, whose amazingly thoughtful reading and probing questions compelled me to reach deep inside and pull out this book's final version. Most importantly, Bill Gladstone found me the perfect publisher. Thanks also to the elegant and efficient Ming Russell who helped me out of many a jam.

A big thank you to everyone at Hampton Roads in beautiful Charlottesville, Virginia. You are so true and real and you feel so much like family, how can anyone miss New York City? I especially thank:

Bob Friedman whose steady and tireless commitment to *Megatrends 2010* means so much to me.

Randy Achee and Jack Jennings whose excitement, support and belief in *Megatrends 2010* always keep me pumped.

Frank DeMarco, my fantastic and very funny editor.

Sarah Hilfer, a very organized and gracious young woman who is a joy to work with.

Jane Katra and Sara Sgarlat in publicity supported my book with great dedication. Thanks also to Kathy Cooper and Linda Huffaker for your good efforts and to Jane Hagaman for the beautification of my charts.

Over the years I have profited from knowing and learning from many Spirit in business colleagues, including Martin Rutte, John Renesch, Richard Barrett, Craig and Patricia Neal, Corinne McLaughlin and Gordon Davidson.

Cindy Wigglesworth and Carolyn Long read the entire manuscript and made extensive comments and recommendations.

I am grateful to Jill Reurs who helped me through this book's fact checking and endnotes which, trust me, are not the most enjoyable parts of the undertaking. How lucky I was to find someone who was both fastidious and fun. Thanks to Niki Vettel for sending Jill and for your support.

Thank you Geoff Fallon for your news clips, which I happily used.

Thank you to my immediate family (East) Barbara Jones and Phil Harter, Jen Jones, Chris Jones and Hunter Jones and (West) Nana Naisbitt and Rory, Lily and Jake Sullivan.

Thanks to my beloved women friends: Donna Coombs, Lynne Sausele, Sousan Abadian, Jeanne Flanagan, Carolyn Long, for your support and love and for putting up with me during the final year of this project.

I thank my dear ones in or from out West: Marsha Bailey, Becky Padilla, Leyla Wefallé, Elizabeth Plamondon Cutler, Sharon Shuteran, Roger Knapp, John and Pamela Lifton-Zoline, Valentina Lert, Harley Brooke-Hitching, Leigh Fortson. Yes, I will be a fun person once again!

By the time *Megatrends 2010* needed to be reviewed for this trade paperback edition, my new assistant Trude Irons was already on board. Trude read and reread the book, tracked down the facts and charmed the sources so successfully that the final result is truly, as we say in the book biz, "Revised and Updated." Bravo, Trude!

If I missed anyone, please know I bless you in my heart.

Finally, I thank the wise and witty man in my life, Alain Boléa, who read and reread the manuscript and made many wonderful suggestions. His steady presence always reminded me that beyond work (and stress) is Life, which is sacred and primary. This is a good thing to know if you take matters a little too seriously and equate your work with your spiritual purpose. Not that I would ever do such a thing.

Preface

I come to the study of Conscious Capitalism as a trend tracker. My number one bestseller, *Megatrends 2000* (William Morrow, 1990), co-authored with John Naisbitt, predicted the prosperous, networked, technology-driven era of the 1990s. Today, however, we live in more perplexing times. In *Megatrends 2010*, I will describe the social, economic—and spiritual—trends transforming free enterprise in this tumultuous decade. But before we begin, I'd like to tell you a little about myself.

I am a capitalist and a spiritual seeker. Every weekday, I dwell in each of these very different worlds. Early in the morning I light a candle and journal with my favorite fountain pen. Then I usually meditate. Before settling down at the iMac, I observe one final ritual, switching on the business-oriented cable station, CNBC. From the sublime to the ridiculous, I suppose, but on July 16, 2002, CNCB finally covers the story I've waited 15 years to watch:

The public denouncement of Gordon Gekko.

Gekko is of course the character Michael Douglas plays in the 1987 film *Wall Street*. The arrogant dealmaker who stands up there at the shareholders meeting in his expensive suit and slicked back hair and shamelessly preaches the capitalist doctrine of the era. "Greed is good. Greed is right. Greed works," Gekko proclaims. "Greed clarifies, cuts through and captures the essence of the evolutionary spirit . . . Greed, you mark my words, will not only save Teldar Paper, but that other malfunctioning corporation called the U.S.A."

Over the years, as we all know, Gekko spawned numerous executive offspring. Except that as I watch CNBC, in the belly of the worst bear market since the Great Depression, the cost of greed is in our collective faces. Trillions of dollars in shareholder wealth have vanished into thin air. The markets are jittery and many look to the man who has come to symbolize the true glory of free enterprise to restore calm. Today he speaks before Congress on the dire financial consequences of Gordon Gekko's favorite vice.

For me this is no ordinary day, no routine testimony. I've spent a decade searching for the facts and figures, the stories and examples to illustrate what I hold as economic and spiritual truth: that transcendent values like Trust and Integrity literally *translate* into revenue, profits and prosperity. As you might well imagine, finding Spirit in capitalism has not been exactly easy.

But now the puzzle piece that has eluded me—the formal admission of the intolerable cost of greed—is rolling across my TV screen, uttered by none other than Federal Reserve Chairman Alan Greenspan.

"An infectious greed seemed to grip much of our business community," he says, which "perversely created incentives to artificially inflate reported earnings in order to keep stock prices high and rising."

Fraud and falsification, says Greenspan—inspired by greed, one might add—"are highly destructive to free-market capitalism and, more broadly, to the underpinnings of our society."

Exactly. Not only has greed already cost us plenty, it keeps would-be investors and their money on the sidelines.

"Our market system depends critically on trust," says Greenspan, as I sit on the edge of my sofa glued to his every word, "Trust in the word of our colleagues and trust in the word of those with whom we do business."

Alan Greenspan, the official voice of capitalism, is connecting the dots, linking, in the most explicit terms I've heard yet, the virtue of Trust and prosperity on the one hand, and the vice of greed and economic self-destruction on the other.

The prime factor predicting whether a company will be honest or not, he adds, is the character of its CEO. "If a CEO countenances managing reported earnings, that attitude will drive the entire accounting regime of the firm. If he or she instead insists on an objective representation of a company's business dealings, that standard will govern recordkeeping and due diligence."

With Greenspan's words, the illusion that greed is beneficial to society is officially shattered and the truth rings out loud and clear. Greed *destroys* wealth. Trust and Integrity, by contrast, foster prosperity.

Gordon Gekko is, at long last, history.

Thank you, Mr. Greenspan, for ringing the opening bell, so to speak, on the age of Conscious Capitalism. Because now out of the ashes of crisis, corruption and public distrust, a grassroots movement to revitalize the ethics and Spirit of free enterprise is gaining momentum and attracting millions. In *Megatrends 2010*, you will meet the investors, activists, CEOs and consumers whose courage and commitment are building a new world where money and morals thrive side by side.

Introduction

In *Megatrends*, published in 1982, John Naisbitt and I talked about the birth of the Information Economy. For millennia, the West's developed economies had been based on agriculture. That was how people made their living. Then came the Industrial Revolution. Sometime in the 1960s or 1970s, we argued, another, more subtle upheaval occurred: More and more people held jobs in which they created, processed or manipulated information.

By 1982, the Information Economy was up and running, but it was still a controversial idea. "Information?" some folks scoffed. "There can't possibly be any economic value in *that*." But by the 1990s, the Information Economy had blossomed into the age of high technology, now a trillion-dollar industry.

Today we are on the brink of another extraordinary revolution. The Information Age is already over and an exciting new epoch is taking its place.

Remember, the key point is this: When wealth is derived from a *new* source—say information rather than industry—a new economic era is born. In time, people's jobs reflect that new activity. That said, consider the following:

It is often argued that the soul of a technology-driven economy is *continuous* innovation. No successful enterprise can pat itself on the back for last year's software, for example, then sit around until customers demand a better product. Corporations must lead the market by initiating change.

But the same is true whether you're a tech firm, a consumer-products company or a public relations agency: Creativity and innovation are the name of the game.

Medical tech device maker Medtronic, for example, invented pacemakers in 1957. Today, for each new product launched, the company is working on *four generations* of upgrades. That steady stream of innovation translated into more than 20 percent a year in earnings growth for over a decade.

How do corporations achieve the challenging but lucrative goal of continuous innovation? The short answer, the *only* answer, is through the genius inherent in human consciousness.

In fact, there can be no invention in business or technology *without* human consciousness.

What is consciousness? I use the term in the spiritual sense, to mean presence or alertness—the awareness of awareness, the willingness to observe without attachment, the gleam of Spirit that animates humanity.

When an engineering whiz is patiently contemplating a complex problem, submerged for hours on end, he or she is living in the Now, dwelling in the realm of consciousness. Consciousness, the prime ingredient in creativity, represents a higher intelligence than the mind. When consciousness guides our mental facilities, the result can be brilliant.

Technology is consciousness externalized.

We've reached the point in economic history where human consciousness—the capacity for quiet, detached observation—*is* the raw material of innovation and, ultimately, of corporate money making. We will return to that point often in these pages. Consciousness is now as valuable to business as mundane assets like capital, energy or even technology. And the best way to cultivate consciousness is through techniques like meditation. As you will see in chapter six, that's exactly what many companies are up to.

To those who claim high tech is dead and that computers have become a replacement industry (like refrigerators), I would reply: One highly conscious individual can—and will—create the "killer app" (a software application that's so popular and universal, like word processing or email, that it drives hardware sales) that will launch a $100 billion industry.

Welcome to the New Economy of Consciousness.

Charting the "Inner" Dimensions of Change

Megatrends 2010 chronicles the social, economic and spiritual trends transforming capitalism into a new, more wholistic version of itself.

What is a megatrend? It is a large, over-arching direction that shapes our lives for a decade or more. Like the megatrends books I co-authored in the past: *Megatrends 2000, Megatrends for Women* (Villard, 1992), *Re-inventing the*

Corporation (Warner, 1985) and *Megatrends* (Warner, 1982) on which I served as John Naisbitt's collaborator, this book is full of the facts, figures and vivid examples that *quantify* social change. But *Megatrends 2010* takes it one step further—it depicts the *internal* dimension of change.

Because the inner world of ideals and belief shapes our actions.

Let me tell you what I mean.

The search for morals and meaning at work, as well as the desire to experience the peace and purpose of the Sacred in the stressful world of business, are "inner" truths, alive in the hearts of millions of people. These internal realities profoundly influence people's behavior—like the choice to invest in a corporation that embraces higher social, environmental and ethical standards than its peers; the decision to work only for a company that honors your soulful, creative instincts; or the pledge to shop only at retailers who refuse to traffic in "sweatshop" labor.

These inner truths are our values—and they play a crucial role in change.

How does transformation happen? In *Re-inventing the Corporation*, John Naisbitt and I suggested a formula that I think is especially useful today. Social transformation, we wrote, "occurs only when there is a confluence of changing values and economic necessity."

Most of us are well aware of the economic factors pressuring capitalism today, such as corporate scandals and the tech bubble. These forces, depicted in Figure 1, drive change from the outside in, from the top down. Figure 2 illustrates values-driven trends, like consumer action or spirituality in business. These forces, by contrast, prod change from the inside out or bottom up. Figure 3 portrays the combined impact of top-down and bottom-up forces.

In *Megatrends 2010*, you will discover that the synergy of changing values and economic necessity is transforming capitalism.

Turbulent Times

Business has yet to recover from the jolting events of recent history: recession, the market crash and corporate accounting scandals. Yet we now face new challenges—growing deficits, soaring energy and healthcare costs,

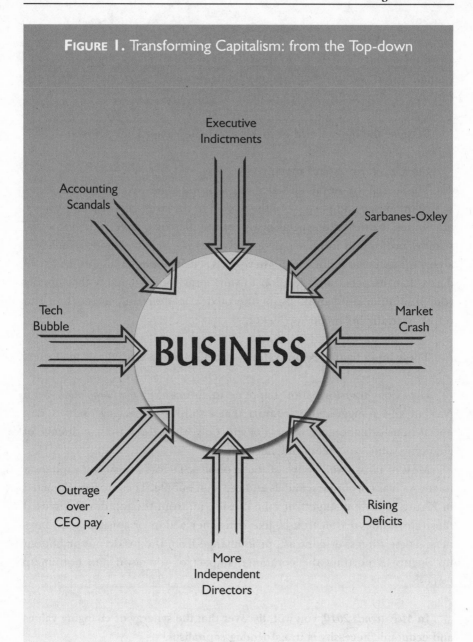

FIGURE 1. Transforming Capitalism: from the Top-down

Executive
Indictments

Accounting
Scandals

Sarbanes-Oxley

Tech
Bubble

BUSINESS

Market
Crash

Outrage
over
CEO pay

Rising
Deficits

More
Independent
Directors

Economic   Transformation
Necessity → of Capitalism

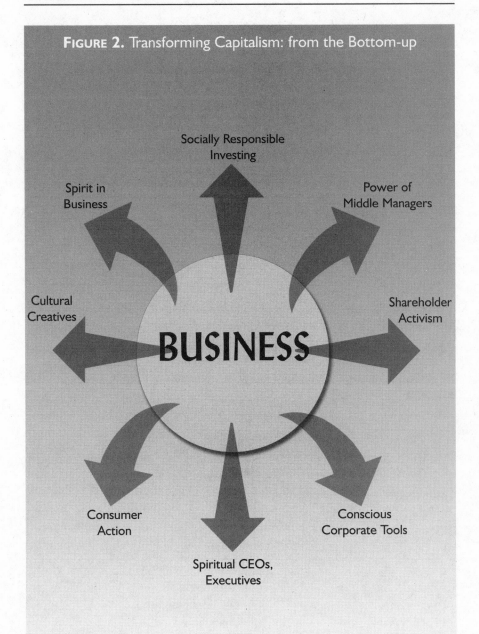

FIGURE 2. Transforming Capitalism: from the Bottom-up

Socially Responsible Investing

Spirit in Business

Power of Middle Managers

Cultural Creatives

BUSINESS

Shareholder Activism

Consumer Action

Conscious Corporate Tools

Spiritual CEOs, Executives

Transformation of Capitalism ← Changing Values

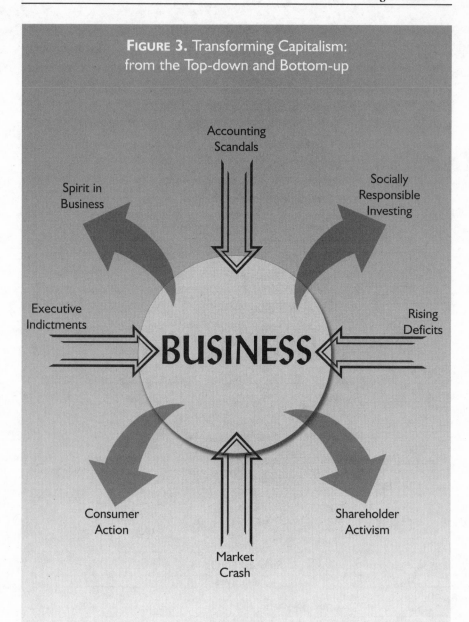

FIGURE 3. Transforming Capitalism: from the Top-down and Bottom-up

fluctuating interest rates, shrinking disposable income and an "expansion" in which corporate spending and hiring remain restrained.

As individuals, too, we live in a time of great uncertainty—the constant threat of terrorism, two recent wars, growing geopolitical tensions, unemployment, fractured IRAs and lost savings. When we find little security outside ourselves, we are forced to look within to search the heart and soul for fresh answers and new directions. That's why "The Power of Spirituality," described in chapter one, is arguably the greatest megatrend of our era.

Whether you call yourself spiritual or evangelical, green or new age, a die-hard capitalist or a soccer mom who shops with her values, you need to know the powerful trends that are already re-inventing free enterprise.

People behind the Megatrends

Before I spell out my seven new megatrends, I'd like to introduce some of the soulful people *behind* the economics. In reading their stories, which I tell in each chapter, you'll feel the powerful personal commitments fueling change.

In *Megatrends 2010*, you will meet:

• The CEO of a red-hot 2004 IPO who's a devout meditator.
• The Dow 40 activist whose adventures in Third World economic development have trickled up into the speeches of her CEO.
• The workaholic, high-tech czar who lost his beloved son, opened his heart to Spirit and now says his Fortune 500 firm has earned hundreds of millions because of the spiritual principles he brought to work.
• A 13-year marketing vet turned meditation guru to the Fortune 500.
• The Silicon Valley entrepreneur working with the California legislature to free companies to be responsible to *stakeholders*, as well as shareholders.

The stories of people *driving* social change bring the megatrends to life.

Megatrends 2010: The New List

Here is my new list of megatrends, each of which serves as one of this book's chapters.

1. The Power of Spirituality. In turbulent times, we look within; 78 percent seek *more* Spirit. Meditation and yoga soar. Divine Presence spills into business. "Spiritual" CEOs as well as senior executives from Redken and Hewlett-Packard (HP) transform their companies.

2. The Dawn of Conscious Capitalism. Top companies and leading CEOs are re-inventing free enterprise to honor stakeholders and shareholders. Will it make the world a better place? Yes. Will it earn more money? That's the surprising part: Study after study shows the corporate good guys rack up great profits.

3. Leading from the Middle. The charismatic, overpaid CEO is fading fast. Experts now say "ordinary" managers, like HP's Barbara Waugh, forge lasting change. How do they do it? Values, influence, moral authority.

4. Spirituality in Business is springing up all over. Half speak of faith at work. Eileen Fisher, Medtronic win "Spirit at Work" awards. Ford, Intel and other firms sponsor employee-based religious networks. Each month San Francisco's Chamber of Commerce hosts a "spiritual" brown bag lunch.

5. The Values-Driven Consumer. Conscious Consumers, who've fled the mass market, are a multi-billion-dollar "niche." Whether buying hybrid cars, green building supplies or organic food, they vote with their values. So, brands that embody positive values will attract them.

6. The Wave of Conscious Solutions. Coming to a firm near you: Vision Quest. Meditation. Forgiveness Training. HeartMath. They sound touchy-feely, but conscious business pioneers are tracking results that will blow your socks off.

7. The Socially Responsible Investment Boom. Today's stock portfolios are green in more ways than one. Where should you invest? This chapter charts the "social" investment trend and helps you weigh your options.

In this book's conclusion, **The Spiritual Transformation of Capitalism,** we explore the underlying values of capitalism. I shall attempt to dispel what I believe is the absurd notion that free enterprise is rooted in greed. Conscious Capitalism isn't altruism, either; it relies instead on the wisdom of enlightened self-interest.

Spirituality or Religion

I use the word Spirit often, so let me define It before we continue. Spirit, for me, is the attribute of God that dwells in humanity, the Great I AM, the Life Force, the aspect of us that most mirrors the Divine.

In a theological sense, you might say Spirit is analogous to the Holy Spirit, but in an ecumenical and nondenominational way. That brings up another distinction: the difference between spirituality and religion. I use the term religion to refer to the formal, and often public, structure through which people worship God. Spirituality is the experience of, or the desire to experience our connection with the Divine. Religion tends to be behavioral;

spirituality, more experiential. Spirituality is often (but not always) a private matter. Some people, of course, are both spiritual and religious.

Money and Morals

Megatrends 2010 explores the quest for morals and meaning in business within the legal confines of capitalism, a world where public firms are bound by law to maximize shareholder return. What is remarkable and largely unheralded, however, is that corporate morality often correlates with superior financial performance. In other words, plenty of corporate "good guys" are trouncing the Standard & Poors (S&P) 500! For example, in 2003, a great year for stocks, the Winslow Green Growth Fund, which holds stock in firms with high environmental standards, soared more than *90 percent* (versus 28.2 percent for the S&P 500).

Several studies by prestigious outfits—you'll read all about them in chapter two, "The Dawn of Conscious Capitalism"—show us that corporate responsibility, far from being a drain on profit, is an important marker of success. The long-standing business myth of "lean and *mean*" threatens not just the morals but the *prosperity* of American business.

I am not saying corporate responsibility *causes* financial success. But there is certainly a relationship. As you'll discover in chapter two, it is a simple one: Socially responsible corporations tend to be well managed, and great management is the best way to predict superior financial performance.

In fact, if you want to invest in or work for a company that demonstrates high moral standards, it is relatively easy to identify many that also deliver excellent financial results. There are thousands of great companies, but let's start with 100. The *Business Ethics* "100 Best Corporate Citizens," published annually in *CRO Magazine,* are companies devoted to ethics, Earth and employees—yet, as one study discovered, they outperformed the S&P 500 by a stunning 10 percentile points.

Then again, suppose you're a Conscious Consumer; you vote with your pocketbook—whether for fair trade coffee, solar panels or that new Toyota Camry hybrid. Well, you're not alone.

Most Americans weigh the moral impact of their purchases. An impressive 79 percent consider corporate citizenship in deciding whether to buy a product, says a Hill & Knowlton/Harris Poll, while 36 percent call it an important factor in a purchase decision.

That 36 percent are your fellow Conscious Consumers. You'll read all about them in chapter five.

In *Megatrends 2010*, you'll see why Conscious Consumers are a $250-billion dollar market that's changing free enterprise for the better.

Success and Consciousness: The Missing Link

"Spirituality" in business sounds lofty. How practical is it?

The answer is "very." There's a fundamental way in which Spirit and consciousness contribute to worldly success—and it has long been ignored. (In chapter six, you'll meet the fascinating individual who clued me in on it.)

As experts, authors and gurus often note, the game of business is to influence the external world. But here's the point: How can you control your environment if you can't even manage your own thoughts and emotions? In other words, how do you rule the world without first mastering yourself?

The cornerstone of effective leadership is self-mastery.

But that's exactly what's missing in business today. Lack of self-mastery is why so many business heroes wind up in court—if not the jailhouse.

The fallen heroes of free enterprise who parade across our TV screens illustrate the irrational, self-destructive choices we make without the grounding, illuminating power of self-mastery.

And the surest route to self-mastery is spiritual practice. Time spent in peaceful reflection or mindful meditation clarifies thought, sharpens intuition and curbs unhealthy instincts. Spirituality, it turns out, is a lot more practical than most of us ever thought.

Am I saying a dedicated meditation practice would have helped people like former Tyco CEO Dennis Koslowski, former AIG chairman Hank Greenburg and many others?

Yes. I certainly am.

Worldly power without self-mastery is the downfall of leadership.

Why Now?

Meaning, morals and self-mastery are what's missing in business, all right. But the legal limits of capitalism warn us that high-minded ideals are no substitute for success. Business is obliged to turn a profit. Besides, without cash flow and profit, how does a company hire people, attract shareholders, pay suppliers or invest in R&D?

In the midst of recession, corporations executed harsh measures to restore profit. But today, the layoffs are behind us. Hiring is finally picking up.

Profits are back, mostly because of cost-cutting. Now business must again start to focus on growth. How do you *grow* a business? With people. You need a strategic plan, of course, but what good is that without the right people to execute it?

People alone drive peak performance.

Studies like McKinsey's much-quoted "War for Talent" show the best people are attracted to companies that fulfill the deep, personal need for meaning while making contributions to society—beyond the profit motive.

That's exactly what the companies cited in *Megatrends 2010* do. Moreover, this is the ideal point in the business cycle to invoke the power of consciousness, values and Spirit. The seeds of corporate transformation grow best when a high performance culture is already in place, says Michael Rennie, the top McKinsey honcho (and powerful corporate shaman) you'll meet in chapter six. In high performance cultures, meaning and morality deliver the elixir of superior productivity, but, says Rennie,

"You actually have to create a performance ethic first."

At this point in the business cycle, corporations have achieved *that* goal. The next step is to recognize the power of their human assets—people who are full of wisdom, consciousness and Spirit. The time is now and the task at hand is the moral transformation of capitalism—while growing prosperity.

This book's message is simple and clear: 1) We the people have the power to heal capitalism; 2) Concious Capitalism has the power to change the world.

Isn't it time we got started?

1

The Power of Spirituality— From Personal to Organizational

As Hewlett-Packard's VP and general manager of inkjet cartridge opera-tions, Greg Merten managed 10,000 people and a multi-billion-dollar busi-ness. Much of his success, he says, grew out of the transformation he experienced when his son Scott, 16, was killed in an automobile accident. He calls Scott's loss "my greatest tragedy and greatest blessing."

Scott was a "real people person," who never had an unkind word for any-one, says Merten. Scott's example inspired Merten to focus on and invest in his relationships including business. "I used the tragedy as a source of learn-ing, an occasion to *see*," he says.

Specifically, every four to six weeks Merten carved out a full day to meet with his eight senior managers and with coaches Amba Gale and Mickey Connelly. "We'd update Amba and Mickey on what had happened since we last met, then together ask, 'So, okay, what are we going to *do* about it?' We explored how to behave differently, find more productive choices, expand our influence and make a bigger difference.

"It was the most concentrated learning environment I've ever known," says Merten, "because it focused on 'the conversation,' that is, how people *operate* with each other. In the face of differences, do we *inquire*? Do we try to understand each other and create value? Or do we need to be right and then defend, disagree, destroy—and waste the chance to generate positive results?"

Armed with these conscious techniques, Merten led his group through several business doublings in a year and expanded operations from one to six sites.

As Merten's spiritual insight blossomed, he learned to "Let go, forgive and suspend judgment," then *applied* these powerful truths at HP. "I quit competing and starting to think of the other person first." He "granted others 'good intentions' even in the face of contradictory evidence."

How do spiritual principles like these impact corporate success? Put simply, Merten's enlightened business precepts changed how things got done internally and externally. They inspired people to trust themselves and others. As Merten's team grew in awareness and consciousness, they "gained access" to actions and options that were literally unavailable to them before.

Merten says these breakthroughs, in his words, "contributed hundreds of millions in incremental dollars to HP's bottom line."

How so? Merten offers this answer.

"We put up our third site [after Singapore and Puerto Rico] near Dublin *twice as fast* as it had ever been done in HP history. The Irish contractors literally laughed at us when we told them our due date. How did we do it? Mickey Connelly helped us take the Irish contractors, the developers, the County Kildare officials and HP's own operations folks through the same protocols on relationship and conversation that we ourselves practice."

The Dublin success alone, says Merten, "netted HP hundreds of millions of dollars. We needed the capacity that much."

"You can create results from fear," Merten admits, "but I came to see that the greatest results come from a more positive place—community, relationship and conversation." Greg Merten retired from HP in 2003 and now consults on something he understands well: the art of outstanding leadership.

Let's start with a simple assertion: business is transforming because people like Greg Merten and other top executives—as well as millions of "ordinary" managers, some of whom you'll meet in chapters three and four—work in corporations! As individuals grow in consciousness and Spirit, so do the organizations they inhabit.

The problem is organizations take longer to change than people do. Why is institutional change more difficult? Because it is so complex. Not only does it require time, vision and leadership, it involves greater numbers of people, their commitment and the development of a shared purpose. Institutional transformation relies on human evolution, grows slowly, then finally hits the mark.

In the years that it takes for all these positive ingredients and uplifting circumstances to catalyze, the people inside companies can grow so discouraged, they fall victim to the lie that "business as usual" would have us believe: the idea that there's an impenetrable barrier between personal spirituality and corporate transformation, between Spirit and business.

The purpose of this first chapter is to dissolve that firewall.

Meeting the Enemy

Meanwhile, the quest for spirituality flourishes in society at large. I'll soon cite plenty of figures to illustrate that point. Yet many people, even those who are spiritually aware, envision the business establishment as an armed fortress that will somehow repel the transformation everyone else is going through.

That is not going to happen. Because business does not possess the power to prevent people from transforming. Yet there's little wonder why we think it does! The business world often portrayed on CNBC and in *The Wall Street Journal* boasts, not just a single-minded passion for turning a buck, but unmatched devotion to assassinating any high-minded ideal that might get in the way.

Well, guess what? Mainstream business is under siege, from activists and regulators, as expected, but even from investors. And all the barricades in the world cannot defend it. Because the most dangerous adversary of all—a transformed individual—lies *within* and we are IT. Whether spiritual CEO, activist middle manager or visionary entrepreneur, we've opened our minds and expanded our hearts and there is no shutting either of them down. So much so that when I edited this chapter in early 2005, both CNBC and *The Wall Street Journal* had just run stories on spirituality or faith in business.

Conscious individuals transform organizations. Period. Consider:

- The Fortune 500 CEO and devoted meditator who championed a corporate meditation room that thrives long after his retirement.
- The glamorous female executive whose lifelong spiritual quest leads her to a hot workshop on HeartMath that she later shares with her customers.
- The third generation CEO of a high-profile public company who disdains "selfish" capitalism and enthusiastically embraces corporate responsibility.

You'll meet these inspiring leaders in this book's first two chapters as we begin to explore seven new megatrends accelerating the transformation of free enterprise and the birth of Conscious Capitalism as mainstream business culture.

We start with some off-the-charts numbers on personal spirituality, then look at how Spirit is already starting to transform the bellwether sector of medicine. Later we'll delve into case studies of CEOs and other top execs whose spiritual journeys are re-inventing their careers and their companies.

Spirituality: from personal to organizational. That's this chapter's theme. Put differently, personal "growth" is about to get a lot less "personal." It is about to spill into—and transform—the collective.

The Passion for Personal Spirituality

The quest for spirituality is the greatest megatrend of our era.

Before diving into some illustrative facts and figures, I should like to raise the larger, more substantive question: What does it mean to be "spiritual"? Or to want more Spirit in your life? Admittedly, it isn't easy to define: Spirit is intangible, after all. Few of us will agree on the exact definition of spirituality. But it begins, of course, with the desire to connect with God, the Divine, the Transcendent. That said, let me throw out the five hallmarks that I think cover most of the spiritual bases: (1) Meaning or Purpose, (2) Compassion, (3) Consciousness, (4) Service and (5) Well-Being.

Many of the things we might call spiritual—inner peace, meditation, wellness, prayer, loving relationships, life purpose, mission, giving to others—fall under one of these headings. I may have missed one of your favorites, but I think you'll agree that all these words have one thing in common: Each and every one of them is sourced in and emphasizes the *immaterial*. We may live out our spiritual inclinations here in the material world, experiencing compassion for a friend—or well-being in our bodies—but the source of our inspiration is the invisible realm of Spirit.

The earthly treasures we all love and enjoy here in the mundane grid of reality—money, hot jobs, gorgeous clothes, a wonderful mate, an Ivy League diploma and a beautiful home—are missing from the "spiritual" list.

Spirituality means you thirst for something else. For the peace, wholeness and fulfillment that, as Grandma would say, "money can't buy." Perhaps you seek also to know the Source from which all else, both material and intangible, flows.

Well, you've got a lot of company.

Spirituality Is "Off the Charts"

Millions have invited Spirit into their lives, through personal growth, religion, meditation, prayer or yoga. The result is a values shift that is measurable and monumental. A 2004 Gallup survey found 95 percent of Americans believe in God "or a universal Spirit." (The 2006 percentages remain about the same.) Western Europeans, by contrast, have a belief rate of less than 50 percent.

Sixty percent of Americans say they have absolute trust in God.

But wait a minute. Haven't Americans always been a religious lot? Maybe so, but in the past decade, the number who call themselves "spiritual" is decisively higher. In 1994, the Gallup people asked Americans whether they felt the need to experience spiritual growth. Only 20 percent said "yes." In 1999, they asked again—and a surprising 78 percent answered in the affirmative. An astounding 58 percentage point gain in five years.

But that was only in 1999. Remember how simple and secure our lives were then? Before terrorism, the market crash, corporate scandals and the disastrous Iraq war. People tend to turn to Spirit in times of stress, trouble and sorrow. In 1999 technology was still riding high; unemployment was low and no one was overly troubled by Enron, Osama or Saddam. Since September 11, 2001, however, 57 percent said they thought more about their spiritual lives, as reported by a *Time*/CNN/Harris Interactive poll.

It is hardly a stretch to conclude that war, recession, layoffs and financial losses since 2001 have strengthened the ranks of spiritual seekers.

Spirit in Action

The quest for spirituality is shapeshifting human activities, priorities, leisure pursuits and spending patterns.

In 2005, some 16.5 million people practiced yoga in the United States, said *Yoga Journal*, up 43 percent since 2002. Ten million American adults say they meditate, twice as many as a decade ago, declares the 2003 *Time* cover story, "Meditation."

• Meditation, the *Time* article reports, is taught in "schools, hospitals, law firms, government buildings, corporate offices and prisons."

- In 2003, Colorado's Shambhala Mountain Center, which hosts yoga and meditation programs, welcomed 15,000 visitors. Today, it is 30,000.
- New York's Catskills hotels "are turning into meditation retreats so quickly that the Borscht Belt is being renamed the Buddhist Belt," quips *Time* writer Joel Stein.

Do some people do yoga and t'ai chi or meditate as a form of stress release or exercise? Undoubtedly, but these ancient practices grow out of such profoundly spiritual traditions that I would venture to say that practitioners are connecting to Spirit whether or not they consciously seek to do so.

Spirit in Print

Spirituality has certainly inspired a megatrend in publishing. Over a five-year period, spiritual and religious books outpaced sales in all other categories, surging from $1.69 billion to $2.24 billion, says the Book Industry Study Group. Bestsellers like *Conversations with God* (Neale Donald Walsch, Hampton Roads, vols. 1–3, 1995–1998) and *The Power of Now* (Eckhart Tolle, New World Library, 1999) attest to our healthy appetite for soulful matters. Joel Osteen's *Your Best Life Now* (FaithWords, 2004) has sold 3.8 million copies since 2004.

Baby boomers, concerned with ethics and their own morality, says *Publishers Weekly* editor Lynn Garrett, are driving up sales in the spirituality and religion categories. Books like *Jesus CEO* (Hyperion, 1996) and *The Seven Habits of Highly Effective People* (Fireside/Simon & Schuster, 1990), which advises people to cultivate spirituality, shows us that Spirit has penetrated the business category.

"All kinds of answers to the question, 'What is the meaning of my life?' are selling," says Susan Petersen Kennedy, president of Penguin Putnam Inc.

The Future of Spirituality

Spirituality is today's greatest megatrend, but where is it taking us? What's the future of our compelling interest in all things spiritual? To discover the answer, we must first clear up a common misunderstanding.

Most of us harbor the belief—reinforced in the media—that a passion for the "inner life" takes us away from the world, rendering us self-obsessed, if not downright selfish.

Well, the truth is: It *does*. But only at first. During the journey's initial introspective chapter, many instinctively withdraw from the daily grind of modern life. Why? Because, seekers grow more sensitive and too much stress will overwhelm the fresh, emerging spiritual consciousness.

Often we detach in order to heal: As we fill with Spirit, we release a lot of old emotional baggage, find peace, discover a new inner voice—and that requires a fair amount of energy. When my own lifelong spiritual journey intensified in 1994, I shut off the TV for two years and rarely read newspapers. Good-bye violence, cynicism, TV commercials. Hello silence, meditation and hearing myself think.

But later the spiral path of Spirit takes a different turn and we plunge into an exciting new phase: our return to the world. Now regenerated, we come back to society and service. That is exactly what millions of people—investors, consumers, managers—and the business leaders you'll meet in this chapter are up to—living their spirituality day to day.

From Silence to Service

The miracle of spiritual healing strengthens and energizes us. Millions of people, long-time meditators, for example, (and people who are . . . ahem . . . age 45 or older) may have spent a decade or more healing negative patterns. They—or should I say we?—have soaked up so much spiritual energy that we are transformed. Sure, we will still face plenty of new challenges, but for this life, we're basically cooked: We will not go back to "life before Spirit."

We are chock full of Spirit and consciousness. We've hit critical mass. Now what would the Divine do with all that consciousness?

Put it to work!

In a project, cause, mission or place—somewhere in the world that attracts our now-higher consciousness. The power of Spirit embodied in people like you and me is pouring out into organizations—including businesses.

Spiritual transformation, triggered at the individual level, is now spilling over from the personal to the institutional.

Before we discover why the transformation of business is at hand, let's briefly explore the discipline of medicine, an important bellwether for business, and a field where spirituality is already revamping many established protocols.

From Medicine to Business

If a wise and advanced being were to gaze upon the drama of human evolution, she might say, "Well, they're finally starting to get it. Humanity at long last is beginning to see that Spirit activates *every* part of life—politics, economics, medicine, psychology, business. Some day soon, they may even quit relegating God to the narrow confines of religion and metaphysics."

So when we talk about transformation, it's not a shift from the profane to the sacred. What is transforming is our *awareness.* We are waking up and smelling the roses—that is, the presence of Spirit all around us—and the scent is both comforting and intoxicating.

Most of all it is a relief to emerge from the fog of separation, where God was God, physics was physics, business was business, and medicine was medicine. Free from the illusion of separation, we're excited about "new" disciplines like God and physics, spiritual healing, and Spirit in business.

We are awakening to the Truth that always was.

Consider the example of medicine, a near-perfect indicator for "what is coming next" to business. More than most other fields of endeavor, medicine is investigating and integrating the Truth of Spirit into daily practice.

During medicine's dramatic metamorphosis, a handful of pioneers spoke their sometimes controversial truth, opened people's minds, touched and healed them and finally revolutionized the institution of medicine itself.

Bernie Siegel, M.D., told us no physician can inform a patient how long he or she has to live. That's between you and God, he declared.

Carolyn Myss, Ph.D., opened our eyes to the bonds linking Spirit, our physical bodies and the seven spiritual energy centers called the chakras.

Larry Dossey, M.D., witnessed the healing power of prayer so often, he decided denying prayer to his patients was like withholding a needed medicine.

Jon Kabat-Zinn, Ph.D., and Herbert Bensen, M.D., demonstrated how meditation lowers blood pressure and promotes well-being.

Christiane Northrup, M.D., underscored the value of spiritual practice at every stage of a woman's life: maiden, mother or wise woman.

As practitioners like these legitimized new ways to perceive Spirit and medicine, half of U.S. adults opted out of the mainstream health system—at least in part—to explore greater well-being and innovative solutions through alternative care, reported a 2002 *Newsweek* cover story. Americans now make more visits to alternative healers such as massage therapists, chiropractors or naturopaths than to traditional M.D.s. Furthermore, since precious little of this "alternative" care is covered by health insurance, we spend more than $30 billion per year of our own funds to partake of these new remedies.

Follow the money, as they say. Is it any wonder that teaching hospitals and universities—from Duke and Johns Hopkins to Harvard—are setting up centers of complementary and integrative (i.e., alternative) medicine?

In chapter six, "The Wave of Conscious Solutions," we'll look at the breakthrough medical research that documents the extraordinary power of prayer in healing—and investigate how other spiritual practices might work in business.

When personal healing, with all of its psychological, spiritual, emotional and physical components, reaches critical mass, people often experience a new or renewed sense of mission or purpose. It is all about critical mass, or as one writer puts it: the "Tipping Point."

Critical Mass and the Tipping Point

I wrote about critical mass in *Megatrends for Women* (Villard, 1992) as a sort of counterpoint to Susan Faludi's popular (but to my mind, pessimistic) *Backlash* (Crown, 1991). The more progress women enjoyed, Faludi argued, the more they suffered a sort of retaliation from society. But I didn't buy it. To my mind women's social progress from politics to business, religion to sports, had achieved such momentum that success was irreversible. Sure, there'd be setbacks along the way—Faludi is right about that—but no turning back.

Now Malcolm Gladwell's bestseller *The Tipping Point: How Little Things Can Make a Big Difference* (Little Brown, 2000) treats the notion of critical mass at book length, and I think he explains it expertly. The "Tipping Point," says Gladwell, is "from the world of epidemiology. It's the name given to the moment in an epidemic when a virus reaches critical mass. It's the boiling point. It's the moment on the graph when the line starts to shoot straight upwards."

Sometime in the 1990s, personal spirituality hit the Tipping Point. Now in the 00 decade, we are translating spirituality into organizations and the collective.

Gladwell, who covered the AIDS epidemic for *The Washington Post* before landing at *The New Yorker*, doesn't stick to epidemiology, though. "What if everything has a Tipping Point?" he asks. "Wouldn't it be cool to try and look for the Tipping Points in business, or in social policy, or in advertising, or in any number of other nonmedical arenas?"

Indeed—and it applies to spirituality, too. For many of us, at some point in the spiritual journey, the Divine energy within us reaches a sort of Tipping Point and a once personal quest becomes more universal:

The wounded become healers. The warriors, statesmen. The victims, advocates. And the managers—corporate activists and change agents.

The Tipping Point and Social Change

The Tipping Point, says Gladwell, explains why social change so often comes "quickly and unexpectedly." It occurs this way because, he continues, "ideas and behavior and messages . . . behave just like outbreaks of infectious diseases."

Invisible one moment, widespread the next. So building on Gladwell's model, a social epidemic—or a roaring new megatrend—might simmer along, just out of official view, until one day it's ready to explode.

That is the case with the Rise of Conscious Capitalism which grows out of the lives of millions of transformed individuals. If it is not quite visible to many people, that's because, like every megatrend I've ever studied, it is largely a bottom-up phenomenon.

Just remember the formula from this book's introduction: When changing values meet economic necessity, transformation takes off.

Later in this chapter, you'll meet Paul Ray, co-author of *The Cultural Creatives* (Harmony, 2000). Ray laments how the media ignores "fundamental change going on just beneath the surface of events in American life, ready to break through in a new level of awareness and concern."

Both Gladwell and Ray explain how maverick notions gradually gain mass and momentum, then suddenly burst onto the scene.

In the 1980s and 1990s, pioneering investors restricted their portfolios to socially responsible funds, those that limit holdings to stocks that can meet certain social, environmental and governance criteria. This trend was largely discounted on Wall Street, until a perfect storm of events occurred. The tech bubble, market crashes and accounting and corporate scandals ravaged mainstream business, provoking reforms, such as the Sarbanes-Oxley Act of 2002, which requires greater financial disclosure, auditor independence, executive accountability and a public accounting oversight board. According to the Social Investment Forum, a Washington, D.C.-based nonprofit association of more than 500 financial professionals and institutions, socially responsible investing (SRI) has soared 5,000 percent in less than two decades.

CEOs and Executive Change Agents

Today we all know that capitalism must morph into a more honest, responsible and wholistic economic system. The question is how to achieve that end while securing financial prosperity. In this book's next chapter, "The Dawn of Conscious Capitalism," we'll delve into that very issue. But first, let's meet the executive change agents whose personal efforts prepare the way for the kind of social epidemic Gladwell and Ray describe—but in this case, a very positive one.

The Spiritual CEO

For years I'd heard about the multi-billion-dollar medical tech firm whose CEO openly defied Wall Street. "We are *not* in business to maximize shareholder value," he stated heretically. Nevertheless, his company won coveted "Buy" ratings from tony brokers up and down the Street. During his tenure, in fact, the firm's market cap soared from $1.1 billion to $60 billion.

How did he pull that off? By masterfully generating the shareholder value he appeared to renounce by committing the company—not to beating the Street by a penny or two a quarter—but to healing patients. Period.

Later, something else caught my eye—a glossy photo of said CEO in his cozy den, eyes closed—meditating. In *Fortune* magazine, no less.

The company is Minneapolis-based Medtronic, which invented pacemakers. The CEO is Bill George, who recently retired, now teaches at Harvard and writes about his exceptional life as a successful, moral CEO. His book, *Authentic Leadership* (Jossey-Bass), was published in 2003.

When Bill George and I talked in 2001, he was still a sitting CEO. Generously, he shared his tales—like the time he staged Medtronic's moving "medallion ceremony" (see chapter four) at 3 A.M. for the employees on graveyard shift at a newly acquired factory.

In fact, Bill George was a lot like his colleagues in the *Fortune* 500, except that he made no secret of passion for Spirit or meditation.

George's private commitment to meditation amplified Medtronic's corporate consciousness.

"I'll tell you a little story," Bill George told me. "The fact that I meditate twice a day was published in a *USA Today* article about the Medtronic innovation machine. The same day, this securities analyst from Morgan Stanley brought in 25 of his largest customers, which represented, oh, maybe $15 billion of our stock, so big shareholders. And this guy [the analyst] started making fun of me. I'd come to talk about where the corporation was headed and he said, a little sarcastically, 'So, it said in the paper this morning that you meditate. Is that how you increase shareholder value?'"

I couldn't help interrupting George's story. So sure was I of exactly how he'd respond. "I bet you told him, 'as a matter of fact, it is.'"

"That's exactly right," said George. "I took him totally seriously. I said, 'You're right.'"

Before George started meditating 25 years ago, he was "a terror in the morning," he says. "I'd get all churned up about unimportant things and by 7:00 in the evening, I would want to fall asleep." Once he started his practice, however, he would get home, meditate, have a great evening and hit the paperwork late at night or go on e-mail. "I had so much more energy," he says. "My most creative ideas came out of meditation. I'd get great clarity about what was really important in the company."

No wonder Bill George enthusiastically supported Medtronic's on-site meditation center.

George, who attends church regularly and is part of a men's group that's met for coffee on Wednesdays for 25 years to discuss family, career and personal issues, always dreamed of leading "a major corporation where the values of the company and my own values were congruent."

In 2002, George retired. Mission accomplished.

High Tech/High Touch: CEO Style

In many ways, CEO Marc Benioff, 41, is a typical high tech success story. His start-up, Salesforce.com, one of 2004's hottest IPOs, put $110 million into company coffers. Salesforce.com boasts the kind of disruptive business model—web-based software—that has enterprise software giants shaking in their boots. Instead of ponying up millions to Siebel or the new

Oracle/PeopleSoft and waiting ages for installation, Salesforce.com clients get customer relations software online for $65 a month per user.

By January 2006, Salesforce.com was a thriving, $310 million company, averaging 7,500 new subscribers a month. By late 2006, paid subscribers totaled 556,000. *BusinessWeek* calls it "one of the few bona fide successes among dot-coms born in the late 1990s."

And many credit the firm's colorful, outspoken leader. Known for a healthy ego, marketing spectacles and intimate client dinners with stars like Arnold Schwarzenegger, Benioff is rarely without the trademark button on his left lapel that advertises, "The end of software."

A Student of Buddhism

But Benioff's public persona hides a surprising alter ego—that of a spiritual seeker with a passion for Buddhism. In 1996, Benioff, then an Oracle salesman, took off on a three-year spiritual journey. He swam with dolphins and traveled to India with his friend Arjun Gupta seeking enlightenment and a vision for his future. There, guru Mata Amritanandamayi advised the young men to give back to society, even as they pursued their dreams of success.

"Spirituality and technology are the yin and yang of Marc," says Gupta, now a venture capitalist. "Most people make their work religion. Marc does both—together."

True enough. In December 2004, *Fortune* ran a photo of Benioff meditating in the woods with several employees, hands folded over their hearts.

But just how much did Benioff's personal journey shape his now red-hot public company?

From his early start-up days, Benioff invoked technology to create positive social change. One percent of the firm's profit, stock and employee time goes to philanthropy. Benioff outlines his philosophy in a book entitled *Compassionate Capitalism* co-authored with Karen Southwick (Career Press, 2004).

How does Benioff stay calm in the midst of success? asks *BusinessWeek*, which calls the 6' 5" Benioff an "overgrown, happy-go-lucky kid."

"He meditates. He doesn't put stress on himself," says his friend Robert Thurman, Columbia University professor of religion. In Benioff, says *BusinessWeek*, "relentless must-win drive is balanced with Eastern spirituality, parties and charity." The combination is clearly working. To celebrate Salesforce.com's 100,000 users benchmark, Benioff hosted a "100,000 Enlightened Users" event featuring none other than the Dalai Lama.

A Parade of Spiritual CEOs

Many CEOs are transforming the workplace with their commitment to Spirit. Before this chapter's in-depth profile, let me briefly introduce several more.

Jay Sidhu, retired chairman and CEO of $90 billion Sovereign Bancorp is a vocal advocate of spirituality in business. "My own personal journey has convinced me that you cannot reach your potential as a leader," he says, "if you are not using your potential as a human being first." Sidhu, whose 17-year stint at Sovereign boosted shareholder return 25 percent a year, chides business for spending $25 billion a year on technical training and "very little" on authentic leadership. Spirituality, by contrast, fosters "character development, love, compassion . . . and a sense of responsibility," he says.

S. Truett Cathy, 84, founder and CEO of the $1.97 billion Chick-Fil-A fast food chain, is a devout Christian. Every Sunday, as the cash registers at Wendy's and McDonald's jingle away, Chick-Fil-A's 1,250 stores in 38 states are closed to keep the Sabbath in silence. Chick-Fil-A's mission vows to "glorify God by being a faithful servant of all that is entrusted to us."

Timberland CEO Jeffrey Swartz, a devout orthodox Jew, reads his prayer book on business trips and consults his rabbi on company problems. Swartz, whose faith inspires him to perform community service, invites Timberland employees to take paid time off to volunteer at their favorite charity. You'll meet Jeff Swartz in chapter two.

Kris Kalra, founder of San Ramon, California-based BioGenex, once a notorious workaholic, was driven to near breakdown. "The higher purpose" was lost, he says, in the stressful pursuit of success. But then he took off three months to read the Hindu scripture, the Bhagavad Gita. Kalra returned to work a changed man. Under Kalra's more balanced leadership BioGenex now employs 120 people and is a leader in the field of cell and tissue testing.

ServiceMaster, the $4 billion firm whose brands include Terminix, TruGreen and Merry Maids, is committed to "honor God in all we do." Still, Chairman Emeritus Bill Pollard, who was CEO from 1983 to 1993 and from 1999 to 2001, says, "We can't and shouldn't and don't want to drive people to a particular religious belief. But we do want people to ask the fundamental questions. What's driving them? What is this life all about?"

Profiles in Commitment: The Priestess of Profit

Ann Mincey—elegant redhead, faithful spiritual seeker and 31-year veteran of REDKEN 5th Avenue NYC—fires up the overhead projector and shows off a drop-dead sales graph, charting the years 1998 through 2002, a time when the revenues of hair-care giant Redken, a division of L'Oréal USA, soared 8, 10, 12, even 15 percent a year—in both good times and bad.

"Want to know our secret?" she teases. "In 1998, we put into place one simple spiritual principle. We call it the 24-hour rule. If I have a problem with you, I promise to go to you to 'face it, solve it and forget it.' We do not talk about people behind their backs. That's our solemn agreement."

Ann Mincey, like HP's Greg Merten from the first page of this chapter, has woven her personal values into her company.

"What's my conclusion?" she asks, eyeing the graphic yet again. "Spirituality in business *works*."

I first encountered Ann Mincey and the "24-hour rule" at the June 2003 Spirit in business conference in San Francisco. But since my passion is the alchemy of how Spirit transmutes into profit, I need more details. Besides, I'm excited about getting to know a successful woman who embodies both Beauty and Spirit. That's why in November 2003, I head to Manhattan with my Spirit in biz buddies, Judi Neal, founder of the Association for Spirit at Work, author of *Edgewalkers* (Praeger, 2006), consultant and retired management professor, and fundraiser extraordinaire and consultant Thad Henry.

So fascinating did I find the Redken executive that I want to take a few more pages to tell the story of Ann Mincey's business-based "ministry" and to cite her advice for tomorrow's business and spiritual leaders.

Tea at the Pierre

To sit with Ann Mincey, as Thad, Judi and I did in the opulent tea room of Fifth Avenue's Pierre Hotel, is to savor a delicious contrast between the inner, invisible world of Spirit and the external allure that Ann's business, the cosmetics industry, celebrates.

Here is a quintessential New York female executive turned out to perfection. The hair—well, of course, the *hair*—swept back and tinted a provocative shade of burgundy. The stylish outfit, flawless makeup and queenly posture. She is, well, almost intimidating. I must confess that even in my favorite black Armani pant suit, I feel a little bit like a Cambridge hippie.

Yet I soon learn that Ann's loveliness, unlike the icy version sometimes associated with her industry, serves to *connect*, not diminish people. Minutes into our visit, she shares a very personal story and we all get slightly teary. Here is a wise woman who's strikingly beautiful, yet authentic, direct and utterly transparent.

And why not? Ann's life mission is to shine the Light of Spirit in a business obsessed with externals. To fulfill it, she's blessed with a down-home warmth that anchors her obvious glamour. Soon I'm totally relaxed, sipping Earl Grey and veering slightly off Atkins to nibble a divine little éclair.

Beauty and the Bible

Ann Mincey was spiritual from day one. A self-described "preacher's kid" who grew up in Middletown, Ohio, Mincey embraced her faith, unlike some clerical offspring who reject it. Yet Ann Mincey was also powerfully drawn to the glamour of the beauty business. So when a Redken rep called on her friend's salon back in the 1970s, Mincey, armed with a home economics degree, announced, "Hey, I want to come work for your company!"

That adventurous spirit is still going strong.

Soon Ann was traipsing from Dayton to Seattle teaching nutrition to hairdressers. That was when her spiritual journey took off. Alone in a hotel room, she distinctly heard the word "LOOK." What could *that* mean, she asked? Then her religious upbringing kicked in and she got it: "Luke."

On a flip chart in her mind, she saw "4:17." So she reached for the Gideon Bible in the nightstand, opened to the passage and read: "The Spirit of the Lord is upon Me, because He has anointed Me to preach the gospel to the poor; He has sent Me to heal the brokenhearted, to proclaim liberty to the captives and recovery of sight to the blind, to set at liberty those who are oppressed; To proclaim the acceptable year of the Lord."

Ann Mincey shut the Bible and exclaimed, "*Oh no!* I'm being called into the ministry!" A path that would have taken her a million miles away from the beauty business she adored. But, never one to shrink from a challenge, she turned back to Luke 4:17 and read the passage over and over.

Then it hit her: You're *already* in the ministry. God needs people in the real world, too!

"For 31 years, this has been my mission, my mantra," she says. "To bring the 'Good News of inner beauty' to an industry focused on outer appearances."

In the Temple of the Body Beautiful

The cornerstone of Ann Mincey's philosophy—preached at Redken seminars brimming with stylists from Taiwan, South Africa, Chile and every other point of the planet—is that a beauty salon is Sacred Space. Mincey's message to stylists is simple: You are healers and never forget it!

"When you settle into a salon chair, what do you do?" she asks us at the Pierre. "You let go. You breathe. This is not work, the gym, church or the doctor's office. You are here to be nurtured. This is a healing place."

Fresh from a hair show in Grand Rapids, Michigan, which attracted 3,200 stylists, Mincey impressed on her audience of 300 the healing power at their disposal. "There's a real live *person* attached to every head of hair you cut. Where is that person? Are they joyous or sad? Even if you've cut someone's hair for 35 years, their life can change radically in the four to six weeks between haircuts."

From Healing to Profit

Redken does business with 70,000 U.S. hair salons and has a presence in 23 countries. Ann Mincey is the firm's highly personal sales channel to the owners, stylists and managers who order Redken shampoo, conditioner, mousse, gel and what-have-you.

Suddenly, the magic of how Mincey's spiritual ways fatten Redken revenue is a lot less mysterious.

But what clients get from Mincey is a lot more than a sales pitch. She preaches, teaches and inspires. "How many people told you a secret last week?" Mincey asks stylists. When people share their secrets in the intimacy of a salon, she believes, there is a sort of healing.

"The danger," she warns, "is for stylists to get overly caught up in the client's emotions." Mincey coaches stylists to set healthy boundaries. "Put on your own oxygen mask first," she jokes.

The Priestess Advises

In the heart of corporate America, Ann Mincey lives and breathes Spirit. If she can do it, so can we. Sure, she has a track record that spans three decades and a long list of achievements. But like the managers you'll meet in chapters three and four, she accepts the fact that Spirit in business often requires diplomacy.

What is your advice, I ask, to middle managers who might think they don't possess enough clout to "be spiritual" in business? Ann mulled it over and offered her thoughts, which I've clustered under several headings:

Take Time for Spirit. Ann Mincey confides that it takes her 45 minutes to achieve the fashionable look she takes out into the world—a must in her business. But lately, Mincey has asked herself, "How much time do I take to prepare my *spiritual* self for the day ahead?"

Her goal is 45 minutes, she says, "but I'm not there yet." Today, she says, it is more like 20 minutes. She journals and reads inspirational works by people like Lloyd John Ogilvie, the former chaplain of the U.S. Senate.

One morning when Mincey was especially pressed for time, she headed out the door without performing her now-customary spiritual routine. Suddenly, the voice of Spirit whispered, "If you take time for me, I will make time for you." Henceforth, she decided she'd better *make* time for her spiritual workout. "When I take time for Spirit," she says, "I wear the armor of God. I'm ready."

Get Personal ASAP. Listen for what people deeply love, then connect with it.

In business, get to the personal level ASAP. If a man is wearing a lapel pin, for example, Mincey immediately asks about it. Tune in to people, she says, by listening for the answers to three simple questions: Who are you? Where have you been? Where do you want to go? Those are the gateways out of mundane business chat and into higher realms of true communication.

Trust. "The business world may seem hard-nosed," declares Mincey, "but everyone is longing for Spirit." In business, of course, you have to get the numbers straight. But then, she says, "people will open to the softer side."

Trust yourself and trust the moment. If you must make a difficult decision, whether business or personal, trust that it's "supposed to be."

Support Your Colleagues. "My openness allows others to open up," says Mincey. The power you give to others is your gift, she adds. "I don't give people any *extra* power, just what they deserve." Says Mincey: "I am an Unconditional Encourager."

Shine. Don't compare yourself to anyone. Get over the lie of insignificance. Your job, your only job, is to shine. In fact, Mincey's new book is called *Get Glowing: You Are a Star Right Where You Are* (www.getglowing.com).

Hug Your Customer

If "salon as temple" is Mincey's first driving principle, "relationship marketing" runs a close second. "Working with *Vogue, InStyle* or *Elle*," she says, "our approach is personal: We cultivate the editors as friends, remembering birthdays and baby showers. We *care*. It's as simple as that."

Mincey is a big fan of *Hug Your Customer* (Hyperion, 2003) by Jack Mitchell, the Connecticut haberdasher and author who advises readers to "know the names of your top 100 customers, their golf handicap and dog's names." Mitchell says his philosophy "can be applied to selling just about anything—from aircraft engines to beanbags."

Not to mention hair care products and corporate culture.

Mincey's latest focus is pampering Redken's best customers. In 2003, Redken's 33 top salon customers jetted off to Santa Fe for a weekend of seminars, spa services and a sneak peak at Redken's plans for the future.

"I am Redken's new CSO," Mincey announces.

"Chief Spiritual Officer?" suggests Judi Neal.

Mincey laughs. "I actually meant Chief Spoiling Officer."

Clearly, Mincey is both.

Notice how "smart" marketing, as in "spoil" your best customers, is rooted in the spiritual value of generosity. I opened my mail in December 2004 and found a $100 gift certificate from Eileen Fisher, the designer and fashion retailer who embraces the values of beauty, simplicity and ease, with a note thanking me for my business that year. Wow! No other retailer ever thanked me quite like *that*, although I've spent a lot more money elsewhere. Of course, it's also terrific marketing: Once I get myself over to my favorite Eileen Fisher boutique, do you think I'll limit myself to a $100 item?

Me neither.

Hug Your CEO?

Mincey, as Redken's longest-serving female veteran, embodies a feminine corporate culture that survives—though not unchallenged—in the modern world of corporate mergers.

Redken was founded in 1960 by Paula Kent, a young actress who suffered allergic reactions to the harsh products then on the market, and her hairdresser Jheri Redding (hence the name Redken from their last names). According to company lore, Kent whipped up batches of shampoo in her bathtub. Shortly after L'Oréal acquired Redken in 1993, Mincey moved to New York and took part in a sort of "It's not my *mother's* shampoo" campaign to convert young, hip stylists and win back market share from competitors like Paul Mitchell and Aveda.

As tribal carrier of Redken's cultural story, Mincey sometimes finds herself in interesting situations—especially with Redken's parent company, French conglomerate L'Oréal.

When Mincey met Lindsay Owen-Jones, the handsome 50-something Welshman who, as L'Oréal chairman and CEO (he retired in 2006), had led L'Oréal Paris to 18 consecutive years of double-digit growth, she asked, "May I give you a hug?" He looked slightly taken aback, she reports, but soon replied, "Is this the Redken way?"

"Yes," she answered confidently.

"All right, then," he said and accepted a "full body" hug.

"Obviously, L'Oréal has its own brand of Spirit," says Mincey. "And it's a little different from ours. One of my L'Oréal colleagues put it this way: 'This is L'Oréal,' he said with his hands in his pockets. Then he opened his arms wide and smiled, 'And this is Redken.'"

Mincey agrees. "Hair care professionals are *very* physical. There's nothing like a hug for heart-opening warmth. But," she adds, "always ask permission."

The Journey Unfolds

Mincey's journey at Redken is a work in progress. "I would love to see more Spirit at Redken," says Mincey, who, when we met, said she wanted to introduce HeartMath to Redken's top salons, that is, best customers, then measure standard business outcomes. HeartMath is a simple but highly sophisticated technique that melts stress and grows performance through the experience of positive emotions such as appreciation and caring. I describe HeartMath more fully in chapter six. Today Mincey is a certified HeartMath trainer who has taught HeartMath at 32 top salons since 2004 and will add 12 more in 2007. Redken's goal is to train all 84 "Elite" salons in HeartMath.

Spirituality, she confirms, is seeping into Redken's corporate culture. Even L'Oréal is intrigued. After Redken showed year after year of double-digit growth, as expressed in Ann Mincey's impressive sales charts, L'Oréal sat up and took notice. What's going on, they asked?

We know Mincey's answer: Spirituality in business—it works!

A New Way

Who are these individuals who so boldly aim their passion and conviction at the armed camp of old-fashioned business? Whether CEOs or executive vice presidents, they're people on the spiritual path. And you'll soon meet their managerial counterparts. But who are we *together*—those of us who vow to express values and Spirit at work? Who are we in the grander scheme of things?

A provocative answer comes from husband-wife team Paul Ray and Sherry Anderson, both Ph.D.s and co-authors of the landmark work *The*

Cultural Creatives. Relying on 14 years of market research, focus groups and polling, the authors describe three distinct "cultures" in the United States and Western Europe, as determined by people's values:

- The "Moderns," the dominant culture, represent the 50 percent who place a top priority on money, success and "making it." Mainstream business epitomizes modernist thought.

- The "Traditionals," about one quarter of the population, emphasize community and the Bible and disdain feminism and sexuality outside of marriage. The Traditionals are shrinking, the authors say, as members gradually age and die.

- The "Cultural Creatives" are the 26+ percent of the U.S. population (30 to 35 percent of Western Europe) who value nature, authenticity, spirituality, peace, relationships, feminism, social justice and social responsibility. Neither modern nor traditionalist, they are literally creating a new culture.

The Cultural Creatives, whose ranks grow by one percent a year, represent more than 50 million Americans. Furthermore they are attracting millions of crossovers from the modernist camp.

In 2000, Ray and Anderson predicted that the Cultural Creatives could be the dominant culture within five to ten years.

This book's next chapter, "The Dawn of Conscious Capitalism," begins with the story of one more CEO—a very spiritual guy whose personal journey most definitely permeates his business. He and his company offer some clear and very definite answers to the one simple yet piercing question that drives the coming metamorphosis of capitalism:

What is our philosophy of business?

2

The Dawn of Conscious Capitalism

Early one October morning I grab a taxi from my home by the Charles River in Cambridge, Massachusetts, and head past the Museum of Science into the financial district. My destination is 60 State Street, home of Hale and Dorr, Boston's very Brahmin law firm and host of a chamber of commerce "Future Leaders" breakfast. Up on the 26th floor I sit in an airy reception room, enjoying walls of windows and a vista that stretches out into Boston Harbor.

I'm here to meet Jeffrey Swartz, CEO of Timberland, the $1.6 billion retailer and manufacturer whose famous yellow work boot is an American icon. Timberland, the winner of numerous "corporate good citizen" awards, is one of *Fortune* and *Working Mother* magazines' "Best Companies to Work For."

Jeff Swartz, 45, works the crowd in an all-Timberland outfit of trousers, shirt and loafers. His only concession to business formal is a checkered sport jacket, which, he tells the well-suited executives, "I wore especially for you." Even in casual attire, Swartz looks more lawyer than lumberjack. And now he's getting down to business.

"[The late] Milton Friedman, who won the Nobel Prize, says the *sole* responsibility of business is to earn money for shareholders," Swartz tells his attentive, young audience. "But when one child in five goes to bed hungry, I find that intolerable. This world *needs* you," he insists.

The third generation owner of a family-led public company, Swartz recalls how his grandfather tutored him in the fine art of boot-making. He then chronicles more recent—and chilling—adventures as a volunteer with City Year, the nonprofit, youth-oriented community service agency that Timberland faithfully supports. Out on the streets, Swartz accidentally found himself in the midst of a drug deal. "I was scared stiff," he said. But mostly he extols the psychic rewards of corporate social responsibility.

This is a man with a new vision for capitalism.

"My grandfather had two goals: to feed his family and to run a shoe business. There was no conflict for him between success and responsibility and there's none today, either. Timberland's philosophy is to 'Do Well and Do Good'—and they're *not* mutually exclusive."

Swartz now serves up the stats to prove his point. For the past 10 years, he states proudly, Timberland has outperformed the S&P 500, NASDAQ and its own competitors. "If I had met Milton Friedman," he says, "I would have said, 'hey, check us out.'"

"Of course, business has to deliver for shareholders," says Swartz. "That's a no-brainer. But in a world where a billion people can't read or write, how can anyone say the sole responsibility of business is to shareholders?"

The Cost of Social Justice

Even Swartz admits "doing well" and "doing good" sometimes collide—at least in the eyes of traditional business. Back in 1995, Swartz, then company COO, got a call from one of his bankers. Timberland, which had recently gone public, had just suffered a disastrous quarter.

"He's going to tell you that you've got to cut all this social justice 'tree hugging' stuff," one Timberland director warned Swartz. Timberland has donated more than $15 million to City Year during their 16-year relationship.

Uh oh, thought Swartz, what now? To Swartz's relief, the board member advised him to hold fast. "This is your bet on the brand," he said. Swartz then began to understand Timberland's financial gifts to worthwhile organizations as a kind of marketing or public relations expense.

"Maybe you can't prove it creates value," Swartz concedes. "But you do it because you're convinced it does." Sure enough, the banker balked at the cost of social responsibility. Only instead of "tree-hugging," he called it "country club crap." Not so, argued Swartz. It's about the brand.

"Prove it," the banker retorted.

Swartz stuck to his guns. "I just did," he replied.

The Rewards of Service

Timberland's favorite cause is the community. Employees get 40 hours of paid time off per year to volunteer for community service. During Timberland's annual "Serv-a-palooza" day, 5,300 employees, vendors and volunteers devote a day's work to nonprofits around the globe. Timberland also offers a six-month, paid sabbatical to employees who want "to pursue a personal dream that benefits the community in a meaningful way."

Swartz loves to talk about the people who really get into service, like the button-down sales executive who quietly "adopted" a fatherless 13-year-old girl from the Bronx and tutors her regularly on the phone.

Or the burly Dutch "warehouse guy" who swims every week with an autistic little girl. She arrives silent. But when her giant of a friend gently deposits her into the pool, she splashes around joyously for a full 20 minutes.

Now after an hour or so of cheerleading, Swartz is winding down.

"When you're ready to make the commitment," he tells the chamber's Future Leaders, "and you want to know how to do it, you call me." Minutes later, in the elevator, Jeff Swartz says, "Let's see how many of them we hear from."

For Swartz, it seems, spreading the gospel of corporate social responsibility affords the opportunity to net a different, but very rewarding, bottom line.

The Dawn of Conscious Capitalism

Timberland CEO Jeff Swartz is not alone.

Hundreds of top CEOs repudiate the dying doctrine of conventional, old-line capitalism, which was brilliantly articulated by the late Milton Friedman, a Nobel Prize–winning economist, in the 1970 article, "The Social Responsibility of Business Is to Increase Its Profits."

"What was most remarkable about that piece," said one CEO, a self-admitted Friedman admirer, "was how wrong it was."

Today capitalism stands at the threshold of Consciousness. That is, we are increasingly *aware* of the untallied cost of capitalism. Now, a perfect convergence of social, political and economic forces compels us to examine the consequences of a financial doctrine that so emphasizes the desirability of short-term profit, that it fails to account for the moral or social costs of achieving it. In 2005, as former Tyco CEO Dennis Koslowski and Adelphia founder John Rigas faced lengthy prison terms, and new scandals erupted at firms like AIG, Merck and

Fannie Mae, investors and consumers alike again wondered how much more corporate wrongdoing capitalism and the public could endure.

As a result, the quest for Conscious Capitalism—that is, integrity, transparency, enlightened governance as well as higher social and environmental standards—is regaining momentum.

Throughout this often painful exercise, we're raising consciousness, renewing hope and setting the stage for free enterprise to evolve into the next, great iteration of itself. Today we are birthing a new and wiser version of capitalism, one that reconciles profit with the values we hold dear. And signs of progress are popping up from Wall Street to Main Street. What might surprise some is how far the process has already come.

Welcome to the Dawn of Conscious Capitalism—a popular, decentralized, broad-based crusade to heal the excesses of capitalism with transcendent human values. Every day Conscious Capitalism wins new converts in the paneled boardrooms of global business. Swartz and the other top leaders are the corporate face of this burgeoning, grassroots movement.

Equally important, the actions millions of us take, "from the supermarket to the stock market,"[1] are drafting a more wholistic brand of free enterprise which will forever outshine the Chicago School—and win someone somewhere a brand-new Nobel Prize.

The Path of Conscious Capitalism

Whether the Dow soars to greater heights or sinks to new lows, will ordinary investors like us cheerfully recommit to business as usual—scandals, crashes and all—trusting Sarbanes-Oxley and the like to protect us from the next round of bad guys? Besides, do we want to support a greedy brand of capitalism that, as Timberland's Jeff Swartz charges, turns its back on injustice to carry out the sole stated goal of making money? Especially considering that the research you'll read in this chapter shows that moral companies often outperform the market?

· Before you decide, journey with me to meet several pioneering firms that set the benchmark in social responsibility and some of the activists who devote their lives to transforming business. In the process, you will discover how much sense it makes to embrace both profit and principle.

---

[1]"Responsibility from the Supermarket to the Stock Market" is the motto of *Green Money Journal,* described later in this chapter.

Corporate Social Responsibility

When Business for Social Responsibility (BSR), the San Francisco-based nonprofit, was founded in the 1990s, it counted just a few members. Today there are 200 organizations, including many firms from the *Fortune* 500. BSR defines corporate social responsibility (CSR) as a "comprehensive set of policies, practices and programs" that earn financial success in ways that "honor ethical values, and respect people, communities and the natural environment."

In other words, CSR firms are *conscious* of how their actions impact their constituencies. Sure, they worry about stockholders, but they're also concerned about "stakeholders" like employees, customers, suppliers, communities at home and abroad—and planet Earth.

In addition to joining outfits like BSR, corporations signal their willingness to embrace Conscious Capitalism by endorsing standards like the CERES (Coalition for Environmentally Responsible Companies) Principles and through the Global Reporting Initiative (GRI).

WHAT ARE THE CERES PRINCIPLES?

In 1989, CERES created a 10-point code of corporate environmental conduct. In 1993, Sunoco became the first *Fortune* 500 firm to subscribe to the principles.

1. Protection of the Biosphere
2. Sustainable Use of Natural Resources
3. Reduction and Disposal of Waste
4. Energy Conservation
5. Risk Reduction
6. Safe Products and Services
7. Environmental Restoration
8. Informing the Public
9. Management Commitment
10. Audits and Reports

Today more than 80 companies—from environmental leaders like Interface, the pioneering carpet and carpet tile manufacturer, and the Body Shop to global giants like Bank of America, Coca-Cola and Nike—endorse the principles.

The GRI issues uniform guidelines for corporations—as well as governments and NGOs (Non Governmental Organizations)—that choose to report on the social, environmental and economic aspects of their operations. About 1,000 organizations have adopted the GRI guidelines.

Why do corporate blue chips rally round the banner of corporate social responsibility? Many want to do the right thing, of course, but there is a practical reason as well. A reputation for corporate responsibility enhances the company's brand, while being deemed "socially irresponsible" damages it. The marketplace implications, not surprisingly, are sizable.

Indeed, the crusade for corporate accountability has already garnered immense public support. When the Conference Board polled 25,000 people in 23 countries, a full *two thirds* said they want business to "expand beyond the traditional emphasis on profits and contribute to broader social objectives."

Top CSR companies, of course, already do exactly that:

- 3M's corporate-wide offensive against carbon emissions is cutting greenhouse gases at 3M facilities in 60 countries.
- General Mills invested $2 million in a joint venture between minority-owned Glory Foods and community organization Stairstep Initiative to create an employee-owned business and 150 jobs in Minneapolis's inner city.
- Procter & Gamble (P&G) technology helps people in developing countries to cheaply disinfect water in their homes. The consumer giant also supports nine minority-owned banks and invests in venture capital funds for minority business. "Diversity is a matter of ethics," says P&G spokesperson Terry Loftus—and a "fundamental business strategy."
- Motorola's superior customer service rests on the firm's commitment to "bionics"—a new field where product inspiration comes from the "simplicity, efficiency and beauty of nature."

Every year *CRO Magazine* (which merged with *Business Ethics)* lists the top 100 corporate citizens. 3M, General Mills, P&G and Motorola all make the grade. Drawing on ratings devised by KLD Research & Analytics, *Business Ethics* ranks corporate responsiveness to seven stakeholders: shareholders, the community, women and minorities, employees, the environment, non-U.S. stakeholders, and customers.

Here are a few more winning examples:

- A Cummins Engine project near its San Luis Potosi, Mexico, facility teaches blind people basic carpentry skills. In Brazil, when kids climbed under a Cummins fence to snitch the sheet metal, Cummins built a school for 800.

• Natural grocer Wild Oats stocks 80 percent organic produce. Work there for
  25 hours or more and get profit sharing. Competitor Whole Foods, whose
  energy is 100 percent renewable, is a regular on *Fortune*'s 100 Best list.
• Chip giant Intel sets the benchmark on safety. If one of Intel's 99,900
  employees misses a day of work due to injury, the CEO had better get an
  e-mail on it within 24 hours. On May 18, 2005, Paul Otellini succeeded
  Craig Barrett as CEO and Barrett became chairman. The *following day*, the
  word went out at Intel: "accident reports will now go to Paul," says Intel CSR
  director Dave Stangis. Intel studies the mishap's cause to prevent another.
  Result: Intel's minuscule accident rate: 0.40 per 100 versus an industry average of 6.6 per 100.

Starbucks: It's All About the Beans

Starbucks is an American cultural icon. Steaming lattes and ink-black
espresso fuel the digital economy. Comfy Starbucks cafes, wired for Wi-Fi, are
modern oases for weary warriors traversing today's urban landscapes. With
some 12,440 outlets and 135,000 partners, Starbucks is a top player in the
transformation of capitalism. Corporate social responsibility, said retired
CEO Orin Smith, who was succeeded by James Donad in 2005, "is such an
inherent part of the business model, our company can't operate without it."
Long a fixture on *Fortune*'s 100 Best Companies list, Starbucks famously
extends benefits, even stock options and health plans, to part-timers.

But how many of Starbucks' 40 million weekly customers realize that the
$7.8 billion firm is committed to stakeholders—from coffee growers to part-
ners (employees)—while growing at a breakneck pace that satisfies shareholders?

Starbucks is making its mark on the planet through its towering impact
on the commodity that made it rich and famous—the noble coffee bean.
When coffee farmers raise the bar on quality, environmental, social and economic standards, Starbucks grants them "preferred supplier" status and pays
top dollar for their crops. In 2005, Starbucks paid an average of $1.28 per
pound for green (unroasted) coffee, 23 percent higher than the average
"free" market price.

That might mean, for example that a Colombian farmer will decide to
grow coffee rather than the coca plant—which becomes cocaine, and in turn
destroys communities North and South.

Starbucks promotes sustainable agriculture and biodiversity by favor-
ing shade-grown coffee—which saves land that might be used for coffee

production as tropical forest. In 2002, Starbucks bought 20 times more shade-grown coffee than in 1999. In 2005, Starbucks bought 1.9 million pounds of shade-grown coffee, up from 1.8 million pounds in 2003. In recognition of such efforts Starbucks and partner Conservation International won the World Summit Business Award for Sustainable Development Partnerships.

The Evolution of Free Enterprise

Capitalism mirrors the awareness of its members. And we capitalists are in the midst of a massive awakening. Thanks to the booming 90s, tech bubble, market crash, recession and corporate accounting scandals, we are all feeling the unhappy result of a business doctrine whose only goal is profit—at any cost. For more and more of us, the moral consequences of unconscious capitalism are intolerable.

What we don't yet realize is that the moral high ground is actually very profitable.

Money and Morals: An Engine of Superior Performance

Before we continue the discussion of Conscious Capitalism, I'd like to expand on one critical point—the relationship between morals and money.

Most of us, no matter how spiritual we think we are, harbor the belief that old-fashioned capitalists—those who invest to make money with no regard for moral considerations—actually earn the highest returns. In other words, if you want to go in for social justice, prepare to suffer financially.

"Socially concerned investors," write Marshall Glickman and Marjorie Kelly in *E: The Environmental Magazine,* were often considered "good-hearted saps, destined for sub-par returns."

Well, decades of research later, it turns out that theory is just plain wrong.

Socially responsible firms repeatedly achieve first-rate financial returns that meet and often beat the market and their peers, proving morals and money may be curiously compatible, after all. For example, Governance Metrics International rated public firms on governance, labor, environmental and litigation policies. Top-ranked firms substantially outperformed the market, while poorly rated firms significantly trailed it. When Morningstar, the revered fund rater, examined socially responsible stock funds over a three-year period, it found that 21 percent had earned its top five-star rating. That's twice the rate of all mutual funds.

Consider these additional intriguing findings:

- A 2002 DePaul University study found that the *Business Ethics* 100 Best Citizens (the 2001 list) outperformed the mean of the rest of the S&P 500 by *ten percentile points*. The DePaul study tracked total returns, sales growth and profit growth.
- When researchers studied firms that honor stakeholders, not just shareholders, the results were particularly striking. Towers Perrin studied 25 firms that excel in relationships with stakeholders—investors, customers, employees, suppliers and communities. From 1984 to 1999 the "stakeholder superstars" beat the S&P 500 by 126 percent. The "superstars," including firms such as Coca-Cola, Cisco, P&G and Southwest Airlines, showed a 43 percent return in total shareholder value versus 19 percent in total shareholder return for the S&P 500.
- Employees are clearly stakeholders. Does it pay to keep them happy? A Watson Wyatt Worldwide survey of 400 public firms found those with the most employee-friendly practices, such as flextime and good training, delivered shareholders a 103 percent return (over 5 years), while those with the fewest gained 53 percent in the same time frame.

What's the simple truth behind these studies? Why do moral companies perform so well financially? The answer, say many experts, is that corporate responsibility is a proxy for good management—and good management is *the* prime indicator of superior financial performance.

Dan Boone, who runs Calvert's Social Investment Equity Portfolio, puts it this way: There's a "huge overlap" between socially screened investments and companies he calls just plain "high-quality."

I will end this section with one last example, a real eye-opener. For the past seven years, the public firms on *Fortune*'s "100 Best Companies to Work For" list earned more than three times the returns of the broader market, says a 2005 study by Great Place to Work Institute (which compiles the *Fortune* "100 Best" list cited above) and Russell Investment Group. Between 1998 and 2004, the public companies on the "100 Best" list returned 176 percent compared to 42 percent for the Russell 3000 and 39 percent for the S&P 500.

If these examples do not convince you that the marriage of morals and money was meant to be, hold on—I've saved my best evidence for chapter seven, "The Socially Responsible Investment Boom."

Spiritual Economics?

Wait a minute, you say, what do social responsibility and all this economics have to do with the "Power of Spirituality" megatrend in chapter one?

That's the question I asked my old friend Cliff Feigenbaum, publisher of the award-winning quarterly *Green Money Journal*. Cliff is a social responsibility wonk with a mischievous twinkle in his eye, a ready laugh and a mystical bent. "There's definitely a link between Spirit and finance," says Cliff. The link is values. "My values don't stop when I hit the ATM or the supermarket. Examine your heart and your wallet and ask yourself if they're in alignment. Make financial choices that are in sync with your values." Not surprisingly, Cliff co-authored a book with father-son team Hal and Jack Brill called *Investing with Your Values* (Bloomberg Press, 1999).

That's why Cliff is still smarting about what personal finance guru Suze Orman had to say about social responsibility in *O: The Oprah Magazine* (August, 2003). Your financial job, she told readers, is to invest to make money. Period. Cliff says a lot of social responsibility types let Oprah and Suze have it in a letter-writing campaign.

But has Orman seen the research, I ask Cliff, that social investments often *beat* the Street—and by a wide margin?

"Well, exactly," says Cliff, for whom the idea of making as much money as you can, any way you want, and then—as some traditional capitalists suggest—giving it to the charity of your choice, is unthinkable.

"That's like earning money on tobacco stocks all day, then giving to the American Cancer Society at night," he says. "*Profoundly* out of alignment."

I've watched Cliff and Hal Brill win the recognition they deserve. I first met the guys at the great Spirit in business get-togethers put on by Santa Fe, New Mexico's Message Company. Sometimes they'd happily mind the conference bookstore for the pleasure of hanging out with kindred souls and spreading the gospel of socially responsible investing. Today, however, those days are over. The phone is ringing and it's either *Barron's* or *The Wall Street Journal*. "Thanks to the whole corporate irresponsibility thing," Cliff says with a laugh, "I went from 'fringe' to visionary."

From a spiritual perspective, corporate social responsibility is love, justice and truth in action. When a corporate activist shines the light on opaque governance rules and increases transparency or exposes a company's poor environmental record, he or she is expanding consciousness as surely as if he or she had built a meditation center.

I believe the "Spirit in business" and "corporate social responsibility" trends represent two sides of the same coin, the inner and outer dimensions of the same phenomenon. Together these new directions will transform capitalism in the next decade or two.

Rewards in the Marketplace: Growing Public Support

No doubt about it: Conscious Capitalist companies are reaping the rewards of accountability at the cash register. Corporate social responsibility— or irresponsibility—profoundly colors the public's impression of a company.

In chapter five, we'll explore how Conscious Consumers are transforming capitalism. For now, take a look at how powerfully people feel about corporate morality—and how much it influences their purchases:

• The majority of people (90 percent) would consider switching products to avoid doing business with companies that have a reputation for poor corporate citizenship, reports a 2004 Cone Corporate Citizenship Study. Most (75 to 80 percent) would also speak out against the company, sell their stock in it and refuse to work there.
• An impressive 79 percent of Americans consider corporate citizenship in deciding whether to buy a product, says a 2001 Hill & Knowlton/Harris Poll, while 36 percent call it an important factor in a purchase decision.
• Forty-nine percent cite social responsibility as a key factor in their impression of a company, says a CSR Monitor survey. When price, quality and convenience are equal, the study found, people increasingly opt to buy from companies they deem socially responsible.

The Biodiversity of Social Change

As consumers pile on the CSR bandwagon, much of the credit goes to grassroots leaders like Alisa Gravitz, vice chair of the Social Investment Forum and executive director of Co-op America, a 70,000-member activist consumer group dedicated to raising public awareness.

Alisa Gravitz, however, is not your average antiestablishment activist. "Business is a fact of life," says Gravitz, who holds a Harvard M.B.A. in marketing and finance. "We have to trade. We have to have an economy." Nevertheless, she's committed to radical social and economic change and to asking simple, profound questions like, "What would a healthy economic system look like?" and "What are the best practices for achieving it?"

I find her both practical and visionary.

An environmentalist at heart, Alisa often invokes images from nature. "We know that ecosystems thrive on diversity," she explains. "At Co-op America, we apply the principle of biodiversity to the work of social change. That is, we rely on a full spectrum of change strategies."

Alisa lays out a multiple-choice menu, including engagement, drama, consumer action and shareholder resolutions (we'll get to those later), that she and others draw on to "do business" with business, all while clueing me in on today's hot issues.

Engagement. "Activists in business suits," as one activist put it, meet with corporate people, discuss the issues and lobby them to adopt more progressive policies. Co-op America successfully persuaded one of the most famous national magazines to switch to recycled paper and helped get Procter and Gamble to sell fair trade coffee in supermarkets under the Millstone and Folgers brands.

But today's driving issue is vendor compliance, better known in the vernacular as sweatshop labor. Not long ago Nike was lambasted in the media for using sub-par overseas suppliers. Today, Wal-Mart is catching lots of flack on the sweatshop front. For years, Amy Domini, founder and CEO of Domini Social Investments, tried to get Wal-Mart to clean up its vendor act. Finally, she gave up, dumping Wal-Mart stock in 2001 because of its overseas sweatshops.

Meanwhile shareholder activist Shelley Alpern of Trillium Asset Management, who dialogued at length with Target on the subject, says Target now does a better job on vendor compliance. (Co-op America, however, still criticizes Target on the sweatshop issue.) When talks with company insiders stall, as they, ahem, sometimes do, it's time to plug in different tactics. "We'd rather work it out," says Alisa, "but sometimes, we're obliged to take the old carrot and stick approach."

Drama. During the old-growth timber campaign against Home Depot (described later in this chapter), the Rainforest Action Network took over the loudspeakers at the famous Do-It-Yourself retailer and announced, "Attention shoppers: There's a special in aisle 23 on old-growth timber."

Consumer Action. The fair trade coffee crusade is a great example of grassroots action. The beauty of the effort is its simplicity. "You don't need a big instruction guide on how to do it," says Alisa. "It's like, here are the names of the fair trade/shade grown companies. Just buy them." Co-op America also invites tens of thousands of its members to ask their local grocer to stock fair trade coffee.

Alisa talks about the unique role the faith-based community plays in the fair trade campaign. In the Lutheran Church, she says with a smile, it is said that the quest for social justice is fueled by coffee.

Co-op America's website is full of ideas on how to get involved in everything from "buy-cotts," as in buy organic flowers, to letter writing campaigns to companies on the "Corporate Hall of Shame," a list of firms deemed socially "irresponsible."

There is great power, Gravitz says, in engaging *several* strategies, as activists did in the Home Depot/ancient timber campaign. But, she adds, there's nothing quite as potent as a shareholder resolution—which we'll soon explore.

The Spiritual Activist

I ask Alisa about the spiritual side of her work. She gestures toward the lush garden behind her townhouse in Adams Morgan—Washington, D.C.'s hip, multi-ethnic neighborhood—and the environmentalist in her speaks. "The power of nature is a great mystery," she says. "The issue for me is do we have the *human* systems to celebrate and preserve nature—to really protect the health of our planet, which all of us humans depend on for life itself?"

Answering that question is Alisa Gravitz's spiritual practice.

Alisa hails from Minnesota and a family devoted to service. Her father was a social worker, her mother, a nurse. The dinner conversation was peppered with comments about social responsibility.

"As a girl," she says, "I assumed I'd follow in my family's footsteps." Then came Alisa's "conversion" experience. "During the long, cold winter, before Earth Day 1970," she says, "I read and was profoundly touched by Rachel Carson's *The Silent Spring*."

When the snow finally melted in early April, Alisa went out for a walk.

"It was one of those days you wait the whole Minnesota winter for. The sun was shining and the smells of spring were everywhere. It was so mild—and this is the turning point up north—that you could take your coat off. I looked around at all that beauty, feeling viscerally connected to nature and the thought came to me, 'we could lose *all* of this.' I knew at that moment what my life's work would be. *My* path would be a little different from my family's. My service would be on behalf of a healthy planet, Mother Nature herself, so that every person on Earth can have the most fundamental of human rights—healthy air, water and food."

Amazingly, Alisa Gravitz was only in the eighth grade at the time. But soon after, she'd banded together with classmates ("my co-troublemakers," she laughs) to form an environmental group and her life of activism began. At Brandeis, she earned a degree in environmental science and economics before ending up at Harvard Business School.

3M

We all love socially aware consumer companies. But let's hear it for the exemplary manufacturers, whose task is a lot more complex. There's the legacy of us-against-them labor issues and the gritty history of smokestack industry and planet Earth.

If anyone can turn the tide and transform the sector into a model for the 21st century, it would have to be Minneapolis-St. Paul-based 3M. (Why, I often wonder, is Minnesota such a hotbed of good corporate citizenship?) 3M, a $21 billion company that employs 70,000, is an environmentalist pioneer of long standing, whose latest foray in the battle for Mother Earth is the visionary yet practical discipline called "Design for the Environment."

"The idea is to slash pollutants, spare landfills and cut hazardous ingredients by considering design, manufacturing steps and recycling efforts before production begins," says Fran Kurk, Design for Environment coordinator for the Minnesota Pollution Control Agency.

"Lifecycle management," as it's also called, is the process whereby engineers simply design eco-friendly features into a product from scratch. But some of 3M's products are older than most of *us*. So it's less a case of design than redesign.

Today 3M reevaluates its products with an eye toward the environment.

Take sandpaper—which 3M has churned out since 1902. The solvents used to concoct this trademark product are environmental hazards that "need to be remediated with pollution controls," says Katherine Reed, 3M's VP for Environmental Operations. Two billion dollars and 15 years of research later, 3M is producing solvent-free sandpaper, adhesives and tape.

Mother Earth isn't the only beneficiary. Earth-friendly changes often go right to the bottom line. Lifecycle management, says 3M, can save 30 percent in materials cost.

"The more I studied, the more I saw that the problems were not on the science side, but on the human side. The issue, as I saw it even then, was with our economic institutions. I look at corporations and ask what role they play in the 'Web of Life.' Do they contribute solutions? Or problems?"

Alisa Gravitz's spiritual practice—healing the relationship between business and Mother Earth—will challenge her for years to come.

A Force for Change: The New Shareholder-Activists

"Aspects of the economy act like an untamed beast that needs poking in the right direction," write Marshall Glickman and Marjorie Kelly in the March/April 2004 issue of *E: The Environmental Magazine*. Their excellent article, entitled "Working Capital," inspired many of the points in this section. And who does a better job of poking the business establishment than the hardy band of activists who raise consciousness, shine the spotlight on firms who do the right thing—or *not*—and keep the hottest issues on the corporate front burner?

These days, however, corporate gadflies are apt to pursue their favorite quarry from within. One SRI fund holds $1 million in Philip Morris (now traded as Altria) stock in order to oblige Philip Morris executives to "do lunch" with them—then listen to fund reps demand that the tobacco giant scrap advertisements aimed at children. The Sierra Club scarfed up shares in oil and auto companies, then launched campaigns against the same companies in favor of solar and wind energy and fuel-efficient cars.

In addition to time-honored tools like letter-writing campaigns and boycotts, activists now invoke the power of shareholder resolutions. It's a case of economic democracy in action. Even if you own just one share of a stock, you can attend the annual get-together, ask questions and vote the issues. Got $2,000 worth of stock? You may be entitled to draft a proposal. No wonder annual meetings, once as dull as dishwater, have livened up a lot lately. Thanks to the efforts of shareholder activists (that is, shareholders who are more, or at least equally, interested in activism as in "shareholding") the following reforms have occurred:

• Pepsico replaced its soda can lids, saving 25 million pounds of aluminum.
• GE will pay $150 to $250 million to clean up PCB pollution in the Northeast's Housatonic River.
• Ford, Texaco and others quit the Global Climate Coalition, which, say activists, undermines efforts against global warming.

And you can't accuse activists of letting corporate "good guys" off the hook, either. In 2005 Trillium Asset Management introduced a resolution calling on Whole Foods, the top natural food retailer and a company considered exemplary by many, to disclose on its private label brands any genetically engineered ingredients. After the vote, Whole Foods told Trillium it would voluntarily comply with the measure.

Shareholder activism is growing by leaps and bounds. The number of resolutions filed surged 22 percent from 2001 to 2003 (from 261 to 320)—and they're winning a lot more votes, from 8.7 percent in 2001 to 11.4 percent in 2003.

In 2003, shareholders voted in favor of proxy resolutions in record numbers. At Intel, for example, 48 percent of shareholders voted to call on the chip giant to expense stock options. (In 2004, 52 percent of shareholders voted for and passed the nonbinding proposal.) At Avon, 80 percent of shareholders voted in favor of the annual election of directors.

What do those huge numbers mean? Trillium Asset Management's Steve Lippman says large institutional investors, who normally rubber stamp management's positions, are beginning to think for themselves and vote *against* management.

Score another coup for Conscious Capitalism.

By April 2005, 348 resolutions on social policy (including environmental and fair employment) had been filed, compared with 350 social-type resolutions in all of 2004, report the Investor Responsibility Research Center and the Social Investment Forum.

But you don't need big wins like the Intel or Avon votes to change things. The Rainforest Action Network hounded Home Depot to stop selling wood from old-growth forests. Its proposal garnered only 11.8 percent of the votes, but Home Depot opted to phase out the controversial wood. Great success— but the story doesn't end there. Soon after, Lowes, Wickes Lumber and HomeBase followed Home Depot's example.

Trillium Asset Management's Shelley Alpern says shareholder activism is "many times greater than the voting results suggest." Why? Because corporations frequently decide to change their controversial behavior after activists have quietly lobbied them behind the scenes.

Then again, the action isn't always *behind* the scenes.

Profiles in Commitment: A Day in the Life of an Activist

April 28, 2004. 6 A.M. Shareholder advocate Shelley Alpern, vice president of Boston's Trillium Asset Management, awakens at a Marriott hotel near San Francisco, bleary-eyed, but pumped. The night before Alpern and her allies from the advocacy group Amazon Watch were up until all hours huddled with human rights activist Bianca Jagger banging out their statements for the annual meeting—now just hours away.

Tired or not, Alpern, a petite, energetic brunette, has *got* to move. Nevertheless, she takes time for her morning ritual: 15 to 20 minutes of silent meditation. Later she will decide that soulful act saved the day.

Outside ChevronTexaco's[2] corporate campus in San Ramon, California, a noisy protest is in full swing. Dozens of local people and labor leaders are chanting "Rainforest Chernobyl" and carrying signs, "Please Clean Up the Amazon." Clearly, this year's annual meeting will be no staid corporate affair.

Alpern and her team—Jagger, Ecuadorian nurse Rosa Moreno, Amazon Watch's Leila Salazar, several clergy members and two indigenous leaders in full Amazonian regalia—greet their enthusiastic supporters.

This is a powerful moment.

Toribio Aquinda, leader of the Cofan people, will soon come face to face with the CEO of the firm whose oil explorations have, say the activists, polluted the rivers his people depend on for water; scarred the land with 627 toxic waste pits; and destroyed the health of thousands through cancer, miscarriages and untold other maladies. Since the tragedy began, the Cofan people have dwindled from 15,000 to 800.

Shelley Alpern is about to set the entire mess before ChevronTexaco shareholders, who, amazingly, are largely oblivious to the moral and possible financial disaster the company faces. Alpern has drafted a resolution asking for a full report on the health and environmental impact of ChevronTexaco's toxic Amazon operations. Such a study would acknowledge a fact ChevronTexaco has long downplayed to shareholders: that it has been trying unsuccessfully for more than a decade to fight off a billion-dollar lawsuit brought by Ecuador's indigenous people.

Alpern checks her watch, rounds up the crew and escorts them through the gated complex, past security guards and into the annual meeting of one of the world's largest multi-national corporations.

How did these protesters get in? Through the miracle of capitalism, any shareholder can attend an annual meeting and vote on shareholder resolutions. Several Trillium Asset Management clients who hold ChevronTexaco stock simply authorized Alpern and the others to represent them.

The Meeting. Inside, CEO David O'Reilly is running through the protocol—business numbers, new corporate directions, the reelection of directors. He and ChevronTexaco's board of directors sit on a platform facing the audience of 200 shareholders, employees and journalists. In the center aisle there's a microphone set up for questions and comments from the floor.

That's where Alpern will lay out her activist agenda.

Alpern, 41, who looks about 25, is petite, genial and wicked smart. And

---

[2]ChevronTexaco changed its name to Chevron in 2005. I use the old name in this section since that was the correct name in 2004.

today she is in her element. A veteran of 19 shareholder meetings at firms like Allied Signal (where she railed against CEO compensation), GE, Staples, Avon and Chubb, Alpern has introduced numerous shareholder resolutions. But somehow this campaign is different. It touches places in the heart that compel her to face the brutal reality of what some call "globalization."

Fact-Finding in Ecuador. The previous April, Alpern joined investors on a tour sponsored by Amazon Watch to the Amazon to inspect firsthand a catastrophe now compared to the Exxon *Valdez*. She had steeled herself for the emotional assault of poverty but hadn't bargained for a week of "Ah-Has" about the shocking impact of "globalization" on innocent people.

"You hear lots of clichés about free trade and human rights," says Alpern, "but it's all rather abstract." Now here it was face to face—the harshness of global economics. "Under IMF debt policy, for example," she says, "Ecuador has practically no budget for people's healthcare, no funds for job creation."

The full magnitude of suffering is staggering even for a veteran like Alpern. Still she fights the fight, not just for the ideals at stake, but to help in a concrete way. Monies from ChevronTexaco would ease some of the people's burdens. But that could be a long time coming. The next step is clear, however. They're at this annual meeting to rock the corporate boat.

Thinking on Your Feet. Alpern sits at the edge of her seat, keenly alert. Her resolution is second to the last of nine. Once it's up, her little team will ask questions and describe what they saw in Ecuador. Except now CEO O'Reilly says that since there are a number of resolutions, they might have to "limit" the time for conversation.

Oh, *no*, thinks Alpern. We've got a problem here. Just because you show up is no guarantee you get to talk. They're going to invoke their power to limit the discussion. That's how they'll get rid of us. I've got to do something!

Alpern promptly takes the microphone, signaling her desire to speak.

"I have a procedural question, Mr. O'Reilly," she notes. "Some of our guests have come all the way from Ecuador. We may need a little extra time."

O'Reilly doesn't promise anything. But thanks to Alpern's quick thinking he will not look very gentlemanly if he cuts them off.

How did she keep her cool and act decisively?

Alpern credits her morning meditation. "It helped me think more clearly and kept me from getting angry," she says. "I'm in a sort of chess game. I can't get too emotional. I have to think, 'Okay, what's my next move?'"

The Resolution. Finally they're up. Alpern reads a statement in support of the resolution. "It's time now," she concludes, "for our company to remove the black eye that it gave itself in Ecuador."

Jagger, who visited the disaster area twice in the previous six months, seconds the resolution. "ChevronTexaco is responsible for the worst oil-related disaster in the history of Latin America," she says, "and it is evading its moral and ethical responsibility."

The resolution read and seconded, Alpern's cohort goes into action.

"My people are on the brink of extinction," Toribio Aquinda tells O'Reilly. "I fear we may not be here in another five years. When the first oil well was built, my people numbered 15,000. Now there are 800."

Next comes Rosa Moreno, a licensed nurse from the region. "Every day I see children with skin irritations, men and women with cancer of the throat and pancreas, woman who have miscarriages," says Moreno, who lost family to cancer in a town near the Texaco oil pits. "They are all in terrible pain."

Two nuns, both shareholders and just back from Ecuador, detail the horrors they witnessed. How, they ask, will ChevronTexaco make it right?

Scanning the audience, Amazon Watch's Leila Salazar sees a shareholder wipe away a tear, but there is no other visible show of support.

CEO O'Reilly defends the company as best he can. ChevronTexaco is not responsible for the damage, he claims, since it occurred as a result of operations by state oil company Petroecuador. Lawyers for the people of Ecuador deny that, of course, and aim to prove their own claims in court.

After the votes are tallied and the meeting adjourns, Alpern and her team review the results. "We spoke for 35 minutes out of a two-and-a-half-hour meeting," Alpern exclaims. "And we won nine percent of the vote!"

Only nine percent? And she's celebrating? "We were absolutely thrilled," Alpern explains. "A vote like this? In its first year? You hope for two, maybe three percent. Tops."

How did they do it?

By winning over powerful allies like the New York State Common Retirement Fund, which holds $350 million in ChevronTexaco shares, and the California Public Employees Retirement System (CALPERS). Typically institutional investors vote with management. Not this time.

"We only needed three percent to come back next year," says Alpern. "We got three times that."

Indeed "coming back" is exactly what Alpern did. By late 2006, Trillium Asset Management had filed its fourth (annual) resolution to appear on the 2007 proxy ballot. Although the resolution has yet to pass, ChevronTexaco now faces a second, related suit. The government of Ecuador is taking the company to court over the legality of the original remediation agreement.

Clearly Alpern knows a thing or two about how to keep issues in the pub-

CHIQUITA BRANDS REINVENTS ITSELF

Think Chiquita is just another lawless, corporate republic?
Think again.

True, Cincinnati-based Chiquita Brands, in its former incarnation as United Fruit Company, was scarred with a history of corruption, brutality, environmental destruction and financial failure that no corporation—let alone a CSR firm—could love. And it's a pretty good bet that the firm's ruthless, meddlesome policies in Central America contributed to its financial demise.

But when the company emerged from bankruptcy in 2002 with a new board and CEO, "Chiquita used the opportunity of bankruptcy to clean up its act," writes Ellen Pfeifer in *Winslow Environmental News*, a publication of the Winslow Management Company, which runs the Winslow Green Growth Fund, about which you'll hear a lot more in chapter seven. The new Chiquita is staging an impressive financial comeback. But it also boasts a superb record in social and environmental citizenship:

- Chiquita embraced vigorous new standards to cut toxic chemicals, control pollution and protect people.
- In 2001, the banana king signed labor agreements based on the SA 8000 standard with the International Union of Food Workers and COLSIBA, a group of banana workers unions.
- Chiquita, which operates in 70 countries, holds *all* units to CSR benchmarks and employs a VP-level CSR officer.

Does this social responsibility success story cost Chiquita a fortune?
On the contrary. Chiquita's Earth-friendly commitments have reaped astounding savings. From 1997 to 2001, the banana giant cut $4.8 billion from its agrochemical budget, then saved another $3.8 billion through recycled materials. By the end of Q3 2003, Chiquita had cut debt to $276 million, beating estimates and exceeding analyst predictions. It is now a $4 billion company.

Meanwhile the kudos from CERES, Social Accountability International and SustainAbility keep rolling in. Chiquita also won activist Rainforest Alliance's first Sustainable Standard-Setter Green Globe Award.

lic eye. "Of course, it did not hurt us with the media that Bianca was working with Amazon Watch and already on board," says Alpern. "Bianca was great— just a total and complete professional."

Shareholder Resolutions: There's Nothing Like Them

"I've had CEOs of *Fortune* 500 companies tell me that they get pressure from all kinds of sources," says Co-op America's Gravitz. "But when the investors get involved they know the issue is not going to go away."

Corporations have ways of getting rid of annoying factors, Gravitz tells me. Bad publicity? Well, stories don't last *that* long. After a while, folks tend to get excited about some new issue and forget to follow up.

Consumer rage? You can usually soothe that with some nice coupons.

But investors never leave you alone. Proxy resolutions, as noted, only need win a small percentage of votes to be reintroduced. So, even though a resolution fails, the activists are "back again next year."

Squeaky Clean versus "Dirty" and Rad?

Different points of view, my friend Cliff Feigenbaum says, are what makes the SRI community go 'round. *Green Money Journal* serves a marketplace of ideas, a forum for SRI types to debate the issues because, says Cliff, "we're often too afraid of offending each other."

In spring 2003, one prominent environmentalist, an advocate of "clean" portfolios, criticized Amy Domini for owning McDonald's, whom Domini has quietly and successfully lobbied to adopt better policies. Feigenbaum believes the Screen vs. Advocacy controversy mirrors SRI's growth and maturation. "In some ways, you could argue that there is not enough advocacy in our community," says Cliff. "That's a danger. If we won't own the advocacy side, we have no voice."

Visionary to Mainstream: The Demographics of Transformation

You already know two reasons why capitalism is in for sweeping change: (1) Personal spirituality, having hit critical mass, is spilling into corporations; and (2) The crisis of capitalism calls out for a new ideology.

These two megatrends, the Power of Spirit and the Rise of Conscious Capitalism, are converging to transform free enterprise. But they might never succeed without one more factor:

3) The demographics of business are changing dramatically.

The Ranks of Conscious Capitalists

Who are today's business people? An executive elite (and an army of yuppies) whose sole passion is lucrative salaries, hefty bonuses and surging earnings per share by any means necessary?

Okay, I admit that it sometimes *seems* that way. But is it the truth?

Of course not. Millions of us passionately embrace vision and values. We demand meaningful work in companies that contribute to society. Who are "we"? A dynamic mix of "ordinary" managers, small-business people, change agents, innovators, activists, socially responsible investors, women entrepreneurs—as well as visionary CEOs and executives.

Yet we're almost invisible in the world according to CNBC and *The Wall Street Journal.* Well, we won't be for long. People like us, once considered "visionary," have moved into the mainstream.

We are the individuals who made *Fast Company* the fastest-growing business magazine in history. After only seven years, it boasted 725,000 subscribers and 3.2 million readers. It took *BusinessWeek* 41 years, *Fortune* 62 years and *Forbes* 67 years to reach that level of readership.

Fast Company's mission states: "We believe that work isn't simply a paycheck; it is the ultimate expression of a fully realized self. We believe that a company's obligations extend far beyond its bottom line and its shareholders—to a wider constituency that includes employees, customers, suppliers and the community."

Millions of us—managers, investors, consumers—are lining up behind that vision—and we are transforming business.

Cultural Creatives versus "Business" Creatives?

Remember the "Cultural Creatives" from chapter one, the 50 million people—more than 26 percent of Americans—who'll be the dominant culture in five to ten years? Well, listen to this.

Fifteen million of them are either managers or professionals, *Cultural Creatives* **author Paul Ray told an audioconference hosted by the Wisdom Business Network.**

Cultural Creatives are the cutting edge of business transformation.

But that's not the whole story. Ray's "Moderns" cohorts, you will recall, are the folks who emphasize money, status and success and epitomize big business. Nevertheless, many are growing disillusioned with those values and they're defecting to the Cultural Creative side in droves.

Twenty million Moderns are "very close" to being Cultural Creatives, says *Cultural Creatives* **co-author Sherry Anderson.**

You can't fight demographics. According to Anderson's and Ray's analysis, there are:

- 15 million business and professional Cultural Creatives.
- 20 million Modernist sympathizers.
- 35 million Cultural Creatives who aren't managers/professionals but *are* consumers and investors.

That's 70 million people who in one way or another are actively transforming capitalism from a system where corrupt CEOs and greedy shareholders call the shots to a new world where free markets thrive while honoring all stakeholders in the name of enlightened self-interest.

As Conscious Capitalism transmutes mainstream business, we stand on the shoulders of some great thinkers and doers. Consider the work of the multi-talented Paul Hawken, founder of Smith & Hawken, the garden and catalogue retailer, host of the PBS series "Growing a Business" and an author whose work has changed the world—and its leaders.

"It was like a spear to my heart," said Ray Anderson, chairman of Interface, the carpet tile maker, when he read Hawken's *The Ecology of Commerce: A Declaration of Sustainability* (HarperBusiness, 1993).

I was in the audience at the 2003 Consciousness in Business conference when Anderson told his story yet again and everyone felt the spiritual power of his commitment to an environmentally responsible company—no small feat for a petrochemical-intensive industry.

"Business people must either dedicate themselves to transforming commerce to a restorative undertaking, or march society to the undertaker," Hawken had written. Anderson's choice was clear.

Hawken later joined forces with Hunter and Amory Lovins, co-founders of the Rocky Mountain Institute, for another landmark work, *Natural Capitalism* (Little Brown, 1999), which envisioned a Green new world where four principles: (1) Radical Resource Productivity, (2) Biomimicry, (3) Service and Flow Economy and (4) Investing in Natural Capital generate prosperity while preserving the environment and eliminating waste.

Natural was the key word as these trailblazers—and others like Dr. Karl-Henrik Robert, founder of The Natural Step, which teaches corporations the

principles of sustainability—demonstrated the critical role business must play
if humanity is to resist the urge to destroy the planet.

Pioneers set the course; innovators stayed it.

Today, we are waking up in a new world where transformation and sustainability are no longer worthy options, but the only sure road ahead.

That's why business people are tuning in to a new wavelength.

Conscious Capitalism means we are becoming aware of the unbearable
price of an unconscious (not to mention illogical) philosophy that would
embrace "profit at any cost." The spiritual dimension of Conscious
Capitalism tells us that the answers to issues as ordinary as business problems
and as extraordinary as planetary survival lie in the Divine realm of
Consciousness and that spiritual practice is the most efficient way to attain
the frequencies where practical wisdom resides.

What Is Conscious Capitalism?

Let's summarize the characteristics of the emerging megatrend of
Conscious Capitalism. It is:

1. Bottom-up—a broad-based, grassroots movement pressing for greater
   accountability and integrity in business.
2. Top-down—espoused in hundreds of the world's leading corporations.
3. Prosperity-oriented—an engine of superior financial performance.
4. Investor-driven—attracting trillions into socially responsible funds, as
   you'll see in chapter seven.
5. Activist—a hotbed of advocacy from shareholder to environmental.
6. Demographic—reflecting of the changing human profile of business.
7. Consumerist—winning growing public support in the marketplace.
8. Spiritual—the real-world manifestation of the quest for transcendent values in business.

As that litany illustrates, Conscious Capitalism is a multi-dimensional
phenomenon. You might think of it as "stakeholder capitalism," or call it the
"Triple Bottom Line," but there's even more to it than that.

**Conscious Capitalism is the dynamic matrix of social, economic—and
spiritual—trends transforming free enterprise.**

3

Leading from the Middle

Who is blessed with the power to transform a company?

What is the driving force behind corporate success?

Conventional wisdom tells us it is the CEO. "In four years," gushes *Fortune*, "Lou Gerstner added more than $40 billion to IBM's market value."

Oh, really? All by himself? Of course not. Yet that is how Wall Street and the media depicted the world of commerce in the 1990s—the manic, speculative decade that exalted the mythology of the superstar CEO.

Everyone knows it takes an *entire* organization to build a company's value—whether measured in sales, earnings per share or market cap. What we still don't understand is what that simple truth means. So here it is:

Leadership does not reside solely in the hands of top executives.

Unelected leaders, the mavericks of middle management, create real change, says Jon Katzenbach, a 40-year veteran of McKinsey & Company, noted author of numerous books including *Peak Performance* (Harvard Business School Press, 2000) and founder of Katzenbach Partners, LLC. Technically skilled and people oriented, these "change leaders," as Katzenbach calls them, are flexible, results-crazy, master motivators and willing to break rules. They are between 25 and 40 years old. One third are women.

"For large-scale transformations, you need a critical mass of change leaders in the middle of the organization," says Katzenbach.

As we stumble through the decade of the "double 0's," a new breed of spiritual leader is living the reality of Katzenbach's astute findings. The stock of the charismatic—and I use the term in the secular sense—CEO is falling and, as this chapter will illustrate, a new star is blazing across the corporate heavens. Business's latest hero—and perhaps its most unlikely—is the honest, hard-working manager.

The Wise CEO

When markets plunged and trillions vanished after widespread accounting scandals, investors and the public wanted to know: Where were the CEOs who stood up and said: "We're not playing this game. It's wrong."

I know at least one. Bill George, retired CEO of Medtronic, insisted his company's mission was not to kiss up to Wall Street, but to serve customers. In Medtronic's case, the ultimate customer was the patient. "If we take care of patients," he said repeatedly, "profits will take care of themselves." At Medtronic, they certainly did. Profits averaged more than 20 percent per year for over a decade.

Sadly, few of his CEO colleagues possessed George's wisdom—rooted as much in the grounding perspective of his spiritual practice (see chapter one) as in his considerable executive skills.

But even a dynamic CEO anchored in the power of Spirit would be hard pressed to single-handedly turn a company around. True leadership is a function of the spiritual energy of co-creation—the energetic dance between top executives and day-to-day managers.

The spiritual power of leadership lies in the act of co-creation.

Top executives source the directive blueprint, but managers and team leaders figure out the nuts and bolts ways to carry it out. Both require initiative, creativity and leadership. It's not a simple back and forth, either, but a spiraling energy exchange. Unfortunately, business often forgets how critical managers really are.

Today, at last, our understanding of the role "ordinary" managers play in corporate transformation has taken a giant step forward.

This chapter describes two complementary trends in leadership—the decline and fall of the celebrity CEO and the emergence of grassroots corporate leaders. Together these changing directions lay the groundwork for a massive power shift. It is upon the lines of this new managerial grid that Conscious Capitalism will flourish.

A New Take on Leadership

We stand at the cusp of a massive shift in corporate consciousness. The future of capitalism—and prosperity—depends on it. At the heart of this sea change lies a fresh mind-set on leadership—an approach that's natural, inspiring, life affirming and already "up and running" in companies near you.

The new take on leadership asks the revolutionary question: What if today's most effective business leaders were not prominent CEOs or swash-buckling entrepreneurs but modest, dedicated managers who, without fanfare and far from the limelight, quietly do the right thing for themselves, their colleagues and their corporations?

You won't read about this trend on the pages of *Fortune* or *BusinessWeek* or hear its praises sung on CNBC. But there's growing consensus that a new and potent brand of managerial power quietly threads through thousands of companies, changing them—and us—for the better.

You might call it the triumph of character over charisma.

What does it mean for *you?* It means that it is high time for grassroots managers; spiritual leaders; middle managers; the rank and file; change agents; doers; practical gadflies; savvy, bottom-up co-conspirators; team leaders; women executives; entrepreneurs; consultants; activists and executive coaches to step up out of the shadows and embrace the not-so-secret mission to transform capitalism.

But if we as managers sincerely choose to assume responsibility, we must first slay a couple of dragons. First, we've got to break the spell of top-down power. Next, we must reject the excuses that thwart our own success: "What can I do? I'm not in charge—well, just my little old department."

The error we're making here is to think that the only way to exercise leadership is through the formal authority vested in a position of power—CEO, U.S. Senator or Marketing VP.

It is time we got initiated into the unique, special power of informal authority.

The Call to Informal Leadership

Our guide is my friend Ron Heifetz, who teaches at Harvard's John F. Kennedy School of Government. In *Leadership without Easy Answers* (Belknap/Harvard University Press, 1994), he analyzes the difference between formal and informal authority and, drawing from examples of leaders like Martin Luther King Jr., Margaret Sanger and Mohandas K. Gandhi (called Mahatma, or "Great Soul," by his people), persuades us that informal authority holds some distinct advantages over formal authority.

What is informal authority? As I read Heifetz, it is the power granted to grassroots leaders by their peers—and later by others. What does it look like? You know those workshops where you end up in a group of, say, four or five people? Remember what happened? Heifetz says that social scientists who study small groups, and assign a leader, report that people pretty much ignore the appointed leader and swiftly pick their own instead!—the informal leader. The group then:

- orients itself toward the new leader,
- expects him or her to "direct attention to the tasks and its themes,"
- increases in cohesion once he or she is on the job.

So, as the scientists observe, informal authority arises out of the "respect, trust, admiration, popularity, even fear" of one's colleagues.

You don't need a lab experiment to figure *this* out, however. This same scenario plays out in offices all around the world. Management experts urge corporate leaders to seek out these informal leaders and the networks they influence. But corporate hierarchies rarely follow through on the idea. Why? Perhaps because the mainstream is uneasy about grassroots leaders, who are often viewed as mavericks who, says Heifetz, can see through "the blind spots of the dominant viewpoint." That kind of vision of course would be an enormous advantage to the system.

So, do organizations seek it out? Rarely.

The Advantages of Informal Leadership

Heifetz describes three benefits of informal (versus formal) leadership. For each benefit Heifetz lists, I offer an example of how corporate change leader Barbara Waugh, whom you'll soon meet, has acted on the principle.

Latitude for creative deviance. Consider Martin Luther King and the civil rights movement. By staging demonstrations, defying racist laws and enduring imprisonment, Dr. King dramatized the injustice he sought to expose. On the corporate front, when Hewlett-Packard blocked domestic partner benefits, Barbara Waugh staged a "Greek tragedy" to dramatize the unfairness of HP's position (you'll read the full story later).

Single issue focus. Informal leaders have the luxury of focusing on their top priority. Dr. King had one passion—civil rights. Lyndon Johnson had to manage Vietnam, the economy and Congress. Similarly, while former HP CEO Carly Fiorina juggled shareholder wars, Q3 earnings and Dell's market share, Barbara Waugh, founder of HP's e-Inclusion project, took time to ponder the limits of technology in much of the Third World.

Proximity to the frontline. Informal leaders are close to the "detailed experience of the stakeholders in a situation," says Heifetz. When Gandhi returned to India in 1915 after 20 years of activism in South Africa, he could have found a leadership post. Instead he went to small villages and learned his people's values, prejudices and the "ingrained habits of servitude and poverty." Dr. King knew the fear, rage and humiliation of black people in America. Neither the British authorities nor the U.S. government could fathom these realities. Before HP even formulated an environmental policy, Barbara Waugh had organized HP's bottom-up sustainability advocates into a potent network.

Heifetz argues that we can't discuss leadership without reference to values. He asks, what if the true measure of a leader were not how successfully he or she influenced a community or an organization to follow his or her vision, but how well the leader got people to face and resolve their problems—which requires difficult changes in values, beliefs or behavior.

That of course is what a lot of grassroots activists are up to. The activists you read about in chapter two, for example, repeatedly hold up the mirror and try to get all of us to see the high cost of "unconscious" capitalism.

The Corporate Activist

"We've been blinded by the image of the heroic CEO," says Hewlett-Packard's Barbara Waugh, who's known as HP's in-house revolutionary. "But," she told a Spirit in business group who grumbled that no CEOs were present, "100,000 employees each doing one small thing differently can shift a company as powerfully as any CEO."

Barbara, however, does not limit herself to small things. With the Grameen Bank, the world's greatest proponent of microlending, she co-founded HP's e-Inclusion initiative, whose radical mission is to bring technology and infrastructure to the world's poorest countries. Barbara Waugh is one of the world's leading corporate activists. You'll learn more about her inspiring activities later in this chapter.

As far as leadership goes, CEOs often run their own tapes, which feature their own pet excuses: "This place has a mind of its own. You'd be surprised how little control I have around here."

Well, maybe they have a point.

Six Reasons CEOs Are in Trouble

Yesterday's larger-than-life CEO is under fire everywhere. Arrogance. Misuse of power. Ego. Cashing out—and worse. To the dismay of honest leaders everywhere, today's CEOs are painted with the same broad—and tarnished—brush.

1. A Matter of Integrity

Did you hear about the next "reality" TV show?

America's Sleaziest CEOs.

Sadly, when bad boys like Misters Rigas, Skillings and Kozlowski turn up in the sordid headlines, the good name of every CEO suffers. In the United States, only 51 percent of employees have trust and confidence in senior management, reports a Watson Wyatt survey, "Work 2004/2005." Not surprisingly, corporate titans fare poorly with the public at large. A 2002 Pew Forum survey found Americans now think more highly of Washington politicians than business executives.

Ouch.

After new scandals at AIG, Merck and Fannie Mae, it's a good bet the politicos are still ahead.

2. The Decline and Fall of the Superstar CEO

Bestselling author Jim Collins of *Built to Last* and *Good to Great* fame (HarperBusiness, 1994 and 2001) debunks the myth of the heroic super-CEO in favor of the glamourless path of hard work and steady growth. "The CEO is important," says Collins, "but just a piece of a much larger puzzle."

Harvard Business School's Rakesh Khurana agrees, warning: "It's so much easier to take complex events and reduce them to an individual."

Look at Ed Breen, the hands-on executive who succeeded Dennis Kozlowski at Tyco. Breen, the former president and COO at Motorola, rolled up his sleeves and set about the daunting task of restoring Tyco's credibility. How'd he do it? Well, it was more a case of courage and hard work than style or pizzazz. In addition to many other moves, Breen:

- replaced Tyco's entire board of directors and executive team,
- relocated Tyco's fancy Manhattan headquarters to an office park in West Windsor, New Jersey,
- renegotiated lower prices for phone bills and other overhead items.

Shareholders have repaid Breen with their confidence. Tyco stock, at around $8 when Breen came on board in July 2002, climbed straight up, trading at around $30 in late December 2006.

"The market wants anti-heroes," says Neil Scarth, manager of hedge fund Symmetry Management.

"I'm always looking for people who aren't too promotional," adds Bob Olstein, chairman and founder of the Olstein Financial Alert Fund.

3. Performance Anxiety

At the crux of today's corporate power shift is a surprising new answer to an oft-asked business question: How much do CEOs actually influence a company's stock price?

Not as much as we thought, it turns out. The research shows CEOs don't impact share value any more than "overall industry conditions or the economic climate," conclude two studies cited in *Fortune*. Margarethe Wiersema, a management professor from the University of California at Irvine, examined 83 new CEOs, 40 percent of whom were brought in to turn the company around. After two years, most presided over *declining* stock values.

Similarly, Constance Helfat at Dartmouth's Tuck School of Business found that CEOs promoted from within fare about as well as those recruited from the outside to shake things up.

So much for the Turnaround Specialist.

"The fundamentals of the company are far more important than the CEO," says Bob Olstein.

4. Merger Mania

But what do CEOs *really* obsess about? Mergers.

Surely, these high-profile deals are the bedrock of rising share value—for which the CEO can legitimately claim credit and success?

Well, not exactly. *BusinessWeek* scrutinized 21 big mergers consummated in spring 1998; 17 *failed* to reward shareholders.

"If CEOs had kept their checkbooks under lock and key and simply matched the stock market performance of their industry peers," concludes *BusinessWeek*, "shareholders would have been far better off."

That is tough talk.

(And as I read the *BusinessWeek* study, I cringed for one of my own business heroes. Then HP CEO Carly Fiorina had recently announced the Compaq merger. I felt sad when she was ousted in February 2005—and the merger topped the list of reasons why.)

When *BusinessWeek* in conjunction with Boston Consulting Group expanded the study to 302 big mergers from July 1, 1995, to August 31, 2001 (including the AOL Time Warner $166 billion mega-merger—or should we say mega-disaster?), it discovered that a shocking "61 percent of buyers *destroyed their own shareholders' wealth*." (Emphasis added.)

Destroyed shareholder wealth?

Conclusion? The minute you see a pair of CEOs approach the podium, advises the prestigious business weekly, *SELL.*

What *is* going on here?

Are investors like you and me to understand that CEOs are squandering their highly paid brain power to screw around with mergers, instead of more mundane duties—like running the company—*and* burning the value of our IRA accounts while they're at it?

It's enough to make you join the nearest network of shareholder activists.

Why, then, do CEOs get so pumped up over mergers? Here's *BusinessWeek*'s explanation: "In the 1990s, growth stocks dominated the market and investors clamored for companies with rising earnings per share. *One easy way to juice earnings was to buy other companies.*" (Emphasis added.)

Here we go again. The dark side of capitalism. Show us the money—this quarter—or we sell your stock short. The unsustainable, unrealistic goal of ever-growing profit. The refusal to patiently grow a company's value over the long haul.

In 2006, mergers were back in the news. Will the latest round be more successful?

At least one expert isn't betting on it. Patrick Gaughan, a professor of economics and finance at Fairleigh Dickinson University and the author of numerous books and articles on mergers, also does business valuations for mergers and acquisitions. His recent book, called *Mergers: What Can Go Wrong and How to Prevent It* (Wiley, 2005), describes high-profile mergers that became mega-billion-dollar flops. "As increasingly more companies look to mergers and acquisitions (M&As) as a source of new growth and income," reads Wiley's description of the new book, "there is an even greater chance that these M&As will go bad."

5. The Tenure Tempest

In response to trends like these, business dumped the stock of CEO superstars as fast as boards of directors could fire them. In 2002, captains of industry were abandoning ship—often walking the plank—at the rate of two a day, calculated *USA Today*. In May 2002 alone, 80 CEOs vanished, says outplacement firm Challenger, Grey and Christmas.

In 2005 the fire-the-CEO trend was back in full swing. By December 2006, CEO departures already surpassed the 2005 record, reports Challenger, Gray & Christmas, which counted 1,347 CEO departures through November 2006, compared with 1,322 in 2005.

In 2005, 15.3 percent of CEOs at the world's 2,500 largest public firms left office—70 percent higher than 10 years earlier, says a Booz Allen Hamilton study. A three-year study by Drake Beam Morin found 57 percent had a new CEO.

Meanwhile, who's minding the store? Good question.

6. CEO Compensation

But if we don't get leadership, it's not like we didn't pay for it. In the 1990s, employee pay rose 37 percent, corporate profits grew a healthy 114 percent, but CEO pay soared 570 percent.

There's no doubt about it: CEOs whose names are now synonymous with fraud got away with the fiduciary equivalent of murder. Over a three-year period, Tyco's Dennis Kozlowski rang out $240 million in stock options while Enron's Jeff Skillings pocketed $112 million in options.

Indeed, executive stock options are often cited as a primary cause of the 2001–2002 crisis in capitalism.

"Stock market capitalizations in the later part of the 1990s . . . engendered an outsized increase in opportunities for avarice," said retired Fed Chairman Alan Greenspan. "Too many corporate executives sought ways to 'harvest' some of those stock market gains."

Meanwhile, CEOs face public criticism over everything from sky-high salaries to outright mismanagement. No wonder many now question the CEO's role in the recent reign of corporate terror.

One prominent guru would severely limit CEO power.

John Bogle, 77, founder of The Vanguard Group, father of the first index fund, The Vanguard 500, and author of *The Battle for the Soul of Capitalism* (Yale University Press, 2005), says no CEO should sit as chairman of his or her board of directors—assigning that powerful post only to an outside director.

As usual, the visionary Mr. Bogle is way ahead of his peers.

Toward a Culture of Values

Where is business headed in the decade of the 00s? Which polestar will guide us? Let's return to the question that animates this walk through these economic and spiritual megatrends: Which philosophy should drive modern capitalism as we try to recover from a series of scandals? The financial affirmation of the 1990s was, "This company will show increasing profit quarter after quarter—and creatively, if need be." Have corporations really forsaken it?

One thing is certain. The myth of steady and predictable earnings growth is exactly what led CEOs astray and took us to the brink of economic disaster. So seductive was the siren song of endless booming growth that even small-time investors like you and me abandoned the spiritual values of Truth and Balance.

As the stock market bounces back, Wall Street is again pressing CEOs to deliver rising profits. What will stop companies from inventing clever new wrongdoing?

Reform and regulation will help, of course. But some are skeptical even of that. Listen to Larry Elliott and Richard Schroth, authors of *How Companies Lie: Why Enron Is Just the Tip of the Iceberg* (Three Rivers Press, 2002):

The "first line of defense" for companies, auditors, politicians and Wall Street, the authors argue, "is to placate investors by creating the illusion of reform—a lot of political talk followed by unenforceable rules.

"Managed mendacity systematically applied to the investing public," they continue, "has become the new science of publicly traded corporations."

Lest you think the authors are completely cynical, they also write: "Companies performing well for their investors do not need to lie."

The question is: Have we learned our lesson? Are we prepared to reclaim Truth and Balance? And to advocate a practical, sane philosophy that says: The wisest route to success is by fostering the long-term growth of an enterprise where profit is the natural, organic result?

It's the sort of stance a Bill George would cheer. Armed with this sensible wisdom, will business find the courage to stand up to Wall Street and proudly carve that liberating philosophy into corporate policy?

Values versus Compliance

In today's marketplace, the outward signs of change are clearly visible—waves of reform aimed at the wholesale cleanup of a corrupt and tired system. But top-down regulation cannot foster a culture of values. A culture of compliance, perhaps, but not a culture of values. Values rely on the spiritual dimension. If free markets are to thrive, ordinary investors—like you and me—must again trust business. That will not happen until we believe the culture and philosophy of business have transformed. And only people can create a shift in corporate consciousness.

All the system knows is how to survive. It *does not* know how to heal itself. But you and I do. We know the only way to save the patient is with an infusion of consciousness and values.

Truth and courage are born in people's hearts. Bottom up. Millions of managers would dearly love to manifest those values and this chapter begins to tell them how. The first step is to get clear about how results are created in business. And I've got just the guy to explain it.

The Great Corporate Leader Shift

Behind the disturbing findings on CEO compensation and merger mania, a quiet revolution is brewing in business. We are once again embracing the practical wisdom that reminds us the key to success in business is the ability to get things done (and I don't mean mergers). In whom, one might ask, is this precious capacity to be found?

You guessed it: "ordinary" managers and grassroots leaders.

What Is Execution?

Even the most dictatorial CEO will agree: Effective leadership depends on commitments from managers who run operations day to day. The power to get things done resides in *people.*

When Larry Bossidy, 71, the highly respected Honeywell chairman and CEO, now retired, sings in praise of "execution," as he does in his bestseller *Execution* (Crown, 2002) co-authored with Ram Charan, read the fine print. A lot of it is about clear, decisive communication with grassroots leaders. "People," says Bossidy, "are the link to execution culture."

My point exactly.

To bolster that link, Bossidy swears by old-fashioned rituals, like follow-up letters, to make sure everyone remembers what they agreed to. He's also big on no-nonsense performance appraisals and generous rewards for top achievers.

Little wonder Bossidy's first (of seven) essential CEO behavior is "Know your people and your business." And he brooks no complaints from CEOs too busy for such efforts. "I'm convinced one big reason all these CEOs get fired is they don't spend enough time on their job."

Amen.

What's Bossidy's advice to managers? "Even if you don't have the final call on things, execution has the same merit for you as it does for a sitting CEO. We're talking about getting things done. Where in business isn't that important?"

Sadly, business and the media forget that (1) managers, not CEOs, carry out the do-or-die task of execution; (2) the soul of execution is commitment, not compliance; and (3) commitment relies on the sacred power of contract.

If you've made it to chapter three, you and I already agree that many managers embody spiritual values. Larry Bossidy shows us how important they are in generating results. Are you willing now to entertain the notion that grassroots managers command the power to create lasting corporate change?

A New Kind of Hero

Consider this statement:

The leadership that millions of managers practice—quiet, modest, behind-the-scenes—is *more persuasive* and *more effective* than the bold, heroic leadership we associate with CEOs and other top leaders.

That's the wonderfully subversive verdict emerging today from the hallowed halls of top business schools. Two new voices out of Harvard and Stanford demolish the "Great Man" stereotype of leadership and lay the groundwork for a new theory—starring, not CEOs, but "ordinary" managers.

This is the intellectual framework we need to "lead from the middle."

The work of Stanford's Debra Meyerson, author of *Tempered Radicals* (Harvard Business School Press, 2001), and Harvard's Joseph Badaracco, author of *Leading Quietly: An Unorthodox Guide to Doing the Right Thing* (Harvard Business School Press, 2002), based on years of study and hundreds of interviews, will inspire and embolden spiritual leaders everywhere. Badaracco and Meyerson record the heroic deeds of "ordinary" people at every corporate level, whose small but important moral choices in the face of everyday dilemmas transform companies.

People like:

Martha Wiley,[3] the senior executive vice president who forges family-friendly work deals to help ease the way for young parents and diplomatically holds up the mirror to her sometimes sexist colleagues.

---

[3]Both authors change the names of the managers and their companies.

Rebecca Olson, M.D., the newly minted CEO who must juggle a board of insiders—and an executive rival embroiled in a nasty sexual harassment case—before she can roll up her sleeves and get down to business.

John Ziwak, the high-tech soccer dad who quietly but deliberately resists drop-of-a-hat travel, evening meetings and Saturday offsites.

This new take on leadership couldn't come at a better time. In the face of public outrage at CEO failure, it offers hope that the soul of leadership lies not in a powerful position or impressive job title but in the millions of conscious acts and daily choices that grow out of the character of a leader's soul.

As this cutting-edge notion gains traction, we'll finally dispense with long-standing leadership myths, discover how companies *really* evolve and accelerate the evolution of Conscious Capitalism.

The new business heroes, however, are practical visionaries. They embrace healthy self-interest, while steering clear of martyrdom and self-destruction. They do the right thing—yet keep their jobs. Elliot Cortez, for example, is a go-getter pharmaceutical marketing rep who smells an ethical no-no, yet consciously sorts through all his options. He wants to honor his conscience, protect patients—and still hopefully make his sales quota.

Badaracco's Quiet Heroes

Difficult problems are rarely resolved with a "swift, decisive stroke from someone at the top," argues Harvard's Joseph Badaracco, but by "careful, thoughtful, small, practical efforts" by ordinary people. Transformation can be a modest, tedious affair, he tells us.

Over a four-year period, Joseph Badaracco distilled 150 case studies into simple guidelines for would-be leaders, such as "Buy a Little Time" and "Bend the Rules" and "Nudge, Test, Escalate Gradually."

Badaracco's "Trust Mixed Motives" precept, for example, explodes the false dichotomy between self-interest and altruism. You need both, he says. "Would-be leaders need to draw strength from a multitude of motives—high and low, conscious and unconscious, altruistic and self-regarding," writes Badaracco. "The challenge is not to suppress self-interests, but to harness, channel, and direct them."

The unsung beauty of self-interest, he points out, is how it sustains you for the long haul—which is exactly what Badaracco's "quiet leadership" demands.

Pick your battles, common sense tells us. Badaracco adds a footnote. Pick an issue you *care* about. Deeply. Quiet leaders don't just think something is wrong. They *feel* it. That sort of passion prepares you, not for a "glorious cavalry charge," but for "a long guerilla war."

Quiet leaders, he says, practice restraint, modesty and tenacity.

Meyerson's Tempered Radicals

"Tempered radicals" do not see themselves as revolutionaries, says Debra Meyerson. Their tone is modest, their moves incremental. They believe patience, persistence and resourcefulness get the job done. Though successful, tempered radicals *resist* the status quo and skillfully navigate creative compromises, eventually playing a role as important as colleagues with more authority.

Peter Grant, an African American, senior executive and 30-year veteran of "Western Financial," for example, got a few minorities hired early in his career. Later, hundreds. After 30 years, he could count 3,500 minority candidates he directly or indirectly hired.

Meyerson's work is rooted in social theories of identity and difference. Tempered radicals have made it as insiders. But something about their identity—race, gender, sexual orientation or values—puts them at odds with the corporate majority—making them, in a sense, outsiders. By honoring both identity and difference, they challenge the status quo yet maintain their status.

"When something is 'tempered,' it is toughened," writes Meyerson. "Tempered steel . . . becomes stronger and more useful."

The ethical renewal of capitalism will not happen by top-down fiat—no matter how many reforms and regulations Congress, the NYSE or any other body legislates. It will be forged in the hearts and minds of everyday businesspeople. The job of spiritual leaders is the massive infusion of consciousness and values system-wide, with or without the imprimatur of The Powers That Be. This chapter sets forth an intellectual context for the moral leadership that will save free markets and transform capitalism.

In the tumultuous "00s" decade, business will finally accept the truth: that leadership isn't confined to the top of the managerial pyramid but is dispersed throughout a company—in competent people at every level. The lesson for spiritual leaders is: You are the leader you always wanted to follow. Start leading by example.

Profiles in Commitment: Grassroots Leadership

January 2003. I'm in Santa Fe, New Mexico, keynoting the Business and Consciousness Conference and there is someone here I'm just dying to meet.

I stand by the elevator. No name tags yet. We register tomorrow. A woman strolls up. She looks nothing like her photo. But I sense it *must* be her.

"Barbara?" I venture. "Barbara Waugh?" She gathers me in a big hug.

Barbara Waugh, a 20-year veteran of tech giant Hewlett-Packard, is a legendary corporate change agent. She sets the benchmark in grassroots activism, in part because Barb's pre-HP career in civil rights, the peace and women's movements and street theater—not to mention a one-night stand as Angela Davis's bodyguard—built up a fine arsenal of tools for spiritual leaders.

And Barbara has taken every one of them inside Corporate America.

"I am Hewlett-Packard employee #210834. I can't believe it. I'm inside." On the first page of Barbara's book *Soul in the Computer* (Inner Ocean, 2001), you know you're in for a good, fast-paced read. Barb is partial to the present tense and to vivid, sparse prose. "Christopher Shockey of HP, who is six-feet, seven-inches tall and who just cut off his pony tail, is an organic farmer."

Barbara advocates what she calls "radical tools and change principles." I've put some of her best precepts to work as this section's subheads.

Amplify Positive Deviance

Barbara is a woman of emotion and fight and not a drop of arrogance. The result? People bond with her almost immediately. They drop by her cubicle, share their deep dark secrets, break down in tears—then sign up for, as Barb puts it, her latest "cockamamie" scheme.

When HP scraps benefits for domestic partners, an outraged Barbara collects stories from HP's gays, lesbians and their straight friends, and weaves their powerful words into a "Readers Theater"—complete with a Greek chorus chanting the names of the trailblazing corporations who already offer domestic-partner benefits. So successful is Barb's corporate drama, the actors "play" the CEO's office and on down the chain of command. And what a run: 60 performances in six months.

Oh yes—and HP's domestic partners *do* win their benefits.

Tap the Strength of Your Relationships

Barbara coaches "quiet leaders" like Tan—the brilliant engineer and former Vietnamese boat person who's trying to help the orphanage back home, except his money keeps getting ripped off along the way—to take more risks. Like approaching his boss, Stan, and asking him to fund Tan's work to dream up high-tech tools for safe money transfers to developing countries.

Tan and Stan do lunch at a certain noodle shop (that's a sweet part of the story) and Stan agrees to fund 10 percent of Tan's time.

Make Impossible Requests

Actually, Barb does *not* list "make impossible requests" as a radical tool, but that doesn't stop her from doing it. Fully expecting to be shot down, she asks the "bigwigs": Why are HP's strategic off-site (versus in-house) meetings just for top execs? To her surprise, they reply, in effect, good point. If the security issues can be worked out, they tell Barbara, the next off-site will be broadcast on the Web and anyone at HP Labs can participate.

Lots of people do and the culture of HP Labs starts "a-changin'."

Back in Santa Fe, Barb and I wander through the Plaza to Pasquale's, Santa Fe's finest funky restaurant. We order piles of gorgeous food, sharing all of it. We chat about life and family—Barbara and her life partner, Anastasia Cusulos, have adopted two African-American children. I happily discover Barbara the Activist is not above girl talk. She admires my purple velvet cape; I am crazy about her colorful, primitive necklace.

Strolling back to the hotel, she confides the story of her dear friend—the activist Lahe'ena'e Gay—who was murdered in Colombia while helping the Uw'a people build schools. The next day, at the workshop Barbara is about to give, she asks me to sit beside her. "I need your strength," she whispers.

My strength?

After all Barbara has endured and accomplished, it is clear to me who the "strong" one is, but at this moment it is the gentleness of Barbara's request that touches me most.

Turn Enemies into Allies

I'm delighted when Barb tells tales on herself. Like breaking her own sacred rule against stereotypes. Someone suggests she enlist the help of a coworker, Rolf, a musician. "I groan inwardly. Rolf is a physicist at HP Labs and I have consigned Rolf to my nerd bucket: very bright, distant, sarcastic, cynical and unavailable for anything I'd ever think of."

Still, she asks for Rolf's help. He refuses, but offers a tape of his music, which Barb pops into the car stereo on the way home. It is so beautiful, she says, "I almost drive off the road." Rolf and Barbara bond and he becomes one of her co-conspirators.

Reframe the Context of What You're Doing

After a few years, Barbara is really cooking. She designs a conference to round up HP's in-house "sustainability advocates." In isolation, these environmentalists are impotent, she says, just tokens. En masse, they're a minority to be reckoned with. Trouble is, once the conclave gets organized, an order comes down from on high: all conferences are canceled. . . .

Except customer visits.

Fortunately Barb's keynote speaker is a VP from treasured client 3M. Whew!

So Barbara "reframes" the get-together as a customer visit and nobody objects. Result: 150 people from all over the globe meet for three days and a potent "minority" goes home inspired that their cause is vital to HP's making a difference in the world.

Remember Whom You Work For

Barbara says her mission is supporting people to "make their dreams come true." Senior scientist Sid Liebes, who's just shy of retirement, has, for 27 years, dreamed of creating what he calls a "One Mile Walk through Time," depicting the evolution of human life—including today's clear and present danger to the environment.

Barbara finds money to fund the initial costs and soon 100 employees, drawing on HP's state-of-the art printing tech, churn out 3-by-5-foot posters. But now "corporate" is freaking out. Hey, what are you doing? they protest. HP hasn't even taken an official position on the environment yet.

Barbara is devastated. How could such a fantastic project fail? She collapses in bed at the end of a long, frustrating day and turns to God. "You figure out how to handle this," she implores and mercifully falls asleep. Remember Whom You Work For. At 4 A.M., she jumps up with a solution.

"This isn't a *content* statement," she announces the next day at work. "The Walk through Time is the *context* in which we should ask our greatest business questions." Corporate backs off. Sid's project is a smash success.

Be the Change You Want to See

I see Barbara as a commanding leader, but Barb the character in her own book is touchingly human—at times, nervous, self-deprecating, tearful, bold, funny—and always blown away by the commitment of coworkers she initially dismisses. Time and time again, nerdy guys and vanilla company women prove to be her greatest allies. Why do they come out of the spiritual closet at work? Because Barbara embodies the Love that supports them to speak their truth.

That is exactly what you and I are going to do.

Grassroots Leadership: An Invitation

I've set out for you where CEOs took a wrong turn, lost our respect and destroyed their stature. You've discovered the new management trend put forth by pioneering academics from Harvard and Stanford. And you've met Barbara Waugh, one of the world's most inspiring corporate activists.

Now it's time to introduce you to the greatest corporate leader you'll ever meet. Your one true soulmate in the daunting quest to transform capitalism: the leader within *you*.

This book chronicles the megatrends that set the stage for that metamorphosis, but without managers like you, capitalism may never become fully consciousness. The question is will you join the crusade?

There have been several major social drives since the 1950s. Civil rights, the peace, women's and environmental movements. Each has earned the right to claim great success. So will the drive for Conscious Capitalism.

BE: Come from a Deeper Place

I hope we who align ourselves with Spirit are strong enough to drop the familiar "us against them" attack mode. Instead of playing the blame game, Spirit invites us to BE the change we want to see happen. To embody the value we cherish most, be it Justice, Compassion or Truth.

But don't stop there.

Take the next step. Shift from Being into Doing. Launch your initiative. This is business, not the monastery. Execute. Make Larry Bossidy proud. Just remember, so long as you are coming from the realm of Being, you will not perpetuate "business as usual." Whatever you do, it carries transformative power, because it comes from your Being and is nurtured by the values you hold dear.

Personify the value that inspires you. Initiate the actions that express your truth. And you'll create the success that's emblematic of your soul.

DO: An Options Menu

What can you *do*? How do you get started? Your next brainstorm might be entrepreneurial, inspirational, managerial, spiritual or educational:

- Start a corporate meditation class.
- Install a hot line for ethical violations.
- Institute a moment of silence in meetings.
- Remind everyone about the company's stated values and mission.
- Launch a corporate book club—starting with books cited in this chapter.
- Speak out at a meeting.
- Grant an award.
- Sponsor an event.

- Host a journaling workshop.
- Bring in an inspiring speaker.
- Tell a story.
- Reward a colleague.
- Humanize a robotic process.
- Cut costs, not service.

Sacred Space

We live in a time of economic crisis and great spiritual opportunity.

This is the moment you and I have been waiting for.

Because of the trends described throughout this book, business has reached a critical inflection point. The system is now more open to creative input, that is, to the medicine grassroots leaders offer: Values and Consciousness. It is time to flood business with these precious, intangible energies.

How?

I hope the options list above gets you started, but it is hardly exhaustive.

We will come up with a billion ways to tweak the system, inspire our colleagues and touch the place in them that only gets off on service and contribution.

But if that cynical voice inside you calls my options menu "superficial window dressing that doesn't change anything," go ahead and thank it for sharing. It's right in a way. That's how it *has* been. You have to give it that.

But so what?

Do it anyway. Because *your* actions arise from a more authentic place— from the patient, quiet depths of leadership that Meyerson, Badaracco and Heifetz speak of. You are in it for the long haul.

How again do we flood the system with fresh consciousness?

I remember the early days of the women's movement, when five, seven or ten women came together to "raise consciousness." But when you broke it down, we really showed up at the local women's group for two simple reasons: (1) To speak our truth and (2) to bear witness to the truth of another. That second step was critical. In bearing witness, we *validated* each other. We coached each other to *feel* the truth of our power. What if thousands of managers today were to convene "circles of consciousness," informal but regular gatherings, perhaps a coffee or a brown bag, to talk about consciousness and values in business?

These get-togethers might begin with four simple questions:

1. What are my values?

2. What are the values of this company or department?

3. Where are we true to those values?

4. Where are we false?

Or, if you prefer, have no agenda at all. Just speak from your heart and allow a topic to emerge. That is exactly what the group you'll meet next does. The result is Sacred Space, which invokes Spirit to create a place where Truth is spoken and heard.

4

Spirituality in Business

Deep in the heart of San Francisco's bustling financial district, it's time for lunch. Bankers dodge the traffic and head to Chinatown, while junior analysts flood the corner cafe for carry-out. But over on Montgomery Street, up in the 12th-floor office of a national organization whose very name is synonymous with American capitalism, you can hear a pin drop.

Here in the boardroom, 14 kindred spirits—a rainbow of ages and ethnicities—surround a massive conference table, their heads gently bowed in a moment of silence. Debra Mugnani Monroe, president of Monroe Personnel Services and one of the circle's leaders, recognizes a few of the regulars: Allison, a 40-ish marketing maven, helped produce the Emmies. Max, 34, is an engineer from dot-com Snapfish. Catherine, 31, advises clients on socially responsible investing. Monroe lights a candle and the strain and worry of the morning begin to melt away.

Public affairs consultant Sarah Q. Hargrave, a former marketing and public affairs executive at Sears Corporate Headquarters and VP at Northern Trust, who cofounded the group with Monroe, hands the trusty talking stick to the Asian man on her left, a 50-something CPA, and invites him to talk about any work or spiritual issue that's "up" for him.

"How do you deal with a culture," he begins quietly, "that's focused only on the numbers and financial results?" One by one, people open up and there's a growing sense of trust and support. Before the hour is over, they will speak their truth, find fresh new insights or offer each other heartfelt advice.

Welcome to the San Francisco Chamber of Commerce's "Spirit at

Work—A Continuing Conversation" brown bag lunch, the monthly get-together that has flourished—during boom times and bust—for more than eight years. Here in one of free enterprise's most important financial hubs, amidst the grinding stress of daily business, people are evoking Divine Presence and creating Sacred Space.

Over the years, well over one thousand people, from administrative assistants to CEOs, have turned to the Chamber brown bag for spiritual sustenance. They are Indian, Caucasian, Middle Eastern, African-American, Vietnamese and Chinese. Bankers, accountants, public relations experts, high-tech guys and executive coaches.

"There are places you can go to talk about 'being spiritual,'" says Sarah Hargrave, "and places you can go to talk about business. But here you get to do *both.*"

We'll return to the Chamber brown bag later in this chapter to discover what it is that brings people back year after year.

Spirit in Business: The Movement; the Megatrend

Spirituality in business, having quietly blossomed for decades, is an established trend that's about to morph into a megatrend.

In true megatrend fashion, Spirit in business is popping up across many geographic regions, as evidenced by recent local headlines.

- "Dallas-based International Organization Offers Spiritual Aid in the Workplace" reports the Fort Worth *Star-Telegram* in 2004.
- "Faithful Are Carving a Niche in the Workplace," reads a 2005 *Los Angeles Times* story.
- "Visibility of Religious Beliefs Grows in Workplace," says the *Charlotte [North Carolina] Observer* in 2005.

In Boston, a secret, invitation-only ecumenical prayer breakfast for top executives is called "First Tuesday." New York's Fifth Avenue Presbyterian Church offered a Faith@Work lecture series. In Minneapolis, 150 business leaders lunch monthly and hear leaders like Carlson Companies CEO Marilyn Carlson Nelson speak on topics like how the Bible guides their business decisions.

In Chicago, some 60 mostly Catholic executives, members of Business Leaders for Excellence, Ethics and Justice (BEEJ), have met for more than a decade to break bread and ponder the sacred and secular sides of work. Bill Yacullo, president of Chicago-area recruiting firm Lauer, Sbarbaro Associates and cofounder of BEEJ, says the group nourishes his spiritual life and helps him be more honest and confident with his clients.

The grassroots appeal of Spirit in business is undeniable. Half of us talked about faith at work in the past 24 hours, reports a Gallup poll. New York's High Tor Alliance, in a study entitled "Applied Contemplative Disciplines in Work and Organizational Life" for the Fetzer Institute and the Nathan Cummings Foundation, found that 81 percent of respondents use individual practices like prayer, silence or meditation on the job.

"The line between business and spiritual life is becoming increasingly blurred," concludes the *Times* of London.

That's for sure. Consider the following:

In the thick of negotiations to purchase New Age ice cream maker Ben & Jerry's, Terry Mollner, a founder of the Calvert Social Investment Funds—who is trying to buy the company—calls a time out. At this point people are ready to give up, walk out and end the discussion over a deal breaker issue. Mollner invites the table of tense, polarized people to be silent for a few moments and suggests that everyone ask themselves, "What is the truth here? What is the highest good for all?" He then opens the floor to anyone to speak. One by one people lean forward and restate their position in a way that accommodates the other side. The negotiations move forward. Mollner repeats the ritual three times during weeks of negotiations, each time achieving the same breakthrough.

"The present spiritual movement is probably the most significant trend in management since the human potential movement of the 50s," says Paul T. P. Wong, Ph.D., a professor at Trinity Western University in British Columbia and president of the International Network on Personal Meaning. And the numbers seem to back up Wong's assertion.

A few years ago, there were a "couple hundred" nonprofits devoted to spirituality or faith in the workplace, says David Miller, executive director of Yale University Center for Faith and Culture, and author of *God at Work* (Oxford University Press, 2006). By 2006, it was at least 1,500. Are Miller's "faith"-oriented nonprofits about religion or spirituality at work?

Let's review my take on each. Religion is the formal, institution-based, denominational worship of God. Spirituality is the more personal and universal experience of the Divine, the Sacred, in one's life.

"For a corporate organization to become successfully faith-friendly, it cannot promote a specific religion," writes Susan Gonzalez in a story about

Miller's Center for Faith and Culture at Yale. "Instead it must provide a setting in which people of every faith—as well as people who have no particular faith—can feel comfortable."

Well said. But as the following list illustrates, it sometimes *looks* as if both spirituality and religion have arrived in business.

- Colorado's Sounds True, an audio, video, book and music publisher listing 750 inspiring titles, honors the Sacred with group meditations, a moment of silence before each meeting and a meditation room.
- Ford, American Airlines, Texas Instruments and Intel support employee religious groups.
- Weekly department meetings at Saint Francis Health Center in Kansas spend 30 minutes in reflection and 30 minutes in dialogue about spiritual issues in management.
- The Billy Graham Evangelistic Association is training people for workplace ministries. In 2004, it ran its first leadership forum in Asheville, North Carolina.
- At Calcutta, India's SREI International Financial Limited, there is a temple in the main lobby and altar space for work teams.
- Charlotte, North Carolina's Coca-Cola Bottling Co. recognizes that "employees have a body, mind and soul." It offers corporate chaplains and a mission statement that "honors God."
- At HomeBanc Mortgage, which won a seat on *Fortune*'s "100 Best Companies to Work For" list, CEO Patrick Flood opens conference calls with a prayer.

Typically, the spirituality in business movement speaks of Spirit as universal and non-denominational. Most people don't want overt piety in the workplace, says Gregory Pierce, author of *Spirituality@Work* (ACTA Publications, 2001) and president of the Chicago-area's ACTA Publications, a nine-person publishing firm. "I'm not going to pray over you before I sell you something," says Pierce. "I'm going to give you a good product at a good price and try to be as environmentally sound as I can be."

But the fact remains, most of the world's major religions are somehow linked to business or work life. You'll soon see how major U.S. companies like Intel and Ford juggle religion on the job, whether Muslim, Christian, Jewish or Hindu.

So, are we talking spirituality or religion at work?

The answer, like it or not, is probably both. In any event, there is often a fine line between the two.

Later in this chapter, you'll meet a former HR executive who says business *can* address the sometimes sticky issue of religion in the workplace with the same blueprint human resource people invoked to deal with diversity.

Meanwhile, there's no denying that it may be challenging to distinguish between spirituality and religion in business.

The Restoration Business

What's the meaning *behind* the Spirit in business trend? Simply this: It grows out of our desire to celebrate all of our Selves at work.

And that is a serious affront to business as we have known it.

We live in a world where Divine Presence is stripped from companies and work life, as if it didn't belong there. But Spirit dwells in all of us. And if you tear the Sacred from humanity, you rip out the heart.

So without a heart, how do you get the blood pumping? You provide a substitute. In the eyes of many, we've certainly found one. Business, it is said, worships the false god of money. Why else do we speak of the almighty dollar? But idolatry can trigger a lot of pain. Enron, WorldCom and the rest show us the shadow side of capitalism—the cost of barring Spirit from the boardroom and glorifying profit instead of Presence.

But even the crisis of capitalism holds a silver lining.

The corporate accounting scandals sent a karmic call out to millions of sleeper cells encoded with the spiritual mission of restoring Spirit, ethics and values to the marketplace of humanity.

One by one, we are waking up.

What business are you *really* in? That's a key question in strategic planning. When it comes to the Spirit in business movement, you might say we're in the restoration business. Our market niche is to reunite the Sacred with the human world of business and work.

"Most of us spend so much time working, it would be a shame if we couldn't find God there . . . ," says Gregory Pierce. "There is a creative energy in work that is somehow tied to God's creative energy."

Spirituality Goes to College

Academia is blessing the emerging megatrend with conferences, courses and new centers:

• At Harvard Business School, a 2003 student-led symposium challenged leaders to reembrace values and explore the bridges between spirituality and business.

- New Orleans' Loyola University boasts an Institute for Ethics and Spirituality in Business.
- Santa Clara University is a hotbed of Spirit in business activity.
- The Centre for Spirituality and the Workplace is housed in the Sobey School of Business at Saint Mary's University in Halifax, Nova Scotia.

Now even M.B.A. programs offer spiritual courses, reports *The Wall Street Journal:*

- Columbia University Business School's Srikumar Rao teaches "Creativity and Personal Mastery," in which students keep personal journals, attend a weekend retreat and "bare their souls" in class. Rao's course gets such rave reviews, Columbia runs a version for alums. "You need the work you do to express your values," says Rao, "and be of benefit to the larger society."
- At Stanford Grad School of Business, William "Scotty" McLennan, Dean for Religious Life, teaches "The Business World: Moral and Spiritual Inquiry through Literature." Among other books, students read *The Great Gatsby* and *Siddhartha* and share their own dreams and failures.
- Notre Dame's "Spirituality and Religion in the Workplace" class invites students to "look behind prestige and salary" and ask if a company is also a good moral and spiritual fit. Although Notre Dame is Catholic, the course draws from Jewish, Protestant and Buddhist sources. Like Columbia, Notre Dame offers a spirituality course to M.B.A. alums.

Spirituality was once taboo in business, admits Thierry Pauchant, the ethics chair at HEC Montreal Business School, but now, "People are suffering by not being able to address that (spiritual) part of themselves."

In fact, many business leaders actually welcome the Spirit in biz trend. Sixty percent of the executives and managers surveyed for the book *A Spiritual Audit of Corporate America* by Ian Mitroff and Elizabeth Denton (Jossey-Bass, 1999) acknowledge the benefits of Spirit at work, so long as it stays clear of imposing religion, says Mitroff, a University of Southern California School of Business professor.

Others agree—especially on the not imposing religion part.

"Folks who feel like they can bring their spiritual values to work," says Rev. Thomas Sullivan, spiritual director at Babson College, "are happier, more productive and stay longer." But, he adds, "we still don't want proselytizing pressure in the workplace."

Religious Networks at Ford, American Airlines, Intel

Before prayer, Muslims perform a ceremonial washing called "ablution," but what if you pray on your lunch hour? Muslim workers at Ford asked Ford's company-funded Interfaith Network for help—and got certain restroom sinks at the Product Development Center available for the ritual, reports a 2004 story in *Workforce Management.*

"We're particularly trying to make sure people feel that they don't have to leave their faith or personal beliefs at the door," says Daniel Dunnigan, a finance manager in the Marketing and Sales Controller's Office and the Network's chair. "The company acknowledges that is part of who they are."

Ford vetoed single faith networks. The Interfaith Network, however, represents eight religions: Catholics, Buddhists, Evangelicals, Hindus, Muslims, Jews, Mormons and mainstream Protestants. It sends a monthly electronic newsletter to 5,000 employees.

American Airlines approved a Christian employee group in 1995. By 1997 there were Jewish and Muslim networks. There's been "no difficulty" with the religious groups, says diversity director Sharyn Holley. American's Christian employees shipped 729 contemporary Christian music CDs to U.S. troops in Iraq.

Intel's Bible-Based Christian Group won company-paid trips to the 2004 Christian Games Developers Conference. Unlike good Christians, computer games are notoriously violent. So I was interested to read that Christian developers ask God to bless the industry—which sure needs it!

Marketplace Chaplains USA

Marketplace Chaplains USA, founded by ex-military chaplain Gil Stricklin in 1984, ministers to the spiritual needs of more than 100,000 employees in 43 states from California to Massachusetts. "Fifty percent of the workforce does not belong to any religious organization," says Stricklin, and 73 percent don't attend regular services. "They need someone to take care of them." That's what the organization's nearly 2,000 chaplains do.

Pilgrim's Pride, in Pittsburg, Texas, employs 43,000 people and is Marketplace Chaplains's biggest client. Says chairman Bo Pilgrim, "This is a third-party, private, independent source of help for them. If they want to talk about anything, they can consider it to be a private conversation."

Stricklin's chaplains are on call 24/7, 365 days a year.

Why Now?

Whenever a new social trend emerges, pundits, journalists and even the average Joe tend to ask: "Why?" I think the question really is: "Why *now?*" What factors are propelling this issue or that, straight into our collective faces?

This year. Today. Now.

You already know my candidate for the number one reason behind the spirituality in business trend, described at length in chapter one: The personal quest for Spirit has hit critical mass. To put it in blunt but spiritual terms, so many people have inhaled and grounded so much God Energy that they're moving beyond personal healing into mission and activism, be it in communities, government or business.

But there are many additional reasons. Here's a list of the powerful contributing factors I've collected from a host of interviews and articles.

The Quest for Meaning. You can be a complete atheist, yet still long for work that is fulfilling. Furthermore, the demographics of the baby boom tell us that more and more people are of an age when they seek more meaning. Successful folks who've enjoyed material comfort often conclude that it is no longer enough: Now they seek greater meaning in life.

Downsizing. Demoralized by layoffs, we reexamine our personal values—and question those of the company we once worked for.

Burnout. We burn out in the boom years; we burn out in the bust years. There is no letup. Layoff survivors are burdened with the added tasks of those let go, not to mention the worry that their heads will roll next. The result is, surprise, more stress. Next time you hear about those stellar U.S. productivity figures, consider the uncalculated costs of stress and burnout.

Accounting Scandals. These disgraceful crimes only confirmed what many have long suspected, that in business, virtue is too often overruled by short-term financial considerations—and the unchecked desire to win at any cost.

Terrorism and Workplace Violence. In troubled times like these, there's no way to check your soul at the office door. Disgruntled employees go on a rampage. The Bureau of Labor and Statistics says that in 2005 (the last year for which figures were available) there were 14,560 employee injuries from assault and 565 homicides. The Centers for Disease Control calls workplace violence a "national epidemic." Most of the people who lost their lives on September 11 were *working*.

Competition. "Downsizing, rapid growth, shortened production cycles and more competitors have brought many people pain—and in moments of pain, people often turn to metaphysics and God," says Yale's David Miller.

But enough with the trouble and pain, already. On the much more positive side, corporate leaders are finally beginning to get that to succeed in a competitive global marketplace, business must figure out how to tap into the creativity and innovation—in other words, the God power—within people.

That is exactly what the following company sets out to do.

Profiles in Commitment: High Tech/High Touch

Imagine a sizzling high tech firm where spiritual principles, values and consciousness are so seamlessly woven into the fabric of daily life that footprints of Spirit echo through communications, corporate change management, leadership development, training and wellness.

The company is TELUS Mobility, the 6,000 person, red-hot wireless division of TELUS Corporation, Canada's second largest telecom company. TELUS Corporation, the parent company, is an $8.5 billion corporation traded on the New York and Toronto exchanges. When TELUS Corporation reported a seven percent increase in 3rd quarter 2006 revenue, the company attributed the growth to the "continued strong wireless and data growth" that TELUS Mobility provided. TELUS Mobility counted 4.5 million subscribers in 2006.

For its devotion to technology and Spirit, TELUS Mobility epitomizes the principle of High Tech/high touch, which John Naisbitt and I talked about in *Megatrends*. The more technology we have in our lives, the more we need the countervailing balance of high touch. TELUS Mobility is so high touch that it also won the International Spirit at Work Award described later in this chapter.

Corporate Transformation

TELUS Mobility is a child of the tech/telecom boom—a time of mergers, acquisitions and countless failed attempts at integration. No wonder "Leading People through Change" is one of the firm's key themes.

What might surprise some business leaders, however, is the practical yet inspiring kit of spiritual tools TELUS Mobility has used to drive success.

Leading People through Change

One year after TELUS Mobility acquired Clearnet Communications in 2000, then-consultant Karen Goodfellow led 600 managers through the daunting task of integrating two different corporate cultures across two provinces. Her goal was simple yet challenging: to arm managers with the right tools to help their people manage change—while the managers themselves were simultaneously caught in the throes of chaos.

That definitely sounds like a job for Spirit.

From February to April 2001, the 600 managers (and later 1,600 employees) studied the spiritual tools of reflection and visualization, then explored the business applications of challenging universal principles like:

• What we resist, persists.
• The stronger our personal values, the more resilient we are in chaos.
• People who trigger us (especially our anger) may reflect the issues, or aspects of ourselves, that *we* might want to work on.
• No one wins until we all win.
• Strength through diversity.

TELUS Mobility's adventures in personal and corporate transformation were a huge hit. Participants rated the program an enthusiastic 4.44 out of 5.

The Power of Wellness

The Wellness Centre, a "place of sanctuary within the working day and workplace," is the heart of TELUS Mobility's spiritual side.

Why does the firm invest in wellness—or for that matter spirituality?

TELUS supports popular, spiritually based workshops to boost energy, decision-making ability, productivity, responsibility, reflection and self-esteem. But TELUS Mobility cites one more factor: Employee willingness to start a spiritual journey leads to better health—which cuts corporate health costs. From 1999 to 2000, the use of wellness services rose 47 percent, while the cost of prescription drugs and sick time *dropped* 16 percent.

Company-sponsored lunch and after-work courses, taught by instructors and employees, feature meditation, t'ai chi, yoga, stress management, flexibility and mental focus—as well as Latin dancing and self defense. In addition:

• "What Is Meditation?" introduces several types of meditation and describes the benefits of spiritual practice, deep breathing and visualization.
• "Unchain Your Brain" revives a commitment to fun, risk-taking and open communication.

• "What's Next in My Life?" is eight weeks of meditation, journaling and visualization to "re-image" where a person has been and where they want to go.

The Case for Alignment

The first spiritual concept to gain acceptance in business was vision, as in "what is this company's vision for the future?" A powerful vision inspires people and organizes priorities. Next came alignment: When individual goals are "aligned with" corporate goals, outstanding performance can result.

But too many companies try to persuade people that by subscribing to corporate objectives, they'll achieve "personal" goals—like being a team player or tough competitor. Few say, "Look, we'll support your personal growth and trust that some good will rub off on us." At TELUS Mobility, 80 percent of team members have a "Personal Development Plan."

Hundreds, maybe thousands, of corporations would enthusiastically sign up those Spirit in biz consultants if they understood, as TELUS Mobility does, the direct connection between spirituality and personal responsibility. Consider the following: 92 percent of TELUS Mobility people agree with the statement: "I am responsible for contributing to our profitability."

Suppose your company is no TELUS Mobility. Where do you find the spiritual sustenance to keep you going until you and your colleagues create the *Extreme* Corporate Makeover that transforms your firm into a trailblazer?

Perhaps in a grassroots organization devoted to people exactly like you.

Spirit at Work

Judi Neal, singer/songwriter, Yale Ph.D., corporate consultant and retired management professor, birthed a network that nurtures grassroots leaders devoted to Spirit in the workplace.

The Association for Spirit at Work (ASAW) counts some 40 chapters and associates, either active or organizing, and hundreds of members. From Boston to Austin, from Toronto to Manchester, U. K., spiritual leaders gather in local cafes or cozy living rooms to hear inspiring speakers and share their hopes for a world in which Spirit is alive at work. The first chapters, founded in New York City and San Francisco, are still active.

ASAW was born at an Institute of Noetic Sciences (IONS) Conference back in 1992, when Judi Neal says she "felt electricity shoot through me, just thinking about Spirit at work." When fellow conference goers shared their

Spirit at work stories, Judi followed up with a newsletter—distributed to about 10 people. But after *BusinessWeek* quoted Judi in a 1995 story on spirituality in business, ASAW blossomed from 100 in 1995 to 200 in 1996.

ASAW's newsletter is still going strong and ASAW's new, twice-monthly author teleconferences, which feature interviews with writers of new books on Spirit at work, are attracting a lot of interest. You'll find more information on ASAW in the appendix (for Judi's own book, see p. 15).

You'll now discover what just might be ASAW's most important contribution to the spirituality in business movement—and what Judi Neal is most proud of.

The International Spirit at Work Award

What do fashion retailer Eileen Fisher, the *Times of India* newspaper and TELUS Mobility, the company you just read about, have in common?

They're all winners of the International Spirit at Work (ISAW) Award, first granted in 2002 to pioneering organizations whose policies and programs explicitly nurture spirituality at work. Created by ASAW, the Award is now co-managed with three other groups, the Spirit in Business Institute, the World Business Academy and the European Bahá'í Business Forum.

The nine winners for 2005, chosen by a committee of activists, executives and consultants, include India's Aarti International, Canada's Providence Health Care, The Netherlands's Van Ede & Partners and two German firms, Elcoteq Communications and Heiligenfeld, as well as U.S.-based Catholic Health Initiatives, Central DuPage Hospital, Mount Carmel Health and St. Joseph Health System. For more information, see www.spirit atwork.org.

You can nominate any organization for the ISAW, so long as it is at least five years old and employs at least 60 people. For more nomination guidelines, visit the ASAW website cited above.

The awards are inspired by the late Willis Harman, Ph.D. (1919–1997), Stanford professor, social scientist, author, founder of the World Business Academy, president of the Institute of Noetic Sciences, futurist and Renaissance man—and the godfather of the Spirit in business movement.

Explicitly "Spiritual"

The International Spirit at Work Award is looking for companies whose sense of Spirit is both "vertical" and "horizontal," says Cindy Wigglesworth, president of Conscious Pursuits, a consulting firm. For two years Wigglesworth chaired the selection committee.

Vertical? Horizontal? What do these terms mean?

Vertical Spirit is an organization's overt acknowledgment of connection to a Higher Power, the Transcendent, God or a Sacred Dimension, says Cindy, a 20-year Exxon veteran, spent mostly as an HR manager. Horizontal Spirit, by contrast, is about service and treating humanity and the planet with love and caring—all of which are the hallmarks of Divinity.

"Lots of great companies embody horizontal Spirit," says Cindy, "They certainly deserve—and get—recognition." Many show up on lists like "100 Best Companies to Work For" or the "Top 100 Corporate Citizens."

"But that's not what we're looking for," she says. "For us, there must be an explicit link to the Transcendent." According to Cindy, many firms qualify on the horizontal, but not vertical side "because their leaders want to *act* from Spirit, but not *talk* openly about it. That's fine, of course. But we specialize in celebrating companies with the courage to fly *above* the radar."

What's Wigglesworth's vision of the future for the Awards?

"Front page of *The Wall Street Journal. The Financial Times. The Times of India,*" she replies. (The latter, a 2003 "Spirit at Work" winner, will probably head the pack.) "What if we were besieged with organizations demanding, 'What does it take to win a Spirit at Work Award?' We'd have to set up a training program to teach them," she laughs. "Now, *that's* my idea of success."

Sound Familiar?

Cindy Wigglesworth's commitment to Spirit at work grew out of her search for wholeness. Her former employer, Exxon, was, she says, "outstanding in many ways—ethical, clean books, tops in training people to succeed." She'd still be there, she says, were it not for a values conflict. "My core value is faith in a Higher Power, yet I spent most of my time in my career." That mismatch spawned a mysterious sense of discontent. "For two years I prayed to be shown what to do."

Then, ten years ago, Wigglesworth went on a three-day retreat at Unity Village in Missouri. "I was sitting in the old prayer chapel, the site of nearly 100 years of constant prayer," she recalls, "when my mind went completely quiet. This *never* happens to me," says the practical and efficient Wigglesworth, "A voice in my head said clear as a bell, 'Jesus with a job. Buddha with a briefcase.'"

Those few words named her pain, answered her prayers. Ever since, she's spoken, written, conducted training and consulted about Spirit at Work. Eventually she worked on a values-based transformation project at The

Methodist Hospital, a 2002 Spirit at Work Award winner described in chapter six.

Why are the ISAW awards so important? "Because we learn by example," says Wigglesworth. "If a leader wants to create a company where Spirit can thrive, you and I can point to another company and say, 'Look what they did.'"

I got so excited about both the Spirit at Work award and ASAW that I launched ASAW's Boston chapter. Let me take you inside one of our best meetings.

The Corporate Shaman

Here in the comfortable club room of my Cambridge condominium, the lights are glowing softly and we're about to start the December 2004 ASAW meeting. It's our last get-together until spring and we are definitely celebrating.

The coffee table, spread with power objects—beautiful fabric, a large feather, sage and a giant shell—is transformed into an altar tonight, because Richard Whiteley, 64, one of our members, is taking us on a shamanic journey to the underworld, where we'll meet power animals with powerful medicine to support our careers, work lives and businesses.

Whiteley, a hugely successful businessman, began studying shamanism in 1992 and now leads workshops all around the world for individuals, corporate clients and high-profile organizations like the Young President's Club. Richard's book, *The Corporate Shaman: A Business Fable* (HarperBusiness, 2002), tells the tale of shaman Jason Hand, who healed PRIMETEC, "a mid-size company in crisis."

This is a special treat. Labyrinth guide Joe Miguez has driven all the way from New Jersey and ASAW founder Judi Neal arrives from Connecticut. There are a few new faces, like Marvin Smith, a partner at Cambridge-based Synectics. Lynn Robinson, the corporate intuitive, is here and so are my dear friend Donna Coombs and her beau, Brett Zacker, an engineer with Allegro MicroSystems near Worcester.

The word shaman, Richard tells us, is Siberian for "one who sees in the dark." For 40,000 years shamans have entered altered states of consciousness, traveled to other realms and brought back the power and wisdom to heal people. Much of that wisdom, Richard tells us, comes from animals who've helped humanity for eons. "Pick an issue to ask the animals," he tells us, then describes what happens next.

"We'll enter the Earth through a hole in the ground of some sort and, well," he pauses, "you'll just go inside any way you like—crawl in, jump, it's up to you.

"Most of you will encounter animals. But some might not, especially if this is your first journey," he cautions. "That's normal. But be sure to notice any animals you meet twice. They're probably your totems."

I wonder if Richard's calm and gentle voice has already worked some shamanic magic, because in no time, we are all pretty relaxed. Several of us are sprawled out on the carpet, eyes closed, ready to go.

Richard starts playing the fantastic drumming tape he created with his sons. The drums take over and we're off.

It's not a long journey, either. Ten minutes, maybe more. Soon Richard is calling us back. Some of us have zero interest in coming back. We're in that much of an altered state. But one by one, we open our eyes, stretch, climb back on our chairs and share our stories.

I'll tell you mine—which I found quite amazing. On a previous journey, I saw a colorful bird—nothing more—and frankly, I was a little disappointed. Not this time.

Now, I am not "an animal person," but I met two huge beasts, Cougar and Rhinoceros. Over the next few months the power, authenticity and practicality of their message struck me again and again. In my career—writing this book, in fact—I was compelled to work with the kind of speed that usually makes me crazy. But after my thrilling shamanic ride on the back of the cougar, I handled it fine. In another situation, involving real estate, I faced a predicament that threatened my feelings and finances. There was nothing I could do but be "thick-skinned" and "charge." Like a rhino.

Spiritual Centers: Washington, Minneapolis, San Francisco

In 1996, my friends Corinne McLaughlin and Gordon Davidson founded the Center for Visionary Leadership in Washington, D.C., whose mission was to nurture the "inner resources" required for effective leadership. For more than 20 years, the two have taught what they call the Ageless Wisdom of East and West.

McLaughlin and Davidson, co-authors of *Spiritual Politics* (Ballantine Books, 1994), are equally engaged with the public and private sectors. Their 2000 conference, "Re-igniting the Spirit of America," featured Congressman Dennis Kucinich (D-Ohio), the U.S. presidential candidate, and *Conversations with God* author Neale Donald Walsch.

In addition to spiritual retreats and courses on transformational change, Corinne and Gordon consult with business, government and nonprofit organizations. In 2002, they opened a center in San Rafael, California, to serve the Bay Area.

San Francisco is also home base to Spirit in business pioneer John Renesch. Publisher (New Leaders Press) and impresario (Presidio Dialogues), Renesch has devoted more than a decade to convening conversations, workshops, luncheon discussions and conferences. His new book is *Getting to the Better Future* (NewBusinessBooks, 2005).

No wonder he's famous for introducing the movement's key players to the Bay Area and to one another.

America's Heartland

The Minneapolis area's Heartland Circle, a community-based, global network co-created by Patricia and Craig Neal, keeps the spiritual fires burning in Middle America and beyond with several creative initiatives:

• A Leader's Journey Retreat offers a time of reflection and quiet conversation with fellow spiritual leaders.
• Heartland's Thought Leader Gatherings—held in Boston, the San Francisco Bay area and near Minneapolis—feature speakers such as Meg Wheatley, author of *Leadership and the New Science* (Berrett-Koehler, 1992).
• The Art of Convening (AoC) tele-training teaches would-be masters the principles of "transformative meetings and conversations" and is clearly producing a lot of fans.

"The biggest gift of the AoC for me was a well of strength to just keep doing what I know I am supposed to be doing and trust, trust, trust," says Wells Fargo's Mary Berry.

The Solace of Spirit

It is 2002. Planning manager Joyce Orecchia, 52, a dedicated 30-year veteran of Agilent, the $5 billion (2006 revenues) testing equipment maker, loves her company but is heartbroken about the doom and gloom that have descended on employees due to downsizing. Agilent has laid off several thousand people in her own division and, as offshore manufacturing increases, there will be more. Agilent severance programs have won kudos for fairness in *Fortune's* "100 Best Companies to Work For" issue and Joyce believes the company has treated those leaving with integrity and compassion. Yet layoff survivors are riddled with fear and stress, she says. Morale is lower than Orecchia has ever seen it.

Orecchia has come to terms with her own grief through "the solace of Spirit," she says. She meditates daily and finds resolutions to business problems in her spiritual practice. But now she wants to help coworkers reignite their dimming Spirit. So she approaches Human Resources with a plan to nurture layoff survivors with: (1) an omni-faith chaplaincy, (2) a meditation space and (3) supportive employee discussions.

Joyce left Agilent in 2006 with the peace of knowing she'd expressed her spiritual side at work. She now works in the area of Spirit in business.

"A lot of companies are convinced of the value of spirituality," says management professor Ian Mitroff. "What they lack is a way to bring the practice of spirituality—spirituality, not religion—into the workplace in a way that won't cause disruption or acrimony."

Inspired by Mitroff's remark, my chat with Cindy Wigglesworth and Joyce Orecchia's story, it hit me that the ideas in this chapter might be of service to HR managers—the folks at the cutting edge of the hottest new people issues.

"HR often carries the heart chakra energy of the organization," says Wigglesworth. "But they can't do it alone. They rely on the championship of senior leaders who create policy."

Once a CEO or top executive decides to act on the Spirit in business trend, the next step is to ask: So what exactly do we *do* about it? Instead of wondering, he or she might turn to the organization's heart energy—the HR department. I hope this chapter helps HR to:

• lay out an options menu of Spirit-based programs that are already integrated into corporate life,
• sort possible policies under user-friendly headings,
• cite firms who've achieved these goals for possible follow-up.

You'll find such a list in Table 1, "Weaving the Sacred into Corporate Life." I hope it suggests where a Spirit-based program might best fit into a company's unique culture.

But first I'll give you fair warning.

The "Dangers" of Spirit in Business, or Human Resources to the Rescue

Cindy Wigglesworth put on her HR hat and broke it to me straight.

"As an HR manager," she said, "I'd immediately ask, 'How could we introduce Spirit at work without triggering a lawsuit?' A harassment suit, for example, brought by an employee who says, 'This company—or my boss—is unfairly trying to force his beliefs or religion down my throat.'

"Right now there are nice, safe boundaries," she adds. "Separation of church and corporation. Is it wise to open up and let in a flood of lawsuits?"

Thanks, I tell her. I needed that. Too many gung ho Spirit in biz types (like me) are oblivious to the thorny issues the movement raises. Cindy is right. In 2004, the Equal Employment Opportunity Commission (EEOC) logged 2,466 complaints of religious discrimination in the workforce, up 85 percent since 1992. In 2005, the complaints dropped slightly to 2,340.

But knowing Cindy is a Spirit at work advocate, I ask her to switch gears and explain how HR might address those objections.

Her answer was a relief—and an eye-opener. "HR can do it," she said. "Thanks to the tools and experience we've gained tackling touchy issues like sexual harassment and diversity, we can deal with Spirit in business."

The trick is *how*. Here are Cindy's step-by-step guidelines, what I like to call her "rules of spiritual engagement."

1) *Get clear on language.* Create a corporate dictionary of spirituality terms. As ISAW Award chair, Wigglesworth required every committee member to write a personal definition of the word "spiritual."
2) *Train people in consciousness raising.* As HR did with affirmative action and sexual harassment, HR can teach folks how to expand their minds to deal with Spirit in business.
3) *Get real about religion.* Unlike many spiritual types, Wigglesworth says you can't erect a barrier between Spirit and religion. One third of people call themselves "spiritual," reports Cindy, but two thirds call themselves *both* spiritual and religious.

Religion is not as difficult as it sounds, she says, if viewed through the model of diversity training. The key is healthy boundaries—knowing what's acceptable and what's not. "It is not acceptable, for example, to proselytize about your religion on the job," she says. "That *is* harassment."

"What about tacking up a calendar in your cubicle that says, 'Jesus is my Lord,'" she asks. "Is that harassment? Is it tucked in a private corner or visible from the corridor? Does it offend a Muslim or Hindu coworker?"

These are the kinds of questions, says the former Exxon HR honcho, corporations will now ask. A company or court might decide religion at work is "fine," if it nourishes your spirit. But not if it seeks to provoke a derisive challenge: "My God is better than your God" or "My religion is superior to yours."

Several recent cases, both reported in *Workforce Management,* illustrate Cindy's point.

An ex-HP employee, fired for repeatedly posting biblical verses condemning homosexuality, sued HP. But the judge ruled that the ex-employee had violated HP's anti-harassment policy. Cox Communications fired an Evangelical Christian for criticizing a lesbian's sexual orientation during a performance review. Again, the company won and the fired employee was cited for violating company anti-harassment policy.

This may be a difficult dialogue, concludes Cindy, but hardly an impossible one. "HR managers know how to do this kind of thing," she says.

TABLE I: WEAVING THE SACRED INTO CORPORATE LIFE

In this chapter, we've explored several models for Spirit at work initiatives:

- Multifaith employee networks such as the one at Ford.
- Corporate chaplaincy—whether outsourced to an outfit such as Marketplace Chaplains USA or in-house as Joyce Orecchia sought to launch.
- Quiet rooms.

Not to mention lunchtime Bible study or after-work meditation seminars. The following are several areas in which trailblazers are weaving spirituality into day-to-day business. The companies cited below are all winners of the International Spirit at Work Award (most from 2004). Contact information for each winner is on the Association for Spirit at Work website, which is listed in this book's appendix.

Corporate Ritual

Medtronic's Medallion Ceremony honors all employees with a medal depicting the company's spiritual logo, "A patient rising from the operating table fully healed." Created by Medtronic founder Earl Bakken, the hour-and-a-half rite has been staged for groups of between 10 and 10,000 people.

Houston-based **Memorial Hermann Healthcare System** celebrates a moving "Blessing of the Hands" ritual for all caregivers. The optional ceremony, which has been offered about 12,000 times, helps nurses, therapists, housekeepers, physicians and others renew their callings. Spoken by a chaplain, CEO or unit manager, the blessing includes these simple, but beautiful words, "May the God who created you bless the care you give others."

Corporate Transformation

Melbourne-based **Australia and New Zealand Banking Group Ltd.**'s

(ANZ) Breakout and Cultural Transformation initiative won the trust of key stakeholders and boosted employee satisfaction. "Breakout" pursued growth through people and values, fostering positive, open, honest relationships. More than 26,000 ANZ employees (out of 30,000 in 40 countries) have undergone a personal development workshop as part of the Breakout program.

Ontario wireless provider TELUS Mobility's Leading People through Change program utilized spiritual tools like journaling, visualization and reflection, and spiritual concepts like "what you resist, persists." This and other TELUS Mobility initiatives are described more fully earlier in this chapter.

Leadership Development

Memorial Hermann Healthcare System features a nine-day Spiritual Leadership Institute training program. Initiated in 1995, it involves three three-day sessions spread out over the year. All leaders are required to attend and more than 1,000 of them have delved into topics like, "What does a spiritual organization look like?" and "On becoming a spiritual person."

Illinois's Wheaton Franciscan Healthcare, the parent organization of more than 100 health and shelter services, has spiritually focused leadership selection, training and 360-degree feedback.

Houston, Texas's Saint Luke's Episcopal Health System features a vocation program that helps employees find their true calling. Saint Luke's devotes 50 percent of its chaplaincy to serving employees and often makes the *Fortune* "100 Best Companies to Work For" list.

Training/Spiritual Practice

Bombay's *Times of India* sees the "ultimate customer" as God and helps employees "catalyse the latent divinity in each of us" through employee training in self-mastery to control the ego and liberate potential. The *Times* is studying how yoga, meditation and breath control impact performance.

ANZ's "Breakout" initiative includes training in a "high performance" mind technique and a "quiet room" for spiritual practice.

Missouri's Ascension Health, which employs more than 100,000 people, aims to create a workplace that deepens personal spirituality. Its Spirituality Scorecard and seven-step ethical discernment process foster self-reflection.

Retreats

In the Netherlands, Windesheim University's Geert Groote Institute offers two-day retreats for Reflection and Inspiration and an advanced retreat entitled, "Search for Meaning and Spirituality."

Wheaton Franciscan Healthcare holds a two-day annual retreat to foster the spiritual life of the company's leaders. Employees evaluate Wheaton's mission, values and leaders.

Washington's **PeaceHealth,** which employs 10,000 people, holds Compassionate Care retreats for physicians and executives, to explore topics like how to honor all spiritual traditions. It also offers an advanced retreat called "The Renewal Experience."

Values/Mission

At **Phenomenex,** a chemical specialty company with 400 people in the United States, United Kingdom, Germany, Australia and New Zealand, nourishing spiritual values is held as a founding principle and top priority—especially important since the company is growing 20–30 percent a year.

Colorado-based **Centura Health** employs 13,000 people. Its leadership training focuses on purpose, passion and how to create truthful, loving relationships. Centura's rigorous Values Impact Analysis keeps the organization in alignment with its core values.

The Methodist Hospital's "I CARE" motto stands for Integrity, Compassion, Accountability, Responsibility and Excellence. Methodist's transformation through the Corporate Tools program is described in chapter six.

U.S. fashion retailer **Eileen Fisher** nurtures and publicizes the values of Beauty, Simplicity and Joy. Its purpose is to "inspire simplicity, creativity and delight through connection and great design."

Canada's **Embassy Graphics,** based in Winnipeg, espouses the values of Truth and Love and styles itself as a "modern day community" where business means more than pursuing profit and people can grow, develop—and make money.

Positions

Houston's **Methodist Hospital System** appoints a Vice President of Spiritual Care.

Wheaton Franciscan Healthcare has a VP for Ethics and VP for Mission Integration.

Prayer

India's **Excel Industries** begins each day with a corporate all-religion prayer.

Saint Luke's Episcopal Health System begins every meeting with an ecumenical prayer.

Calcutta, India's **SREI International Financial Limited** begins meetings with a silent prayer.

Planters Development Bank in the Philippines regularly invokes the Planters Bank Family Prayer.

Seminars, Workshops, Gatherings
Geert Groote Institute sponsors Sandwich with Substance lunches.
Ascension Health will host a Spirituality Symposium in 2007.

Spirit in the Soul of Capitalism

Before concluding, let's revisit the story that launched this chapter's discussion of the Spirit in business trend, the San Francisco Chamber of Commerce brown bag lunch, which has endured since 1998. Why is it so successful? Here are a few thoughts from founders Sarah Q. Hargrave and Debra Mugnani Monroe:

- **It sets the right tone.** The brown bag honors diversity and all spiritual and religious belief. "We're not here to talk anybody into or out of anything," says Sarah.
- **There are no speakers.** "Talking heads are fine for some spiritual gatherings, but that's not what we're about. We come together as equals, in an unstructured, open space."
- **There is no agenda.** Every meeting is a new adventure, says Debra, who admits she's had to learn to relax, trust and go with the flow. Once everyone has had an opportunity to share, a topic seems to emerge. And, like magic, so does the wisdom to address it.

A woman in her 20s once complained, "I've found my dream job! But I work 60 hours a week. I have no time for Spirit—or even my marriage. How do you do it *all*?" The perfect person—a 50-something career consultant—offered her seasoned experience. Work/life balance, she said, is like a bicycle. "When it veers too far to one side, you have to tip it back."

Magic aside, Sarah and Debra have crafted a few guidelines over time that might prove useful to other similar get-togethers:

1. Be concise in what you say.
2. Honor confidentiality.
3. Don't try to solve people's problems; just share your own stories.
4. Cool it on networking. It happens organically, as people get to know each other, but it's not a priority. It's okay to put your materials on a side table.

In Praise of the Practical

Although the brown bag is seriously spiritual, work takes center stage every month. What sorts of questions do people ask? How do their colleagues respond? Here are a few exchanges. How do you:

- **Find time for spirituality when you work 60 hours a week?** Take a moment or two of silence each hour.
- **Apply your spiritual practice on the job?** You needn't even talk about it; "just do it." When the phone rings, for example, you might bless the unknown caller with a silent "Namaste," which means, "The Divine in me honors the Divine in you."
- **Maintain a spiritual perspective in those tough times and dry periods—like endless job searches—when it seems like nothing is happening?** Remember that just because the "field lies fallow," it doesn't mean nothing's happening. There's a lot going on below the surface.
- **Keep your soul intact among difficult people in a stress-filled office?** Post an inspiring message on your desk or the marquee scroll of your computer screen.

Several years ago, the brown bag maxed at 35 people. Too many, says Debra, for the intimacy most seek. When the gathering settled down to between 12 and 15, "the conversation deepened."

Regulars call it "an oasis" of tranquility; a chance to "let down the barriers and just be yourself"; an "opportunity to speak from the heart"; and a chance for "deep, soulful communication." Many report they return to work feeling renewed and with a better perspective.

Getting Started

How might *you* replicate this exciting model—partnering perhaps with the Chamber, Rotary, YWCA or local place of worship? Maybe Sarah Hargrave's and Debra Monroe's stories will give you some ideas.

Sarah, a corporate veteran and ordained minister, regularly spoke at "spiritual breakfasts" near San Francisco. When Chamber membership VP Kristin Sivesind showed up at one, Kristin and Sarah decided to survey the Chamber's Women in Business Roundtable (WIBR) to see if there was any interest in an event with a spiritual theme. The response was enthusiastic. So in 1997, Sarah gave a talk on "Spirit in Work and Business: Seven Keys for Success," which drew a standing-room-only audience.

Then Debra Monroe, the WIBR co-chair, and Sarah decided to follow up with a "one-time" brown bag—and it's been going ever since. Although spon-sored by the WIBR, brown bag is completely open to men. And—attention bargain hunters—after eight years, it is still free.

U.S. business and finance, hung over from the excesses of the 1990s, are in excruciating pain.

And the system does not know how to heal itself.

But we *do*. We know that if greed, fraud and speculation got us into the crisis of capitalism, it is going to take character, trust and spiritual leadership to get us out. The spirituality in business trend will foster each of those traits—and lift our hearts in the process.

Gregory Pierce, the author and businessman, puts it perfectly, "By trying to run our company with a spirituality that says God is present in the midst of the hustle and bustle, we'll be a lot happier and do better work."

Exactly.

5

The Values-Driven Consumer

Christiane Perrin waltzes into the October 2004 meeting of the Association for Spirit at Work Boston chapter with a big smile on her face and energy to spare. I assume she's excited about our little get-together. But as we gather in a circle and begin to share, it is clear that something *else* is getting Christiane's heart pumping. Soon the truth comes out: It's her brand-new Toyota Prius—a gas-and-electric hybrid.

"I just love driving it," she enthuses. "There's this display on the dashboard that shows you how the mileage improves when you shift from gas to electric. I watch how it changes and I learn to drive more efficiently every day."

Perrin, 50, a single mom with two teenage sons, is in the midst of a major shift herself. The owner of an HVAC engineering firm, she is launching a new career as an executive coach. "I definitely did not have a lot of extra money lying around," she explains. "But I just *had* to have this car."

So in spring 2004, she drove her 1998 Chrysler Concord to Westborough (Massachusetts) Toyota and ordered the hybrid. In September, five months later, she shelled out $23,000 for a burgundy Prius. "Now you have to wait nine months," she says.

Why did she go ahead and buy the car, even though money is tight? "Mileage and the environment," Perrin replies without hesitation. The Toyota Prius gives off 30 to 50 percent fewer emissions and is 40 to 60 percent more fuel efficient than a gas-only car. Perrin reports she gets twice the mileage she did in her old Concord and now she fills up every two weeks instead of once or twice a week.

Plus, the Prius mirrors her values of practicality, frugality and quality—without showiness. "I despise cheap things that end up in a landfill," she says, "like those toys in the kid's meal at the fast food joints." Christiane Perrin won't stop at McDonald's or shop at Wal-Mart. And don't get her started on gas-guzzling SUVs. "What really gets me," she gripes, "is seeing them parked outside Whole Foods or a Sierra Club meeting."

She does, however, get a kick out of the camaraderie hybrid owners share. "We kind of nod and wave at each other," she says. But for Christiane the bottom line is clear: "I'm just doing what I can to minimize the environmental impact."

Christiane is one of a growing wave of Conscious Consumers who are making their presence felt in car dealerships and at gas pumps all across the country. Their passion for green automotive technology is what energizes the hybrid success story.

By 2010, the hybrid market could hit one million cars, says one expert you'll meet later in this chapter, totaling about six percent of the new car market.

- Hybrid owner Bill Evans, 67, an architectural illustrator, brags that he spent only $40 on gas during a 1,000 mile trip. For an SUV owner, the bill would be several hundred dollars, he calculates. "I feel pretty smug about that," he adds.
- Seattle's Adam Schmidt, 25, and Megan King, 26, traded in their 15-mpg Mustangs for a couple of Honda Civic hybrids and *tripled* their fuel efficiency.
- The hybrid headquarters of the U.S.A.—on a per capita basis—are Washington, D.C., San Francisco-Oakland-San Jose and Seattle.

But the hybrid trend, dramatic though it is, represents only the most celebrated facet of a larger direction, whose potential we haven't even begun to grasp.

What Is a Values-Driven Consumer?

That trend is the emergence of the Values-driven (or Conscious) Consumer. Conscious Consumers, whose ranks are estimated at 63 million, vote with their pocketbooks every day of the year. Consumer spending represents more than two-thirds of the Gross Domestic Product of the U.S. economy.

That means consumers are right up there with investors as a potent force in the transformation of capitalism.

Who are today's Conscious Consumers?

No one puts it better than *Green Money Journal's* Cliff Feigenbaum: "My money is a voice in the world. I want it to express my values." But Cliff doesn't stop there. "I want total coherence between what I believe and do with my money." Cliff speaks for a new generation of consumers who are not only affluent and discerning, but values-driven.

What do I mean by "values-driven"? Simply this: If *values*, more than income, demographics, geography or other factors, profoundly influence your choices at the cash register, whether you purchase fair trade coffee, solar panels or that new Honda hybrid, you're a Conscious Consumer.

This chapter examines three product categories where Conscious Consumers are driving the market: hybrid cars, natural food and green building. Gas-electric cars. Organic produce. Zero Energy homes. What next? Sector by sector, Conscious Consumers are insinuating their energy-stingy, life-affirming, eco-savvy ways into the marketplaces of free enterprise.

Values-driven Consumers have the power to transform capitalism through the classic formula of supply and demand. We demand organic tomatoes, insulated glass, fuel efficient cars—and many more conscious commodities. At first the market is slow to furnish these values-laden products, but as we reward the pioneering businesses that *do* meet our needs with the dollar power of our spending, we compel more companies to accede to our terms or lose the order. It's a twist on the capitalist maxim, "Find a need and fill it." The problem is that mainstream business is so wedded to the status quo, it hasn't got a clue about what our needs are, which makes filling them pretty difficult. That's why we must keep supporting innovative green businesses while shunning products that fail the values test. Call it demand-side economics.

Conscious Consumers often predict where much of the market is headed, not the entire market perhaps, but a sizable portion. Even traditional shoppers are drawn to products that embody and broadcast values. Later in this chapter, you'll hear brand guru Elsie Maio explain how conscious companies project their values through the corporate brand—and why these companies will rule.

The Biggest Market You Never Heard Of

By 2000, the market for values-driven commerce, from organic food and eco-tourism to Earth-friendly appliances and alternative medicine, had reached $230 billion, according to a report in *The New York Times,* and was growing by double digits every year. No wonder the *Times* called it, "The biggest market you have never heard of."

Natural products, from food to personal care items, were a $51.3 billion market by June 2006, up 9.1 percent from 2004, says Boston-based international investment bank Canaccord Adams.

Conscious Consumers are often categorized as "LOHAS" (Lifestyles of Health and Sustainability) customers. In 2006, the Natural Marketing Institute's LOHAS Trends Study counted 35 million—or 16 percent of U.S. adults—as core LOHAS consumers, devoted to "personal and planetary health." Another 53 percent, they noted, are focused on natural/organic items, but not as committed or "driven to eco-friendly goods."

The LOHAS market is comprised of five sectors: (1) Sustainable Economy (green buildings, renewable energy, socially responsible investing); (2) Healthy Living (natural and organic food, nutritional supplements and personal care); (3) Alternative Healthcare (wellness, complementary and alternative care [e.g., homeopathy]); (4) Personal Development (mind, body, spirit products and services from CDs to seminars) and (5) Ecological Lifestyles (ecological or recycled products, ecotourism and travel).

But here is the key point:

Ninety percent of LOHAS customers prefer to buy from companies that share or reflect their values, says *LOHAS Journal,* a publication for conscious businesses and consumers.

Not surprisingly, there's plenty of overlap between the LOHAS consumer and the Cultural Creatives, and the key to both is values. *Cultural Creatives* co-author Paul Ray, who worked for decades in market research and applied social research, says he spent two years trying to figure out how to predict consumer behavior. The answer isn't demographics, income or psychographics, Ray concluded, but *values*—and lifestyle.

A Bit of a Paradox

Values-driven Consumers remain a mystery to mainstream business—and it is little wonder why. Some Conscious Consumers are comfortable, even rich, in disposable income (although Paul Ray describes Cultural Creatives as of "average" income). Still they all disdain consumerism and want no part of the mass market—whether discount, designer or anything in between.

But when these quirky customers find what they *want,* they go wild.

They'll cheerfully wait months and pay a $3,000 premium for a Honda Civic hybrid, then drive 50 miles out of their way to the nearest Whole Foods for the absolute *best* organic $7.98 a pound baby spinach this side of Kansas City.

What's the secret behind their purchase decisions? You gotta know their values. Mainstream companies are gradually catching on—showing up at LOHAS conventions like the one in Broomfield, Colorado, in June 2003. That's where Sheri Shapiro, then assistant marketing manager for the Ford Escape hybrid SUV (which hit the market in 2004), discovered "the values and attributes of the LOHAS customers matched our own research." Time Warner, Sony and General Electric joined Ford at the 2004 LOHAS get-together in Marina del Rey, California.

How does a company reach Conscious Consumers? By understanding the importance of positive uplifting values, of course, but also by *living* those values in business.

Three Concentric Circles

Conscious Consumers represent the cutting edge but more mainstream shoppers are also given to moral qualms.

In fact, most Americans weigh the moral consequences of their purchases—at least somewhat. Several surveys cited in chapter two illustrate that point. I recap them here, because as I reflected on their findings, I developed a theory about how values influence the marketplace as a whole. Here in brief are the kind of results I'm talking about:

- 36 percent call corporate citizenship an important factor in deciding whether to buy a product.
- 49 percent say that when price, quality and convenience are equal, they prefer to buy from companies they deem socially responsible.
- 79 percent consider corporate citizenship when buying something.

Don't focus too much on percentages, as these vary quite a bit from poll to poll. Just think of these perspectives as the rings of three expanding concentric circles, each representing a different level of commitment to conscious consumption.

At the center is the dyed-in-the-wool values-driven shopper. I've seen this hard-core percentage estimated at anywhere between 16 and 36 percent. So let's say 25 percent, roughly the same percentage as the Cultural Creatives. They are the environmentalists, organic food buyers or vegetarians, hybrid enthusiasts and green-home lovers. *Values determine many, if not most, of their purchases.*

Around them is the second circle, what I call the conscious "followers," people who are becoming more interested in organics or environmentalism, but switch on and off. *Values determine a growing percentage but not all of their purchases.*

A RoperASW study found 33 percent beyond the hardcore (which it put at 16 percent) "can be persuaded to base their spending on their environmental values," says *The New York Times* story cited earlier. I would love to think of myself as a dedicated Conscious Consumer, but the truth is I may be a pioneer in Spirit in business, but when it comes to conscious consumption, I'm not there yet. I shop at Whole Foods; I recycle. I finally bought a Honda Civic hybrid in 2006. But I'm not a trend-setter. I'm a follower (as my sister Barbara Jones of Portsmouth, Rhode Island, the family vegetarian, environmentalist, hybrid driver and animal rights advocate, can attest).

Finally, there's the public at large. The vast majority consider the moral implication of their choices. They are reflected in the 79 percent cited above. *Values influence their behavior—sometimes.*

There you have it: the hard core, the followers and everyone else.

Conscious Consumers Unite

Whether you're a die-hard enthusiast, late adapter or mainstream and curious, Co-op America's *National Green Pages* (NGP) is your guidebook to conscious consumption. This data-drenched resource puts shoppers in touch with businesses—listed under categories from beauty to pet care, from computer services to toys—that pledge to do business in a way that promotes social and environmental transformation.

That said, Conscious Consumers, by definition, are hardly shopaholics. NGP suggests you screen purchase decisions with three simple questions:

1. Do I really need this?
2. Can I reuse, barter for or borrow it instead?
3. Is this purchase in alignment with my values?

NGP's practical "Green Step" checklists offer concrete, homey tips for areas like:

- the kitchen (Buy in bulk to save packaging waste),
- spring cleaning (Use 1/4 cup of vinegar in your washing machine's rinse cycle to avoid the chemicals in fabric softener),
- the garden (Invest in a modern reel lawn mower; they're light, easy to use, generate zero pollutants and give you a great workout).

NGP is supported by a who's who of pioneering conscious businesses such as Aubrey, the organic beauty firm; Eden Organic, the natural food company; AMF Safecoat, which makes nontoxic, zero-VOC paint; and Ecover, whose cleaning products are free of harsh chemicals and phosphates. As well as:

- Seventh Generation, the leading natural household product maker, whose recycled, nontoxic and environmentally safe items fill the shelves of conscious outlets like Whole Foods.
- GAIAM, which produces a collection of organic clothing, natural home products and health and wellness items that invite you to "Live in harmony with yourself and the world."
- AVEDA, which works with the Yawanawa tribe in the Brazilian Amazon, where Aveda grows the red-seed pigment the Yawanawa use to decorate the body—and Aveda uses in eye, lip and cheek makeup.

Not surprisingly, these conscious businesses run advertisements that are informative, beautiful and thought provoking.

Beyond Hybrids

The *Green Pages* are full of inspiring stories on topics like green investing and alternative energy. But my favorite item in the entire 2004 directory was the sidebar about Rod Miner's Lightfoot Cycles, which manufactures the Greenway cycle, a mega-tricycle or "trike"—complete with backrest (a thrilling feature in my book), windscreen and a huge back section designed to haul up to 100 pounds of camping gear or groceries. You can customize your human-powered trike with a canopy or passenger space.

As someone who has never found bicycles comfortable or practical—since you can't carry much—I found it easy to picture myself cruising around town on errands peddling a Greenway trike. Who knows, maybe I'll become a hard-core Conscious Consumer after all?

Now let's look at an area of conscious consumption that's grown by leaps and bounds of late—environmental and energy-efficient construction.

Green Building

Once upon a time, green homes were for pioneers and committed environmentalists.

- Judy Cunningham of Manistee County, Michigan, built her home in four years with 300 straw bales of Benzie County-grown rye. "I didn't own anything but a hammer when I started," says the 54-year-old recycling coordinator, who contracted out the electric, plumbing and drywall work.
- David and Jean Wallace produce more energy than their 2,800-square-foot underground, light-filled home near Billings, Montana, can use. Thanks to ten-inch-thick concrete walls, a 1,240-watt solar array panel and a 50-foot tower with a wind generator on top, the Wallaces actually feed energy *back* into the grid. "Using electricity for heat is like using a chainsaw to cut butter," says David.
- Teresa McMahon and Garth Frable of northeastern Iowa rely on a 1,000-watt wind turbine and solar panels to run the pump, lights, microwave, fridge, computer, washer and dryer in their heavy oak beam home.

We respected the heck out of these trailblazers, but when it came to following in their footsteps, most of us wouldn't even know how to begin. Where do you find green designers, contractors—and suppliers? And, furthermore, how much does all of this cost?

But today, the passion for—and practice of—energy-saving, Earth-loving construction is finally about to renovate mainstream construction.

"Ten or 12 years ago, [green building] was truly a fringe movement," says sustainability expert Mark Wilhelm, principal of Green Ideas, president of the Arizona chapter of U.S. Green Building Council and a sustainable building expert with two decades of experience. "Now it has become more mainstream . . . a way of doing business."

"By far, the most talked-about topic in the architecture universe," concludes *The Wall Street Journal* in January 2005, "is how to reduce the environmental impact of everything from summer cottages to skyscrapers."

In fact, green construction has come to stand for efficiency and quality, and it is springing up all over America.

- "Green building is taking root across Arizona," said the *Arizona Republican* in 2005.
- "Green building will save homeowners, businesses, money," declares a 2003 story in the *Daily Texan*.
- "Chicago gives lessons on appeal, practicality of green buildings," reads a 2004 headline in the *Chicago Tribune*.

The U.S. Green Building Council

Much of the movement centers on the U.S. Green Building Council (USGBC), a coalition of architects, builders, suppliers and environmentalists that provides data on all aspects of green construction.

USGBC's membership has skyrocketed from 1,137 in 2001 to more than 6,400 today, illustrating the growing power of the green building trend.

But USGBC's greatest success may well be having established a benchmark for green building, with its LEED (Leadership in Energy and Environmental Design) certification, described later in this chapter. LEED revolutionized green building. "Before LEED, anybody could call anything they wanted to green," says Natural Resources Defense Council's Robert K. Watson.

"Now we have a credible way of saying what green means," adds Robert B. Krasa, former CEO of office furniture firm Haworth Inc., a USGBC member.

But how much difference can green building make in the world's massive energy and environmental predicament?

A lot.

Why Build Green?

When most of us contemplate the cause of a deteriorating environment and rising energy consumption, we usually point the finger at automobiles and heavy industry. Granted, each is responsible for its terrible share, but there's another culprit that often gets let off the hook. In the United States, buildings squander 39 percent of total U.S. energy, says the Department of Energy, more than factories and automobiles. The construction industry accounts for 40 percent of the waste in U.S. landfills.

And there's more. Buildings, says the Green Building Council:

• consume 70 percent of electricity,
• emit 38 percent of greenhouse gas,
• devour 40 percent of raw materials.

Who's the energy and environmental bad guy now?

Green design and construction dramatically slash energy consumption, protect the environment and enhance people's health. Remember sick building syndrome? Working in a sealed building, breathing stale air at best—toxic fumes at worst—literally makes people ill. Building green fosters physical well-being, boosts productivity and reduces absenteeism and turnover.

And I haven't even gotten to the part about how much money it saves.

LEED: Success Stories

Bank of America, Reed Park Zoo and Giant Eagle supermarket are, at first blush, about as disparate as three construction projects might be. But they all showcase breakthroughs in Earth-friendly, energy-saving construction. And each building has achieved—or is aiming for—coveted LEED status—exclusively certified by a USGBC-accredited auditor.

By fall 2006, 550 buildings had been certified as LEED; 3,400 more await certification.

USGBC grants four levels of LEED status: standard, silver, gold and platinum, depending on the number of points a building accumulates. LEED is like a "Chinese restaurant menu of environmentally friendly goals," such as energy efficiency, water conservation and recycled materials, says *The New York Times*. Buildings get scored on these and other Earth-friendly categories.

- Giant Eagle, an 80,000-square-foot market in northeastern Ohio, is the nation's first LEED grocer. It consumes 30 percent less energy than its peers, saves 100,000 gallons of water a year and uses no ozone-depleting refrigerants in the freezer section or anywhere else.
- Tucson, Arizona's Reed Park Zoo doesn't "just" want to improve energy efficiency by 20 or 30 percent, says zoo curator Vivian VanPeenen. "We're going for 50 or 60 percent." In addition to solar roof panels, insulated glass and state-of-the-art HVAC, every material in the zoo's $3 million education building has been used before, including recycled steel, walls of recycled polystyrene blocks and carpets of recycled cotton. *Reed Park is aiming for the LEED "platinum"—USGBC's highest rating—achieved so far by only 26 buildings in the world.*
- Bank of America's One Bryant Park, a $1 billion, 52-story skyscraper scheduled to open in 2008, is also going for the platinum. Constructed mostly from reused materials, the building will recycle rain and waste water, will heat and cool itself with its own $10 million power plant and will use energy-efficient dimming and lighting options.

But one of the few LEED platinum buildings outside the United States is in Hyderabad, India. The Godrej Green Building Center, which achieved a total of 56 points out of a possible 69, is an exhibition and training center for environmental businesses.

A Question of Cost

Of course, commercial clients and homeowners alike want to know how much all this wonderful energy and environmental efficiency actually costs.

U.S. Green Building Council CEO S. Richard Fedrizzi says green buildings pay for themselves, often in energy savings alone. Specifically USGBC says green construction cuts utility bills 20 to 50 percent on average. Green construction can hike costs by two percent, says sustainability expert Mark Wilhelm, but it saves 20 percent of total construction costs over 20 years. And the way energy prices are rising, payback should be even sooner.

But now green building itself is more efficient, as contractors gain experience and suppliers churn out better products. Take energy-efficient glass, for example, which lets in more light, cutting electricity use, but keeps out heat, reducing the need for air conditioning. As a result, the synergies multiply. Standard LEED-certified buildings, USGBC's baseline designation, now cost about the same as other buildings, which means they reap energy savings immediately. In the hands of experienced design-build teams, going green may well be even cheaper.

In 2004, the state of California studied 33 LEED-certified buildings. They cost $4 more per square foot to build, but in 20 years, standard and silver buildings save $48.87 a square foot. Platinum buildings recover $67.31 per square foot. Much of the savings—75 percent—comes from lower turnover and absenteeism and higher productivity, says Gregory H. Kats, a former Department of Energy official and the study's lead author.

What about the Home Market?

Today, the private home building industry trails the nonprofit, corporate and municipal sectors. So does the commercial market in general. But now Conscious Consumers increasingly demand green homes, as a National Association of Home Builders (NAHB) Research Center study recently discovered. Nearly half—46 percent—of consumers who plan to spend more than $10,000 on renovations said they were "eager" to add green products. The survey found that most consumers would pay more to build green: 64 percent would spend up to $1,000 extra and 20 percent would invest up to $5,000 to meet higher energy and environmental goals.

What's in the way? Builders. Only 14 percent of survey respondents said their builders offered green options. NAHB's new "Model Green Home Building Guidelines" may change that. Developed with 60+ architects, builders, government agencies, suppliers, environmentalists and trade associations, the new directives help buyers and builders go green—yet keep costs down.

Meanwhile, green building is blossoming because of both bottom-up and top-down initiatives from builders, environmentalists, energy firms—and the government.

Zero Energy Homes

The U.S. Department of Energy's (DOE) Zero Energy Home designation, awarded to houses that generate as much energy as they consume, sets an exacting standard for homebuilders. In 2004, at the International Home Builders Show in Las Vegas, NAHB exhibited a 5,300-square-foot Zero Energy Home built by Pardee Homes.

At Watsonville, California's Vista Montana community, all 257 single-family homes and town houses have earned DOE's Zero Energy Home certification, the largest housing development to qualify. Each unit comes with solar power, a "tank-less" on-demand water heater, energy-efficient furnaces and windows, special insulation, a radiant roof and bamboo flooring. Developed by Clarum Homes, the houses reduce energy bills by a whopping 90 percent.

Grassroots initiatives are also springing up in the bellwether states of Washington and Colorado.

"Build Green, a program of the Master Builders Association of King and Snohomish Counties [in Washington state]," writes Ben Kaufman, co-owner of GreenWorks Realty, in the *Seattle Daily Journal of Commerce*, "offers home-building checklists that include more than 254 items for which builders can score points to meet criteria for a one-, two- or three-star Built Green home."

In Fort Collins, Colorado, the Colorado Energy Science Center, DOE, The City of Fort Collins and local green suppliers jointly sponsored Zero Energy Home Workshops in 2004. The all-day seminars—one for homeowners and another for building professionals—looked at solar technologies and energy-efficient construction and culminated in a local tour of green building examples.

Affordable—and Green?

The Build Green movement is working to explode the myth that eco-friendly, energy-saving construction is only for the upscale market niche. Austin (Texas) Energy's Green Building Program helps construct green, environmental, healthy homes. "Some of our greenest houses in Austin are in the lowest price range," says Austin Energy's Mary McLeod, a residential program coordinator.

The Green Communities Initiative is a five-year, $550 million pledge to build 8,500 affordable green homes by getting developers the financing, grants and technical assistance to build green, healthy homes. "For many families, asthma, injuries and lead poisoning are just symptoms of the underlying problem," says Boston University's Dr. Megan Sandel, an expert on children's health and housing. "Inadequate housing is the real disease. Safe, decent, affordable housing is the best preventive medicine."

The green building trend is yet another case of "changing values meet economic necessity." We want buildings that honor the environment and save energy, because it mirrors our values. But now soaring energy costs make the concept increasingly cost effective. Add the health benefits and the allure of green building is downright irresistible. As *The Wall Street Journal* puts it, "Green is proving itself a potent trend. And high energy prices should keep developers thirsty for frugal digs."

Natural and Organic Food

When I'm not in Cambridge, Massachusetts, I live in Telluride, Colorado, one of the most beautiful places on Earth. When it's time to leave the rugged mountains, glorious red rocks and pine forests, I always feel a little sad. Until I remember one thing back East that's *so* unbelievably fantastic that I head for the airport singing a happy song.

What is it? The grocery store!

In Cambridge, I get to pick from *three* Whole Foods Markets (there are many more in and around Boston). On the plane, I daydream of wandering through the aisles, collecting every item I've done without for weeks or more: organic raspberries, fresh wild salmon, real red tomatoes, flawless haricot verts, unsweetened Silk soy milk, hormone-free pork, Artisan Italian sheep cheese . . . I could go on and on. Not to mention Seventh Generation 100 percent recycled tissues and all 36 Bach Flower Remedies (plus Rescue Remedy), the plant and tree essences that balance and heal almost every human emotion.

Clearly, I am not the only one who's bonkers for Whole Foods, the first grocery chain to be certified organic. In the past five years, as the economy staggered through recession and a fits-and-starts recovery, Whole Foods—committed though it is to all things natural—has been expanding like an athlete on steroids.

From one store in 1980, it has swelled to nearly 200 in the United States, Canada and the United Kingdom In 2004, Whole Foods employed 26,000 people. But by 2006, it was 39,000.

Whole Foods' track record is extraordinary, especially considering the grocery sector is flat, growing one or two percent a year and sometimes shrinking. In 2004, Whole Foods sales soared 23 percent to $3.9 billion. In 2006, sales hit $5.6 billion.

By 2010, Whole Foods envisions 260 stores and $10 billion in sales.

Name any method grocers use to take the pulse of business—margins, comparable same store sales, sales per square foot—and Whole Foods leaves the competition in the dust. Whole Foods' margins, for example, at around three percent, are twice those of Safeway.

Until recently, Whole Foods was one hot stock, hitting $78 (split adjusted) in late 2005 before dropping in autumn 2006 over concerns about slowing growth. In early 2007, Whole Foods traded at around $45. A good time to buy?

You Are What You Eat

The reason is, of course, Values-driven Consumers. After all, "you are what you eat," as early naturalists admonished. Conscious Consumers, who take that advice very much to heart, are mad for organic food; that is, food grown without toxic pesticides, harmful chemicals or irradiation. And whom do we thank that fresh, natural foods grace our tables today? The mom-and-pop natural food stores, consumer co-ops and farmer's markets that kept the organic movement alive for decades.

Chances are pioneers like these were active in one of the two groups I'll now describe.

The Organic Consumers Association (OCA), an 850,000-strong, activist group, aims to represent the nation's millions of organic food lovers.

OCA's political agenda, cited on its website, is simple and radical:

• A global moratorium on genetically engineered food and crops (more about that soon).
• A phase-out of the most dangerous industrial agriculture and factory farming practices.
• The conversion of American agriculture to at least 30 percent organic by 2015.

The Organic Trade Association (OTA), founded in 1985 by a circle of trailblazers, now boasts 1,500 members. In 1986, it established its Guidelines for the Organic Food Industry, the basis for many future standards. OTA updated its provisions, stayed involved every step of the way and finally worked with the U.S. Department of Agriculture (USDA) to create USDA's National Organic Program implemented in 2002.

So hats off to the visionaries without whose hard work values-driven organic shoppers might have a lot fewer options.

For reasons of quality, flavor, health and environmental impact, Conscious Capitalists are willing to pay a premium to go organic.

Consider:

- The organic food and beverage sector exceeds $13 billion a year, says the Organic Trade Association, and is growing an estimated 16 to 20 percent a year.
- More than half of Americans (54 percent) have sampled organic food, says a 2004 Whole Foods survey.
- Nearly six in ten Americans are concerned about pesticides, reports a 2005 Earth Day survey.
- Nearly one in ten use organic products "regularly or several times a week," the Whole Foods survey reports.
- Forty-four percent of the U.S. population consumes organic food—at least sometimes, says the Earth Day survey.

This enthusiasm—and the success of Whole Foods—is not lost on mainstream grocers. A 17-member retail coalition, including Kroger, City Market, Food Lion and Giant Eagle, participated in the 2005 "Go Organic for Earth Day" campaign.

What Is GE? Why Is It Boosting Organic Food Sales?

As if pesticides and chemicals were not enough, Conscious Consumers also worry about genetic engineering (GE). What are the chances you already consume GE food? Unless you're obsessively organic, about 100 percent.

Coca-Cola, Hershey's bars, Campbell soups, Quaker rice cakes, Swanson frozen dinners, General Mills cereals and hundreds of other products contain GE ingredients, according to tests by Greenpeace reported in the July/August 2003 issue of *E: The Environmental Magazine.* Some 80 percent of soybeans and 38 percent of corn are genetically engineered.

The only way to elude GE food, say natural food advocates, is to buy organic. That's a major factor in today's organic food boom.

The food industry insists GE food is safe for people and for the Earth. Others are not so sure. When scientists add a bacteria gene, for example, to make corn more pest-resistant, it weakens the plant's ability to synthesize its own *natural* pesticides, say some experts. That's just one of many arguments opponents marshal against GE.

Genetic engineering is a huge issue, with compelling arguments on both sides. I will not take the time to explore it fully here (this is the occupational hazard of a generalist writer). But the *E: The Environmental Magazine* story cited above thoughtfully presents the case *for* as well as *against* GE. That's admirable, since its agenda is clearly environmentalist.

But at least one topic in the whole uproar is pretty clear-cut. People want to *know* what they are getting. They want GE food labeled as such, but it is not. The food industry has successfully lobbied against GE labels.

In fact, even Whole Foods sold GE food without labeling it. With the help of shareholder activists, however, Whole Foods decided to come clean, as you read in chapter two.

Whole Foods; Whole People

Even though no company is perfect, Whole Foods Market symbolizes an ethic many Conscious Capitalists can endorse. That said, unions, shareholder activists and animal rights advocates have gone after Whole Foods and CEO John Mackey, 53, whom the media loves to paint as a vegan, libertarian, hippie oddball.

What's surprising is Mackey's response.

When Lauren Ornelas, then director of Viva! USA, which worked to improve conditions for farm animals, made a speech at the 2003 Whole Foods annual meeting about the terrible treatment of ducks, CEO Mackey was initially defensive and even dismissive. Whole Foods has the highest animal standards in the world, he told her. "Go bother somebody else." But later Mackey took it upon himself to read a dozen books on how animals are raised and concluded, "Damn, these people are right. This is terrible." Mackey then invited Ornelas to help him change things.

"I just about fell on the floor," she says.

Mackey has not changed his mind one bit, however, about unions and you might be tempted to jump on the guy for his anti-union stance, except that Whole Foods sets the benchmark for democratic leadership and economic democracy. For example:

- Nonexecutive employees hold 93 percent of stock options.
- Performance-based profit sharing is distributed every other week.
- Individual stores and the departments within them—the seafood or deli team, for example—make lots of decentralized decisions, including customizing the offerings with local products and for local taste.
- Every store has a book that lists how much money everyone made the previous year—from employees to executives.
- A two-thirds majority of team members is required to ratify a new employee (who's on board provisionally for four weeks prior to the vote).
- Every three years employees get to vote on the benefits they want.
- One hundred percent of health insurance costs for full-timers is paid.
- Full-time team members get 20 paid hours off a year to volunteer.
- Executive salaries are limited to 19 times that of workers.

That litany explains why Whole Foods repeatedly earns a strong spot on *Fortune's* "100 Best Companies to Work For" list. The company's strong financials (despite the stock slump) match its ideals, so Whole Foods Market also makes the Sustainable Business 20, a list of the *world's* most sustainable companies. Thanks to energy credits, Whole Foods runs on pure wind energy.

Now that I've researched the company, shopping there is even more satisfying than before. Not only do I get to buy the most gorgeous food around, it thrills me to know the cashiers, produce guys and deli managers—many of whom are hard-working immigrants and minorities—are earning profit sharing and stock options.

This is what capitalism should be and what Conscious Capitalism *is*.

Let's return now to the hybrid trend to see how Conscious Consumers are re-inventing the auto industry. Because the hybrid story is about toxic emissions and the environment, fuel consumption and rising gas prices, global warming and U.S. dependence on Middle East oil.

But it's also about the transformation of capitalism.

The Hybrid Tipping Point: 2005?

Despite their tiny presence in the U.S. market, hybrids were the talk of the January 2005 Detroit Auto Show, says a report from MSNBC News.

Why? It's awfully hard to ignore exponential growth. By the end of 2003, there were well over 100,000 hybrids on the road. In 2004 Americans registered 88,000 new hybrids. In 2006 U.S. hybrid sales were around 250,000 units. Admittedly, hybrids made up only 1.5 percent of vehicle sales in 2006. But you can't blame weak demand for that. Until 2005 three companies— Toyota, Honda and Ford—sold just a few hybrid models in the U.S. market. As those multi-month waits illustrate, there were never enough gas-electric vehicles to satisfy hybrid-hungry Conscious Consumers (not to mention other green options like biomass or biodiesel).

In 2007, new hybrid sales may reach 350,000 units, driving the market share up to about two percent of vehicles sold. For one thing, Toyota will pump up 2007 shipments to the United States to 300,000 vehicles. For another, a lot more models are coming on line. By January 1, 2007, 650,000 Conscious Consumers were driving hybrids.

Coming to a Showroom near You

So far, the Toyota Prius and Honda Civic hybrid dominate the hybrid industry. (Honda also makes the lesser-known Insight model and the new Accord.) But between 2005 and 2007 the market featured a lot more hybrid options. In 2005, U.S. car manufacturers stepped up the competition:

- The Ford Mercury Mariner hybrid SUV debuted in October 2005, with 33 mpg city and 29 mpg on the highway—30 percent better than the gas-only Mariner.
- Ford, the top U.S. hybrid maker, also launched the Escape hybrid SUV in September 2004, which gets 35 to 40 mph in city driving (versus 20 mph for a gas-powered Escape).
- So-called "mild" hybrids like the Chevy Silverado and GMC Sierra pickup truck may sell, although fuel savings are only half that of full hybrids. ("This is a hybrid?" asked *Wired* in 2005. "How can you tell?")

Not to be outdone, market leader Toyota debuted two high-performance SUVS—the Lexus RX400h and the Toyota Highlander in 2005. America's top-selling Toyota Camry debuted in a hybrid model in spring 2006. By December 2006, 21,400 Camry hybrids were sold.

The Camry's entry into the hybrid sector marks the turning point, say analysts, when the hybrid trend hit "mainstream."

The Top Three Hybrid Myths

That said, hybrid dealers still have three myths to dispel if they want to maximize sales:

1. The Plug. Toyota market research shows almost half of consumers still think hybrids need their own nearby electric socket. Signs all over a U.S. auto show boldly announced: Hybrids don't have to be plugged in!
2. Power. Early hybrids weren't very zippy, and the image stuck, even though the reality did not. A Prius hybrid hit 130 mph at Bonneville National Speed Week in August 2004 in Utah. Do not try this at home.
3. Size. Plenty of drivers, it is certainly true, like roomy cars. Can hybrids overcome this factor? The SUVs certainly can. But so can some of the smaller models. "The Prius may look compact," says Christiane Perrin, "but it's spacious inside." Even in the back seat, she reports, there are no complaints from her son, a six-footer.

Meanwhile, what role should state governments play?

• One Minnesota state rep, a hybrid owner, introduced a bill to give hybrid owners state tax breaks.
• A Wisconsin bill would grant hybrid owners a $1,000 tax exemption.
• California, Virginia and Florida allow solo hybrid drivers into High-Occupancy Vehicle (HOV) lanes.
• For more on state incentives, see the endnotes for this page.

Before 2006, the federal government offered hybrid owners a tax deduction of up to $2,000. No more. Starting in 2006, U.S. hybrid owners (as well as cars powered by other clean fuels) can claim a tax credit of up to $3,400— a better deal financially. But how's this for a "strange" law? Only the first 60,000 vehicles sold (per manufacturer) fully qualify!

A Hybrid Future

Where is the hybrid trend headed? Experts are divided, *really* divided on that call.

In 2010, there will be a dazzling array of 50 hybrid models to choose from, said Thad Malesh of Automotive Technology Research Group LLC in 2005, and one million hybrids will be sold, about six percent of the market.

J. D. Powers begged to differ. By 2010, predicted one Powers analyst, hybrids will plateau at 535,000 new vehicles. Why? Because more fuel-efficient gas and diesel vehicles on line after 2006 will cool the hybrid trend. And people will be wary of the $3,000 to $4,000 premium for hybrids.

This analyst may know his cars, but he does not understand the Conscious Consumer. Why do I say that? Because his analysis is based on fuel efficiency and cost and ignores the added values factor: Hybrid owners are committed to the environment.

I think J. D. Powers is wrong. So does Bill Reinert, U.S. manager for Toyota's advanced technology group. He says that by 2025, hybrids will comprise half the U.S. market.

How Conscious Consumers Transformed the Auto Industry

If Reinert is right, the reason is threefold: (1) Conscious Consumers, (2) Visionary businesses such as Honda, Toyota and now Ford and (3) Demand-side economics.

Two big auto makers have already reversed policy to satisfy the growing demand for hybrids. GM—once a vocal hybrid skeptic—did an about-face and declared it *would* make the gas-electric cars—in partnership with DaimlerChrysler. Nissan's Carlos Ghosn wasn't keen on hybrids either. They're a "nice story," he said, "but not a good business story." But Nissan's first hybrid, an Altima sedan, will debut in 2007—with technology licensed from Toyota.

Automakers who sidestep hybrids say they're holding out for hydrogen-powered fuel cell vehicles. FCVs, as they're called, run on electricity generated by fuel cells and air. Emissions? Zilch, just a little water vapor. Even the CEO of hybrid pioneer Honda, Takeo Fukui, agrees. "I think we'll see FCVs taking over in the end game," he says.

There are just two problems. (1) The Hydrogen Vision is very expensive. "Building a network of filling stations will cost hundreds of billions of dollars," writes Brendan Koernen in "The Rise of the Green Machine," in *Wired*'s April 2005 issue. (2) A marketable hydrogen car is *at least* a decade away— maybe two! The question is not hybrids versus hydrogen. The question is what are we going to drive for the next 15 or 20 years?

If hybrids are "only" an interim solution, so be it. Conscious Consumers will take it *now*, thank you very much. Did Detroit expect us to drive toxic gas-guzzlers for the next couple decades? I leave *you* to ponder that question. Meanwhile, the people have spoken. Until something cleaner and more energy-efficient comes along, the answer is hybrids.

Our Values; Our Selves

Early on, I promised that this megatrends book would go one better than my past efforts and depict the *internal* dimension of change.

Because the inner world of ideals and belief shapes our actions.

Well, the Values-driven Consumer illustrates exactly how values alter spending patterns, triggering a thriving market for whichever goods and services reflect those values.

If 16.5 million people practice yoga, yoga mat sales will surge.

If there are an estimated 70 to 80 million Evangelicals, is it any wonder $7 billion worth of Christian and gospel albums were sold in 2004? (Religious music enjoys double-digit growth rates, so in 2007 that figure is billions higher.)

If 10 million meditate, there's a market for meditation tapes.

If most Americans want more spirituality in their lives, is it any wonder that sales of spiritual and religious books hit $2.24 billion in 2005?

Our values, those inner truths that dictate our actions, compel us to go the extra mile—or 50 miles—for organic cotton T-shirts, wait weeks for a Toyota hybrid, put Rick Warren's *The Purpose-Driven Life* (Zondervan, 2002) on international bestseller lists, demonstrate against Wal-Mart setting up shop the town over. Still many wonder: Where are the values in mainstream business?

The Spiritual Power of Corporate Brands

If values are the hallmark of enlightened capitalism, how do the companies that espouse them broadcast their virtues and beckon discriminating consumers to the cash register? Often, it is through the power of brand—that precious, yet intangible asset that symbolizes what a corporation stands for.

More than a name, logo or "iconic" CEO, a brand is a place in the heart where employees, investors, suppliers—and Conscious Consumers—meet to tell a company's story, says brand guru Elsie Maio. "When a brand reveals authenticity, values and humanity's drive toward consciousness, it's a powerful strategic advantage."

That said, let's not underestimate the *financial* power of brands. The Coca-Cola brand, for example, is worth $67 billion, says Interbrand Valuation (all figures for 2006), which puts the value of Mercedes at $21.8 billion; Dell, $12 billion; Harley-Davidson, $7.7 billion. Interbrand arrives at the valuation through an analysis of what the brand is likely to earn in the future, including projected sales and profit. Interbrand's "Global Brand Scoreboard" is published annually in *BusinessWeek*. In 2006, the company that showed the highest percentage increase over its 2005 brand value was Google, up 46 percent.

When a brand is tarnished, the balance sheet suffers. Nike stock and sales tumbled after "sweat shop" exposés. But with those troubles behind it, Interbrand Valuations counted the Nike brand's worth at close to $11 billion.

Through brand, companies discover how values drive performance.

Branding 101

Elsie Maio, president of Maio and Company and designer of the SoulBranding℠ technology, spent decades teaching corporate America how to position its identity—or brand—to consumers, investors and the public. Maio did stints on Wall Street, at McKinsey & Company and *Institutional Investor*. In 1983, she joined the firm that helped Walter Wriston craft the identity of nascent Citibank and later worked with *Fortune* 500 companies like Raytheon, Sun Life, International Harvester and IBM. But today Maio's mission is unlocking the soul power in brands.

Elsie Maio talks my language, but before I can grasp SoulBranding, I have to ask, so what is "ordinary" branding? Elsie offers a classic definition: It is the process of "building preference for a unique set of characteristics associated with a unique set of identifying symbology."

Huh?

Why do you buy Coke versus Pepsi? Why choose this kind of brown sugar water over that? Because one or the other promises a certain lifestyle, fun, peer approval or a cool image. *Brand is a promise that creates an expectation.*

That's true whether it's traditional branding or Elsie's more soulful alternative.

What Is SoulBranding?

Maio and Company offers clients a revolutionary service: It shows them how to position a brand to embody transcendent values. In fact, the firm's tag line is "Aligning Human Values, Corporate Strategy and Brand Experience." SoulBranding identifies 12 core values that consumers, employees and conscious investors expect companies to stand for: Compassion, Humility, Justice, Courage, Respect, Humanity, Empowerment, Integrity, Wholism, Broader Good, Responsibility, Excellence. "The values are *there*," says Maio. "They live in people." But how do you draw them out?

SoulBranding employs a self-auditing tool that gives employees (and other stakeholders, depending on the client's needs) the chance to rate how the corporation scores on these core values. Imagine evaluating your company on Compassion—or Justice, knowing that your opinion will reach the executive suite? The resulting scorecard benchmarks which values a company and its brand broadcast and how well it lives up to them.

But Soulbranding doesn't stop there. It also calculates what companies must do to win credibility. "We ask, 'What specific evidence would convince you that the company had changed—or improved?'" says Maio. In the end, clients get a detailed report card, a set of goals and a "snapshot of the milestones of credibility."

How did brand, Spirit and values get so connected? Much of the answer lies in the Conscious Consumer trend—and the cataclysmic changes in today's corporate landscape.

A New Day for Brand Managers

Time was, a brand manager could tell consumers just about anything and they'd pretty much "buy" it. PR and advertising mavens would concoct a top-down brand campaign, flood the marketplace with messages and successfully dictate the public's impressions. But those days are over—and so is traditional brand management.

Today, thoughtful, conscious customers and media-savvy activists carefully analyze corporate behavior. Result? These days companies had better *deliver* on their promises—or face a possible backlash. That's why Elsie Maio issues this stern warning to corporations: Invoke values and social responsibility authentically and honestly. Because your promise will be scrutinized.

When British Petroleum positioned itself as an "environmental" firm, says Maio, the company opened up lots of opportunity, but also grew more vulnerable. One slip and watchdogs—or competitors—will enthusiastically point out any inconsistency between a company action and its stated values.

"The promise of a brand, no matter how creatively scintillating," says Elsie, "is a liability unless the company delivers to all stakeholders."

Whose Brand Is It?

If experts no longer *control* a brand the way they once did, who does? I would argue, to a large extent, the answer is Conscious Consumers—and, Elsie tells me, I'm partly right. A brand is co-owned by a corporation and its stakeholders, she says, including, and perhaps especially, consumers.

Elsie cites the example of Monsanto in Europe. "Monsanto had a visionary CEO and great brand managers, but failed to recognize how strongly consumers felt about genetically modified organisms in the agricultural system," says Elsie. "So, when Monsanto went into Europe, they were shouted down."

Conscious Consumers hold corporations morally responsible.

How could Monsanto have prevented the debacle? A company can't avoid people's reactions, cautions Elsie. "But it *can* sit down with critics, find shared goals and establish milestones toward achieving them."

In Elsie Maio's vision, brand is a living, dynamic, energy fed by stakeholders, especially Conscious Consumers.

Demand-Side Economics

For better or worse, Values-driven Customers are willing to pay more for products and services that reflect their values, as this chapter repeatedly illustrates:

- The NAHB survey that showed 20 percent—the hard-core Conscious Consumers—would spend up to $5,000 for an energy-efficient, environment-saving, healthy building.
- We all know a hybrid lover who waited months to pay $3,000 more for a clean car.
- Or a natural food advocate who regularly and enthusiastically shells out more bucks at the cash register for organic produce.

As Conscious Consumers compel more producers to satisfy their demand, supply will increase and prices should fall. Meanwhile, Values-driven Consumers remain an unserved market and the next great opportunity for business. But exploiting that opening requires vision—a commodity "business as usual" can't seem to get its head around.

Listen to *Fortune* magazine: "Detroit snickered when Toyota first unveiled its Prius sedans, powered by hybrid gas-and-electric engines. But it's Toyota that's laughing now: Its hybrids are a runaway hit, outstripping Toyota's ability to keep up with demand. Smart products and a sterling reputation for quality have lifted Toyota's share of the U.S. market to 12.2% last year, from 6.4% in 1986."

As I wrote this in March 2005, the debt of General Motors was growing and sales were slumping. One reason sales were off, said commentators, was because GM had no real hybrids to offer (GM's "mild hybrids" do not compare in either environmental or energy standards to those set by Honda, Toyota and Ford). But by late 2006, GM showed signs that restructuring was yielding results.

Admittedly, Ford has its own financial issues to worry about, but Ford *has* taken a leadership role in the hybrid sector and that vision may help save the company. Furthermore, when Ford executive chairman Bill Ford (he stepped down as CEO in 2006) needed to revitalize the River Rouge car plant, where Henry Ford started making Model Ts 90 years ago, he turned to Bill McDonough, the world's leading green architect.

Result: a $2 billion grass-roofed showplace that cost no more than an ordinary factory and is cheaper to operate. The McDonough-designed natural water-drainage system has already saved Ford Motor $35 million—all the while purifying rainwater of manufacturing toxins so effectively that when the water hits the river, it is completely clean.

Bill Ford calls McDonough "one of the most profound environmental thinkers in the works." But McDonough is not your typical, anti-growth environmentalist. He's a green capitalist. His book *Cradle to Cradle* (North Point Press/Farrar, Straus and Giroux, 2002)—printed on waterproof, recycled plastic—describes a world where free enterprise and ecology live in harmony.

"The argument in commerce about growth versus no growth is a stupid argument," says McDonough. "Of course you have to grow; nature wants you to grow, and businesses want to grow." How, in McDonough's vision, do capitalism and the environment co-exist? Clearly it is through creativity and innovation, both of which are sourced in the Divine realm of consciousness.

Where did Bill Ford find the power and vision to enter the hybrid market *and* build one of the world's greenest factories? Well, it turns out, Bill Ford meditates. How do I know that, you ask? I read it in *Time* magazine!

Go ahead, laugh, if you want to. But I was once a researcher at *Forbes* magazine, where my primary responsibility was fact checking. My fellow researchers and I were frequently treated to hair-raising tales about what happened to fact checkers who got it wrong. Believe me, it was not a pretty picture. So I report to you with a high level of confidence that Bill Ford meditates—and with total confidence that Ford manufactures hybrids and builds green factories.

Very interesting, huh?

And now with Ford CEO Alan Mulally running the company day-to-day, Bill Ford will have more time for his visionary interests. That will contribute to both Ford and the environment.

6

The Wave of Conscious Solutions

As AOL's director of business strategy, Joel Smernoff, 40, called his work "frantic and intense." The endless deluge of e-mails, phone calls and instant messaging was brain-numbing, nerve wracking and overwhelming. "You're always putting out fires and you never really solve anything."

It is an affliction millions of managers can relate to. But Smernoff, an athletic, competitive six-footer, whose weekend passion is amateur car racing, found the perfect antidote. Four or five times a week, he ducked out of his seventh-floor Manhattan office and headed to the 20-by-25-foot conference room AOL employees dub "the Gym" for a company-sponsored class in yoga or meditation. Smernoff calls it an "escape from his brain," a "sanctuary"— and a "big advantage."

Do meditation and yoga boost his productivity? I ask. "In terms of the number of calls I return?" Smernoff replies. "Not really." But is that the right way to measure productivity? By counting output only, instead of also analyzing the *caliber* of what we achieve? When it comes to quality, Smernoff harbors no doubt as to the power of his highly conscious practices.

"Out of the fight, I can see the big picture. What's really important? What are my priorities? It's like when you're in the shower in the morning and you get this great brainstorm." Besides, he adds, "It lowers my blood pressure and prevents burnout by giving me a daily outlet for stress."

Smernoff compares yoga and meditation to the weekend car racing he has enjoyed for seven years. Both require total and complete focus. When he races with the BMW Car Club of America or the Sports Car Club on tracks like Danville, Virginia's International Raceway or Connecticut's Lime Rock Park, he says, "You can't think of anything else. What are the tires doing? Am I taking this corner too fast?" It's the same thing in yoga and meditation, he says, except the focus is all within. "Everyone *talks* about living in the moment. But this is *it*."

When I caught up with Joel a year after we first talked, an old AOL boss had recruited him to Paltalk, a leader in the multimedia (voice, video, text, chatroom) space and the fourth-largest Instant Message company. "It was hard to give up those great yoga benefits at AOL," he says. "But I'm so sold on yoga, I've adjusted pretty well."

Which is a good thing since Smernoff's stress level hasn't dropped one iota. In his new job as Paltalk's COO, he wears a lot of hats—revamping the website and product design, upgrading customer service and fraud detection—and, of course, doing his share of sales and marketing.

"I don't even take a lunch anymore," he admits. Nevertheless, Smernoff discreetly closes his office door each afternoon for five to ten minutes of sun salutations and other yoga flows. Then three or four times a week, he'll do yoga at one of Manhattan's Equinox gyms.

"Sitting for too long in a chair is the worst," he tells me.

That's for sure, replies one of the world's worst offenders.

"But you can do yoga in your chair."

You can?

"I do it all the time," he says. "There was a piece on it in *Yoga Journal* by Cyndi Lee, who is a great yoga teacher. I'll send you the link."

You will find that information in this book's endnotes. Cyndi, the founder of OM Yoga Center in New York City and a practitioner of Tibetan Buddhism, has taught yoga for more than 20 years and says you can do almost an entire yoga routine at your desk. Check it out.

Smernoff, a four-year yoga fan, wasn't always such an enthusiast. Prodded by a girlfriend to sample the spiritual side, he was skeptical at first. But a few classes later, Smernoff was hooked. "She and I broke up, but I went hard core into this stuff." Today, he says, "I'm an evangelist."

Coming to a Company Near You

We've entered an exciting new era that will welcome the widespread application of "conscious" techniques in business. The first wave of companies is embracing these techniques, as the proof of their positive, concrete results is substantiated by studies.

- Scores of top firms and hundreds, if not thousands, of other workplaces—high tech, traditional and nonprofit—sponsor meditation seminars, often billed as "stress management."
- American Express experimented with "forgiveness training" and watched sales soar.
- 100,000 people in some 100 blue chip firms have experienced HeartMath, a technology that monitors the positive influence of emotions like joy and love on productivity, performance, health and well-being.
- Some 8,000 EMC salespeople have been initiated into fire walking.
- Corporate Transformation Tools, an exciting new survey instrument, inspired by the seven levels of corporate consciousness and implemented at IKEA, Microsoft and Ford, aligns personal and organizational values, triggering a host of welcome results.
- At Xerox, a Native American-style "Vision Quest" helped dream up the 265 DC, an environmentally friendly, hot-selling copier.

Why is business invoking conscious tools to drive success and productivity? I'd ask the question in another way: Why *wouldn't* business, which is ever the patron saint of the practical, embrace any technique—mundane, spiritual or Martian—that generates results?

The Trends behind the Trends

The "Wave of Conscious Solutions" is headed to a company near you because of several interesting new directions.

Plenty of managers and executives successfully practice techniques like meditation in private. They're already sold on how brilliantly the peace of contemplation penetrates the fog of stress to sort out tricky work problems. "Relax into high performance," reads the brochure of one executive meditation teacher.

Relax and performance in the same sentence? You bet.

In the wake of downsizing—and spiraling workloads for layoff survivors—productivity (as well as human stress) is off the charts. Meanwhile companies, still touchy about ethics concerns, are receptive to solutions based on creativity and integrity. If new answers venture into previously taboo territory like spirituality—well, at least there's no criminal intent!

Besides, the price is right. Meditation and yoga cost "peanuts," says one insider, compared to the big bucks business shells out for team building or sales training. And after a meditation seminar, employees report feeling relaxed, alert, productive and motivated.

Finally, scientists, artists and engineers have always found solutions to intractable problems in the intangible realm of consciousness. Einstein discovered the Theory of Relativity, it is said, in a daydream. The corporate creativity that is nurtured through spiritual solutions may show up as productivity gains, but it is sourced in the Divine realm of consciousness.

The New Economy of Consciousness

Remember, the Information Age is yesterday. Economic wealth is increasingly derived from a new source:

Technological innovation, in fact, *all* business invention, grows out of consciousness—the awareness of awareness, the capacity to observe without attachment.

Human consciousness is the new raw material. This priceless resource is arguably as precious as financial capital, oil or technology. One single conscious engineer—or a small team of them—can discover the unique, universal application that will launch the next $100 billion industry.

That's how it goes in the New Economy of Consciousness. And that's in large part why the tools and techniques that enhance consciousness will continue to find their way into business.

I'll describe several conscious techniques embraced by mainstream business, but first I want to tell the personal story of one high-profile businessman who endured a very challenging spiritual initiation—and later brought the insights from his spiritual journey into one of the world's most famous companies.

Profiles in Commitment: Personal Healing and Corporate Transformation

It is December 1998. I'm in Puerto Vallarta, Mexico, for the International Conference on Business and Consciousness. Down by the pool, I run into my old Spirit in business buddy Martin Rutte, one of the movement's earliest and greatest advocates. Within moments, Martin is introducing me to a youthful, dark-haired fellow with a slight Aussie accent.

"Michael Rennie," Martin promises, "will be the hit of the conference." Diplomatically, Rennie shakes off the compliment, offers some kind words about my book *Re-inventing the Corporation* and heads back toward the hotel.

As Martin and I settle into our beach chairs, he tells me that Rennie and his colleague Gita Bellin will present some dramatic findings about the power of Spirit to grow corporate productivity. I'm all ears—especially when Martin mentions that Rennie is a partner at McKinsey, the world's top consulting firm, an outfit better known in the 1990s for advising clients on slash-and-burn tactics than for anything that smacks of spirituality.

Now I'm *really* curious.

"Yeah, McKinsey and spirituality," laughs Martin. "It's like Nixon going to China."

Michael Rennie, I soon learn, is a super-achiever. The youngest this, the brightest that. Rhodes Scholar. Oxford. McKinsey. The whole nine yards.

But there is something about Rennie I do not know. Perhaps it is a truth that reveals itself when the time is right. I don't discover it for six more years. Researching this book in 2004, I "Google" Michael and get an intriguing story by Australian personality columnist Maxine McKew that begins, "At age 30, Michael Rennie decided to live. It is as straightforward as that." In Maxine's article I find the missing link between Rennie's "dress for success" bio and his more obscure identity as a modern corporate shaman.

At age 30, Michael Rennie was diagnosed with lymphoma. He had two massive abdominal tumors and was given a 40 percent chance to survive. Rennie underwent aggressive chemotherapy, then threw himself into "mind-body" studies, applying his considerable intellectual skills to the hottest scientific discoveries about the mind's surprising power to enter deep meditative states and heal the body through rest and visualization.

Rennie activated and commanded the power of his brain waves—alpha, beta, theta, delta—to heal him of cancer.

During chemo, "a cold, horrible process," while fighting off nausea, Rennie summoned up the painstaking discipline to replace negative thoughts with positive ones. "I'd create scenes . . . being on top of a mountain in Switzerland with friends," he says. "And it worked. If I could hold these thoughts, the nausea started to go down." He boosted his white blood cell count so steeply, his skeptical doctors demanded retests.

Rennie took a year off to think himself back to health, then returned to work—a changed man. He embraced the part of him that loves the "real" world and wants to make a contribution, yet never forgot the self "that had gone down another path of understanding."

Rennie was determined to integrate them both—and succeeded.

But the new Michael Rennie gave up the 70-hour work weeks, limitless work demands and dangerous desire to please others. He learned new habits—eating right, getting a good night's sleep, saying no and taking time for himself. "I work less since I had cancer," he says. "But I get more done."

At least once a year, he goes off alone for reflection and solitude.

By invoking Spirit to command his body back to wellness, Rennie earned a clean bill of health. But the story doesn't end there.

Illness is one of the Universe's most transformative initiations. In the case of Michael Rennie, Spirit tapped a potent force for corporate change. Cancer transformed Rennie's work life and taught him to find peace and stillness in the midst of boardrooms, clients and travel. It gave him "clarity and purposefulness."

Spirit opened Rennie's eyes to the power of transformation and taught him by personal example which techniques would achieve it, the conscious tools that business is increasingly adopting.

Back in Puerto Vallarta, Michael Rennie and Gita Bellin wow us with their fascinating findings. They screen an exciting video about how visualization and other spiritual tools help employees raise the bar and set new personal bests.

Rennie and Bellin have applied conscious technologies to clients such as ANZ Bank, the recipient of a 2004 International Spirit at Work Award.

ANZ's Breakout initiative, a three-and-a-half year, companywide adventure in culture transformation, featured personal development workshops for some 26,000 employees, a "high-performance mind technique" and several quiet rooms in which to practice it.

As the effect of the Breakout program took hold, ANZ went from being a "least-preferred employer" to an "employer of choice." In addition:

- Staff satisfaction rose 35 percent in four years.
- ANZ won Australia's "Bank of the Year" three years in a row.
- ANZ's stock price doubled.

Former breakout program manager Sonia Stojanovic summarized the power of conscious business: "We're giving people hope—the hope to find meaning and not to compartmentalize their lives into home and work and self. We're inviting people to ask the questions: Why am I here? What is my contribution? How can the work I'm doing and the service I'm providing bring forth the best I can be in every moment? People really want to be accountable; they want to take responsibility; they want to feel that what they are doing is being counted as contributing to the success of the organization."

As Michael Rennie masterfully melts the firewall between personal spirituality and corporate transformation, he is increasingly recognized as one of the world's true business masters. And Rennie powerfully illustrates the theme we explored in this book's first chapter: that individual healing is spilling out from people into companies to catalyze corporate transformation.

You'll hear more of his wisdom in this chapter's final pages.

The Productivity of Spirit

From yoga to HeartMath, from fire walking to forgiveness, the full spectrum of spiritual and conscious techniques that have benefited individuals for decades is, one by one, winding up in mainstream business.

Meditation: Gateway to Corporate Consciousness

The Guinness estate in Normandy, France, might seem a peculiar place to test the limits of human potential. But here in July 2001 two Buddhist monks are rigged up to a complete array of Western medical paraphernalia. The room is about 40 degrees Fahrenheit, and the monks are wrapped in bedsheets dripping with ice water. Once they reach a deep, restful state through the advanced yogic meditation called "g Tum-mo," technicians measure their vital signs. Then, once, twice, three times, to the astonishment of onlookers, the holy men raise their body heat and literally dry the sheets off their backs.

Who's behind such an experiment? None other than Harvard Medical School associate professor Herbert Benson, M.D., who took meditation mainstream with the publication of his acclaimed bestseller *The Relaxation Response* (expanded and updated, HarperTorch, 2000).

Though few corporations will capitalize on meditation's sheet-drying potential—as if your average customer service rep could repeat such a feat!—there's no question business is reaping other well-known benefits. Meditation, as Benson and others have proven, decreases blood pressure, heart rate, respiratory rate and oxygen consumption.

As corporations are discovering, meditation is the alchemical cure to the malady ruining us all—stress—which costs U.S. business $200 billion a year, according to the National Institute for Occupational Safety & Health.

Time Warner's AOL unit brought in meditation to help the sales and marketing staff, which was cut from 850 to 500 members, to "deal with the new 12-hour days." (I hope it helped but companies should not invoke meditation to justify stress levels that are just too high.)

After only four months of meditation, scientists report, levels of the stress hormone cortisol drop. People grow more stress-resilient; that is to say, external factors don't trigger as much stress.

But better health is only one of meditation's many wonderful gifts.

Corporate Meditation: How Companies Benefit

In the New Economy of Consciousness, where one talented person may well birth the next hundred-billion-dollar industry, it is no wonder that business is exploring the creative power of meditation:

- Successful high tech companies like Apple, Google and Yahoo! as well as mainstream firms like McKinsey and Hughes Aircraft sponsor meditation courses.
- Pharmaceutical company AstraZeneca's three meditation courses are designed to energize the company's 6,000 employees.
- California-based Clarity Seminars has offered meditation and stress management seminars to more than 13,000 people at some 200 workplaces, including at IBM, 3Com, Cisco, Solectron, Nokia, Yahoo!, NASA, Sun Microsystems and the Pacific Stock Exchange.
- Eric Biskamp, cofounder of Dallas's WorkLife Seminars, has taught meditation to execs at Texas Instruments, Raytheon and Nortel Networks.

The logic behind today's corporate meditation trend is clear. Meditation fires up alpha, theta and delta brain waves. It increases concentration, boosts intuition, relieves fatigue, juices up creativity and enhances organization skills. What's not to like?

Besides, after a modest initial cost, it's *free*.

No wonder, as *BusinessWeek* put it, "Companies increasingly are falling for the allure of meditation, offering free on-site classes."

A Brief History of Corporate Meditation

Meditation hit the U.S. scene in the 1960s when Beatles guru Maharishi Mahesh Yogi gained widespread prominence. Over the next few decades, the

Hindu teacher's Transcendental Meditation (TM) expanded its U.S. presence. Since 1970, there have been 500+ research studies on meditation; TM-related research appeared in the American Heart Association's *Hypertension*, the *American Journal of Cardiology* and *Anxiety, Stress and Coping*.

TM trained "tens of thousands of business professionals" in hundreds of companies, says Robert Roth, author of *TM: Transcendental Meditation* (revised and updated, Plume, 1994).

After three months of meditation at a *Fortune* 100 company identified only as a "large Midwest manufacturing plant," employees registered:

- less anxiety, tension, insomnia and fatigue,
- reduced use of tobacco and hard liquor,
- greater effectiveness and job satisfaction,
- improved health and fewer health complaints.

When TM arrived at H. A. Montgomery, a Detroit chemical manufacturer, results were so dramatic, they may have fueled more skeptics than converts.

Owner "Buck" Montgomery introduced TM in 1983, reports a 1996 story in *The Washington Post*. Three years later, 52 of the company's 70 workers meditated 20 minutes twice a day—at home before work, then again in the afternoon on company time. Results were astounding:

- Absenteeism fell 85 percent.
- Injuries fell 70 percent.
- Sick days dropped 76 percent.
- Productivity soared 120 percent.
- Quality control rose 240 percent.
- Profits skyrocketed 520 percent.

What happened next? Buck sold the business in 1987 and went to work for TM, and the new owners of H. A. Montgomery discontinued the meditation program!

Admittedly, this is an old study, but I report these findings rather than dismiss them because, as amazing (even questionable) as these numbers sound, they're consistent with the results meditation practitioners report.

Furthermore, what other protocol can you follow to achieve numbers like those? You can slash, burn and cut costs like crazy, but you're not going to reduce sick days, raise productivity or boost quality control to the tune of the percentages cited above.

If meditation were a machine, every CEO in America would buy one!

Besides, I have a not-so-hidden agenda: I hope to stimulate *new* research into meditation and productivity. I'll tell you more about my idea later in this chapter.

The Forgiveness Project

The first pioneering experiments into the productivity of Spirit, now coming to light, are very promising. Consider the spiritual value of forgiveness, a blue chip financial firm and a typical objective—sales growth.

Fred Luskin, Ph.D., director of the Stanford Forgiveness Project, took the spiritual techniques he's long taught individuals into financial giant American Express. The results spoke volumes.

Three vice presidents and 13 financial advisors from the Upstate New York Marketing Group signed on for a year's training in emotional competence, stress management and forgiveness. Luskin and company kicked it off with a one-day workshop and some homework: Luskin's own book *Forgive for Good* (HarperCollins, 2002) and an article by best-selling author Stephen Covey. Later, Luskin crafted individualized plans to focus on areas where an advisor was seen as "weak." There were conference calls and biweekly coaching sessions.

In time, Luskin measured the results. Stress fell 25 percent. A test that gauges positive feelings soared 20 percent, and sales—measured by an AmEx metric called "Time of Sale Gross Dealer Concession"—shot up 18.3 percent.

But here's the kicker: The Upstate New York Marketing Group, as a whole, grew sales 11 percent, compared with the 18+ percent for Luskin's group. That means the "forgiveness"-trained advisors beat their peers by 60 percent.

Luskin's experiment was just the beginning. He repeated the "forgiveness training" for three additional cohorts, and the results just got better. The second and third groups showed a 24 percent rise in sales and the fourth registered a 46 percent uptick.

All in all, the average AmEx participant increased productivity by 25 percent (compared to ten percent for his or her peers). Stress levels overall fell 29 percent and the "positive emotions" metric, again on average, grew 24 percent.

Luskin modestly and scientifically reports his findings in a memo entitled, "The Training of Emotional Competence in Financial Services Advisors." Finally he permits a hint of enthusiasm to slip into his conclusion.

"Remarkably, the advisors who participated in this project demonstrated a 60 to 400 percent improvement in productivity over their peers," he writes.

Maybe he can't say it, but I can: Wow.

HeartMath

What if Love, Courage and Joy could be scientifically measured and linked to employee vitality and productivity? Would *Fortune* 500 firms jump at the chance to apply this cutting-edge technology in day-to-day business? The answer is they already do.

Thanks to a revolutionary technique called HeartMath, more than 100 companies, including Hewlett-Packard, BP, Genentech, Cisco, Boeing, Motorola and Liz Claiborne, have clocked productivity gains in areas like leadership, sales and customer service. HeartMath's Inner Quality Management program was featured in *Harvard Business Review.*

How does it work? To simplify a complex body-mind-spirit link: When the heart is beating smoothly and rhythmically, people think and perform better.

Specifically, HeartMath has created technology that enables a personal computer to measure heart rhythms, then actually allows people to observe how stress and negative thoughts or emotions clamp down on heart rhythms to produce a choppy, turbulent graph.

Positive thoughts, however, and the emotions associated with uplifting values (like Love or Joy) *calm* the jagged lines into a nice even pattern. These more harmonious cadences, it has been scientifically shown, correlate with lower blood pressure, reduced arrhythmias—and improved productivity.

So HeartMath teaches people how to observe, monitor and balance their heart rhythms—the key to intelligence, vitality and high performance.

Since 1998, HeartMath has garnered an impressive track record:

- The customer service unit of a *Fortune* 50 tech firm cut stress 50 percent and improved customer listening 33 percent.
- A healthcare firm reduced turnover 50 percent, raised customer satisfaction 27 percent, saved $1.5 million in two years and was ranked #1 nationwide in employee satisfaction.
- 75 percent of executives saw dramatic improvements in performance, resilience, health and leadership.

What's behind these results?

HeartMath taps into the "intelligence of the heart," a wise, intuitive source of guidance that, as HeartMath puts it, can "lift us from chaos to clarity" and fulfillment. "The heart is the central tower of the body's systems and overall health," says HeartMath executive VP Howard Martin.

Fire Walking

During the tech boom, data storage giant EMC was famous for an aggressive corporate culture. Not surprisingly, the $9.6 billion *Fortune* 500 company based in Hopkinton, Massachusetts, liked its conscious business on the macho side. Since 1995, some 8,000 EMC salespeople and others have performed the ancient ritual of fire walking—trekking over a 14-foot-long "carpet" of red-hot coals.

But first they attend a four-hour corporate seminar taught by Mark Magnacca, president of Insight Development Group in Upton, Massachusetts. Magnacca, who says he has personally performed more than 150 fire walks, has taught fire walking to sales folks at Columbo Yogurt, Metropolitan Life Insurance and Pitney Bowes.

Magnacca's job is to prepare would-be coal walkers for the daunting task ahead. How? By changing how people *think* about the experience. Thoughts, says Magnacca, alter body chemistry to empower people to withstand the sizzling, 1,000-degree embers.

"Cold calling is going to be a piece of cake after you do this," Magnacca told one group. That's for sure.

"We're always looking for new ways to challenge them," says EMC VP Jeff Goldberg, who calls fire walking "tremendously uplifting." Goldberg, himself a three-time fire walker, offers no proof that fire walking *directly* translates into fulfilled sales quotas. But EMC clearly thinks fire walking changes behavior—in positive, productive ways. For openers, salespeople who face their fears dissolve limitations and boost self-confidence.

More importantly, fire walkers are more likely to "go over the head" of traditional sales contacts and call CEOs or CIOs, says one EMC sales manager. My sources at EMC tell me the company has changed a lot since the tech crash and is working hard to foster consultative, trust-building relationships—especially with customers. But one thing has not changed. Fire walking remains a time-honored corporate tradition.

Transformation, Success and Metrics Too

In 1998, The Methodist Hospital in Houston, Texas, a 7,000-employee/1,000-bed operation, was at a crossroads. Methodist had lost touch with its faith-based values, the board declared, and was growing more secular every day.

Too bad, some would say, that's life—or at least business.

The Methodist Hospital instead named Tom Daugherty to the new post of vice president of spiritual care, jump-starting cultural transformation and in time superior performance.

By 2004, Methodist had racked up impressive metrics and kudos:

- Turnover fell from 24 percent in 2002 to 15 percent in 2004.
- Vacancy rates dropped from 6.7 percent to 3.1 percent.
- Methodist won a "Spirit at Work" award in 2002.

Methodist's breakthroughs celebrate a fascinating new assessment tool inspired by the seven levels of organizational consciousness.

"You can't always identify a clear line of sight between cultural change and operational performance," warns Daugherty, who is now retired. Even so, the results speak for themselves. The Methodist Hospital was also named by *U.S. News & World Report* one of the top 100 U.S. hospitals.

Corporate Tools

Committed to revitalizing its vision, mission and values, Methodist hired spiritual business consultant Cindy Wigglesworth in 2001. Cindy is the former Exxon executive you met in chapter four. Armed with "Corporate Transformation Tools," a values-driven survey instrument that has successfully mapped corporate and personal values at Ford, Microsoft, Corning, IKEA, Siemens, and ING Bank, Wigglesworth carried forth the journey to transform Methodist's culture.

The Corporate Tools, created by Richard Barrett, a veteran Spirit in business guru and founder of the World Bank's Spiritual Unfoldment Society, expands Abraham Maslow's famous "hierarchy of needs" to seven levels—which, as I read it, parallel the seven levels of the human chakra system. (I'll get to that part in a minute.)

The idea is simple: People feel fulfilled when companies reflect their personal values. Barrett's tools help align individual and organization values, which is great in and of itself. But there's often an added benefit in that positive, productive effects later follow.

Barrett & Co. customizes a list of 90 values for each client. Every employee who takes the survey selects ten values that best reflect his or her experience. The Corporate Tools survey measures: (1) the employees' personal values; (2) the values they now experience in the workplace; and (3) the values they *want* to see in the organization—the *desired* values. This dynamic mix of diverse values is plotted on a grid that portrays the "Seven Levels of Organizational Consciousness." Each level reflects the issues dealt with in the parallel human chakra. Security, for example, is a first chakra value (for both people and organizations), while self-esteem relates to the third chakra.

Now it's all there in black and white, the Big Picture—a matrix that compares and contrasts: (1) employee values, (2) current organizational values, (3) desired workplace values.

What did Methodist Hospital discover? Among other findings, that employees highly valued "compassion" (not surprisingly since they are drawn to the health field), but rated the organization as lacking it. A discrepancy. By contrast, employees ranked "accountability" high on the personal, current and desired scales.

"People intuitively know where an organization needs to grow," says Wigglesworth. Tom Daugherty and senior Methodist managers had already chosen Integrity, Compassion, Accountability, Respect and Excellence as core values and adopted the acronym "ICARE." These "espoused organizational values," as Corporate Tools calls them, were measured against the employee values that emerged during the survey phase.

Wigglesworth then huddled with small groups to interpret and ground the values at the grassroots level. How might a value like "respect"—which employees widely admired—translate into specific behavior, she asked them. People responded with statements like, "We will value our differences in background, experience and lifestyle and listen to others' opinions."

"Each work group ended up with 15 behaviors specific to their areas of expertise and responsibility," says Wigglesworth. People signaled their commitment by literally signing their names to a chart of the values and behaviors.

By 2003, when Methodist resurveyed employees, values were already much more on track. The *current* culture, said employees, was more aligned with personal and desired organizational values—on 33 out of the 35 values measured.

But that wasn't all. Financial benefits had already started showing up.

The Methodist Hospital and the Corporate Tools organization are cautious and modest about the results. That's admirable but I think it's possible to see a clear, unequivocal connection between consciousness and economics. Morale for nurses improved, so vacancy rates for nurses—which were sky-high because of widespread shortages—fell to a historic low of two percent. Methodist not only shaved the high cost of hiring contract nurses, but also improved patient satisfaction—a key metric in hospital management. From December 2001 to December 2002, patient satisfaction rose from 80.5 to 88. By 2004, Methodist employees said that "90 percent of the time," the values in their workplace reflect their own. Today, Methodist Hospital is on *Fortune's* "100 Best Companies" list.

That's a stunning success by any measure and a great example of how spiritual-based tools and cultural transformation raise productivity.

Vision Quest

In the 1990s Xerox sponsored vision quests—a corporate version of the Native American coming of age ritual—to seek inspiration and guidance in making better products. From the boardroom to the mailroom, 300 Xerox employees braved 24 hours of solitude, armed only with water and a sleeping bag, in New York's Catskill Mountains or the New Mexico desert.

"For almost everyone," said then chief engineer John F. Elter, who led Xerox's $400 million product development initiative, "this was a real spiritual experience."

One breakthrough came when a team of engineers out in the wilderness came upon a Xerox paper carton floating in a puddle of motor oil at the bottom of a pit. Appalled to see the company logo amidst a scene of such environmental degradation, they vowed to devise a pollution-free machine.

Out of this extraordinary adventure was born the 265 DC, Xerox's first digital copier-printer-fax, a "green" product that became a top-seller. Impressed by Xerox's success, top honchos from Nike, Ford and Harley-Davidson visited Xerox's Rochester offices to study the project's success.

Former lead engineer Ed de Jong says, "We changed our corporate culture . . . we designed a machine that was different and we did it faster than earlier programs. . . . Did we get a return on our investment? Absolutely."

Says software manager Kathy Berretta, "I couldn't see myself in the woods chanting or banging a drum, but away from work in a new environment we learned to trust each other. When we came back, everyone was willing to help each other, rather than compete."

Berretta is still talking about her 1995 vision quest, but Xerox is not. The vision quests were halted during Xerox's painful reorganization.

On the brink of bankruptcy in 2000, Xerox is in the midst of a powerful comeback. By January 2005 Xerox had shown a profit in 10 of the previous 11 quarters. CEO Anne Mulcahy is widely admired for *that* track record and for cutting Xerox's secured debt in half since 2005. No wonder *BusinessWeek* in 2005 named her one of its "Best Managers of the Year." No doubt Xerox is still in the market for a breakthrough product like the 265 DC. Isn't it about time to redeploy the successful vision quest?

Spirit and Business: The Missing Link

There's something about the link between Spirit and business that I've always sensed, but could never quite put my finger on. My insight, when I find it, will show hard-nosed go-getters the practical power of Spirit, yet take them to a depth of truth that no one, however ambitious, can manipulate.

As I research this chapter, a guru arrives to teach me. She is Tevis Trower, the founder of New York's Balance Integration Corp., which teaches yoga and meditation to TimeWarner, Yahoo!, Google, Apple and many other companies large and small. After 13 years in business development at companies like Coca-Cola and UPS, all the while pursuing her own inner path, Tevis went out on her own as a spiritual entrepreneur. Her last employer, AOL, became her first client.

I am happily chatting with Tevis, jotting down her remarks. She is about to teach a course to 30 executives at the world's largest public relations agency and was just quoted in the *BusinessWeek* story entitled "Zen and the Art of Corporate Productivity." Then something she says gives me goose bumps. "In business, the goal is to manipulate the *external* world," Tevis tells me and I can almost anticipate what she is going to say next.

"Stephen Covey [of *Seven Habits* fame] talks about 'expanding your sphere of influence,'" she says. *"But how can you exert control over your surroundings without first mastering your own thoughts and emotions?"*

As Tevis's words ring in my ears, I finally "get" it.

What business leaders need more than anything else is exactly what Spirit offers: The power of self-mastery.

Self-knowledge and personal mastery, the fruits of spiritual practice, are also key to the worldly pursuits of leadership, high performance, power. Yet self-mastery is sorely missing in business (not to mention politics).

The failure of self-mastery is often the downfall of leadership.

And the most reliable route to self-mastery is personal spiritual discipline—reflection, journaling, meditation—the sort of activity designed to force busy, stressed-out, Type A people to sit still and simply *be*. True, spiritual practice will lift your consciousness and bring you closer to the Divine—but there's a mundane benefit as well: The clear thinking it nurtures will prevent you from making costly mistakes!

Tyco's Dennis Kozlowski, Enron's Jeff Skilling, the Rigas of Adelphia and many others might have avoided the courthouse—and worse—were they as skilled at self-mastery as they were at business. Sadly, each made what looked like reckless, self-destructive errors. I'm not judging them. Who *hasn't* made terrible mistakes? A jury may have pronounced them guilty. But who knows what was in their hearts? What I *am* saying is the spiritual power of self-mastery could have alerted each of them—and can save the rest of us from ourselves—by increasing their awareness of the consequences of their actions.

But back to Tevis's and my conversation.

"Corporations reorganize; they bring in McKinsey or Accenture," Tevis says. "That's like moving the furniture around. You can create some very cool space by doing that. But ultimately, what good does it do you to change the decor when there are cracks in the foundation?"

The crack in the corporate infrastructure, of course, is the profound and widespread lack of self-mastery. Without people who possess expertise in self-knowledge and self-regulation, how can you create a sustainable, high-performance culture?

"Imagine how beautifully we could manage people—and the world," Tevis tells me, "if we could only master ourselves."

Calling All Consultants

Say you're a soulful business consultant or spiritual coach. How do you teach the potent tool of self-mastery and turn corporations into clients?

Tevis gives me several ideas. One reason she's so successful at selling spiritual tools to business is that, as a marketing executive, she has mastered basic sales principles—simple skills that few spiritual types would ever study. Most of us are so skeptical of the word "sell" that we call it "hype" and run the other way. It is, I believe, high time we got over *that* one.

For openers, the best sales methods are grounded in the wisdom that it's impossible to manipulate any intelligent person to buy something. Furthermore, if we are serious about transforming capitalism, we'd better figure out how to "open the corporate doors."

Tevis succeeds in synthesizing both marketing and spiritual practice. I've summarized her wisdom under three headings.

1. Sell the Benefit: What are you, as a spiritual leader, selling to business? What's your "product"? Meditation? Yoga? Corporate transformation? Great! But how does your customer know what those practices will do for them?

Enter the core sales precept: Sell the benefit.

The best saleswoman isn't hawking a cell phone or Swiffer mop. She is selling what those handy little devices will *do* for the customer. She's selling the benefit: be it a warm chat with a loved one, a sparkling floor or time to kick back and read a magazine. The best salespeople sell the benefit.

Tevis's mantra is, "I take mindfulness tools into corporate America to support creativity, productivity and well-being." In her case, yoga and meditation are clearly mindful practices, but when Tevis talks to clients, she extols the benefit: She talks about what she calls "peace of mind at any time."

Peace? *That* they get.

Furthermore, by naming her product "peace of mind," instead of stress management, a popular euphemism for meditation, Tevis shifts the context from the negative of stress to the uplifting benefit of peace.

2. Know Your Customer: To those who say Spirit in business advocates should "tell it like it is" and *speak* the word "Spirit," Tevis offers this warning: *"If it's not relevant to the customer, it won't work."*

Rather than impose an agenda on the client, Tevis asks questions: "What is everyone concerned about here? What sort of changes are going on? Have there been any mergers, downsizings, management changes?"

3. Use Sales as a Spiritual Discipline: All the while, Tevis engages in active listening, which, she says, "compels me to hear the client's needs, tune in to where they are open to spiritual solutions, then figure out how to 'language to' their comfort level. It forces me to be very present."

Keeping the Faith

Tevis has endured many defeats in her quest to bring mindfulness to business. Once she won approval for a one-year program only to have the company president declare that it sent "the wrong message."

Then there was the time she was set to launch a ten-week initiative—and top managers vetoed it. Did they freak out about the spiritual content? Not this time. They were afraid people would get so in touch with their creativity that they'd quit their jobs!

Yet Tevis remains philosophical—and respectful of the huge step it is to bring Spirit to business. "If you invite consciousness into corporations," she says, "there's no telling what will·follow. Companies should consider how to support the high frequencies they're liberating."

Tevis is devoted to "mainstreaming" consciousness in business, to transmuting ancient wisdom into valuable modern nuggets and to reaching people who "would never do this." Her goals are modest yet extraordinary.

Tevis looks up at the Manhattan skyscrapers all around her and the windows that have been sealed since the day they were built. "If I can crack open a window to consciousness," she concludes, "anything can happen."

Business Turns to Spirit

Let me rephrase the question I posed earlier in this chapter: Why should business turn to Spirit to fulfill mundane goals like sales quotas?

When *Fortune* ran a July 2001 cover story provocatively entitled "God and Business," writer Marc Gunther, a wonderful voice for conscious business who later authored *Faith and Fortune* (Crown, 2004), went out of his way to say what the story was *not* about. "It's not about deploying spirituality in your company to boost productivity . . ." Hmm, I remember thinking, why *not?* Does Mark's editor at *Fortune* (to say nothing of *Fortune* readers) deem the productivity of Spirit so preposterous that the magazine refuses to touch the notion?

Possibly. Mainstream business is firmly rooted in the physical world. Is it any wonder then that the marketplace of man is skeptical of solutions that rely on an intangible source? If you could pick up meditation, fire walking or forgiveness training at Staples, they couldn't keep the stuff in stock.

But business is practical—and willing to try almost anything. By 2003, *BusinessWeek* was extolling the strategic benefits of meditation in its story "Zen and the Art of Corporate Productivity."

Conversely, a dear friend who's devoted to the Spirituality in business movement turns her nose up at companies who seek Spirit to bolster profit or performance. These motives, in her words, are "all the wrong reasons."

I disagree. Seekers on the spiritual path turn to Spirit for anything and everything. Peace, compassion, love, a new car or a healthier bank account.

American business already invests a gold mine in training designed to teach business people how to think out of the box. The mystery is why business hasn't gone a lot further. I believe the problem lies not with business but with the advocates of consciousness in business. (I'm not criticizing here. I include myself.) Daunted by the strict face of the business establishment, we've lacked the courage to drum up the research funds, conduct the studies and celebrate the results in business. We need a coach, a role model.

We need to study the bellwether sector of healthcare.

Medicine: A Bellwether for Business

Back in the 1970s, registered nurses began experimenting with a spiritual energy technique called Therapeutic Touch, which involves scanning a patient's body. "Therapeutic Touch has been derived from the ancient practice of the laying-on of hands," writes Janet Macrae, Ph.D., R.N., in *Therapeutic Touch: A Practical Guide* (Knopf, 1996).

Many RNs felt sure the treatment helped people, but there was no proof. Then in 1975 one trailblazer, Dolores Krieger, Ph.D., R.N., who with her colleague Dora Kunz pioneered the modern practice, submitted Therapeutic Touch to scientific protocols and published the findings in the *American Journal of Nursing*. Patients who received Therapeutic Touch, she discovered, showed "significantly greater increases in mean hemoglobin" levels than a control group who received routine nursing care.

The experiment was a "milestone in the development of Therapeutic Touch into a recognized clinical method," writes Janet Macrae. For decades now, nurses have routinely studied Therapeutic Touch in nursing schools and healing centers and the practice is widespread. Therapeutic Touch has helped heal indigestion, headaches, high blood pressure, ulcers, wounds, infections and burns, says Macrae.

Today, as we witness the dawn of an era that will mark the wholesale importation of scores of spiritual approaches into business, medicine will serve as the bellwether. Why? Because it has already subjected the most common spiritual "technique" imaginable to rigorous scientific study.

Under the Microscope: The Power of Prayer

Ninety percent of Americans pray; 80 percent believe prayer heals.

Now it looks as if all those prayers have triggered one heck of a miracle: the widespread, well-funded scientific study of the healing power of prayer. Today hundreds of documented studies about prayer, faith and healing have been published in medicine's most prestigious journals. Researchers study prayer at Johns Hopkins, Duke and the University of Miami.

At Memphis's Baptist Memorial researchers are studying patients who've received "prayer intervention" before and after bypass surgery. At Baltimore's Johns Hopkins, Dr. Diane Becker, the recipient of two National Institutes of Health (NIH) grants, will examine African American breast cancer survivors who'll say a meditative prayer twice a day and/or participate in prayer groups.

A decade ago, it was heresy. Now it's scientific protocol.

That's exactly where research on the impact of spiritual tools like meditation on corporate productivity is headed this decade.

The Healing Power of Prayer

Many studies already demonstrate that prayer heals:

- Dartmouth Medical Center observed 232 heart surgery patients and found their survival prospects could be predicted by how much comfort they drew from faith and prayer.
- Georgetown University's Dr. Dale Matthews, author of *The Faith Factor* (Viking, 1998), says 75 percent of studies show the health benefits of prayer.
- A review of 23 prayer studies involving 2,774 patients published in the *Annals of Internal Medicine* showed positive results 57 percent of the time.

There are documented findings of prayer having helped heal AIDS, heart attack, depression, alcoholism, hip surgery, drug addiction, stroke and bypass surgery.

Medicine doesn't know why prayer works. But says one physician, "We cannot explain why beta-blockers reduce death rates after a heart attack either, but we know that they do."

Exactly.

Similarly, does American Express care *why* the New York state "forgiveness-trained" brokers beat their peers by 60 to 400 percent? It's the results that matter—and that's where business can learn a thing or two from medicine.

MANTRA

Cardiologist Mitchell Krucoff performs several coronary catheterizations a day and before each one, he prays. Not surprisingly, perhaps, Dr. Krucoff and nurse-practitioner Suzanne Crater also direct Duke University's MANTRA (Monitoring and Actualization of Noetic Trainings) prayer study.

In 1998, Krucoff and Crater conducted a double-blind prayer study at Durham, North Carolina's Veterans Administration Hospital and the results were published in *American Heart Journal.*

In the study, 150 cardiac patients who had undergone "invasive diagnostic angiography" were divided into three groups. Researchers tracked heart rates, variability and ischemia (a shortage of oxygen) as well as length of hospital stay and need for added surgery.

The control group got standard medical care; the second, music, imagery and touch therapy (also called "noetic" therapy). The third were the recipients of distant prayers from seven spiritual communities—Buddhist monks in Tibet, Carmelite nuns in Baltimore, Baptist and Monrovian churches in North Carolina, Jewish groups and members of the Unity Church. The prayer groups got the names, ages and illnesses of those they prayed for.

The patients who got touch, imagery and music enjoyed a sizable 30 percent reduction in complications like stroke, heart attack, heart failure and death.

But the prayer group registered even bigger benefits—50 to 100 percent fewer adverse episodes.

Krucoff and Crater later expanded their investigation to 1,500 patients in several different sites. That study is currently being reviewed for publication, but the word is the results failed to establish a clear connection between prayer and healing.

Some prayer advocates—or should I call us believers?—might be disappointed, but not all. Sister Patricia, from the Carmelite Monastery in Baltimore, says, "A person can be healed in ways we're not aware of. Maybe their heart wasn't healed in this particular study but . . . maybe they're meant to be ready for death in a fuller way . . . That's healing in itself."

Some researchers cite the difficulty of structuring a prayer study itself. How do you account for others—perhaps a whole congregation—praying for a subject? One thing is clear, however: the need for more in-depth study. Why? Because prayer possesses at least two enormous advantages over standard care: cost and toxicity.

Patients are routinely prescribed medicines that introduce terrible side effects. We are still reeling from revelations that Vioxx and other arthritis drugs may increase the risk of heart attack and stroke. (The stock of Merck, which recalled Vioxx, dropped precipitously in 2004—from around $45 to around $27.) By 2007, the stock traded at around $45. But Merck still faces thousands of Vioxx lawsuits.

If prayer were a drug, it would spawn an instant $100 billion industry and Spirit Pharmaceuticals would be the hottest stock on Wall Street.

Except for one thing: At a time of surging health costs, prayer is free.

And hundreds of prayer studies, some cited earlier, have established the efficacy of prayer. Consider one more:

Dr. Elizabeth Targ, then director of the Complementary Medicine Research Institute at California Pacific Medical Center in San Francisco, studied 40 AIDS patients, 20 of whom were prayed for—"six days a week for 10 weeks by experienced healers from Christian, Jewish, Buddhist, Native American, shamanic and other traditions," reports *Hippocrates*, the online newsletter of *The New England Journal of Medicine.*

After six months, the "prayed-for" patients had fewer, that is, *substantially* fewer of the following:

• "AIDS-defining" illnesses (2 vs. 12).
• hospital visits (85 vs. 260).
• days in the hospital (10 vs. 68).

"It is crucial for this work to be replicated to be more confident that the effect is real," said Dr. Targ.

What medical experiments on prayer have repeatedly shown, business has only started to explore: The potent techniques of consciousness and Spirit have a profound and positive impact on people.

If prayer can help heal AIDS, depression, heart attacks and cut heart surgery complications, what can meditation and other mindful tools do for the creativity of engineers?

If the Spirit in business movement cannot claim the same concrete results as medical researchers, maybe it's because until recently we didn't conduct any studies. That's why the American Express Forgiveness Project is so critical. We know meditation lowers blood pressure and prayer heals the heart, but these techniques also do wonders for people who thankfully are well and on the job.

In the midst of all those magnificent brain waves generated and harmonized by the power of conscious contemplation are the solutions to humanity's most intractable—and business's most mundane—problems.

As Bill George, the retired Medtronic chairman, says, "I get my best business ideas meditating."

Okay, I admit it. I'm fixated on my fantasy about the *corporate* version of all this great medical research—the story, already written, at least in my mind, of how IBM, Citibank, Procter & Gamble or 3M documented the surprising surge in productivity of salespeople, accountants and engineers, as a result of two 20-minute sessions a day of meditation.

Think it would be impossible to find funding? Consider the following:

In July 2000, the Duke University Medical Center was the beneficiary of a $1 million grant from the Medtronic Foundation, the nonprofit arm of the medical device firm, to bring mind-body-spirit techniques to patients with chronic heart failure.

I have to think it would cost a lot less than $1 million to study how meditation increases creativity, productivity and performance in Medtronic's own employees. Besides, Medtronic already has the quiet/meditation rooms. And a matchless champion of meditation. Come on, Mr. George, how about a meditation study at Medtronic?

The blessing of prayer—in the operating room and research lab—will not rescue each and every patient. But it is reducing suffering, saving lives and changing how doctors practice medicine. Physicians who pray before surgery yet still lose patients can at least say, "I did my very best—on every level." And that helps comfort families.

Similarly, the transformation of capitalism won't halt every layoff, abolish fraud, guarantee quarterly profits or neutralize stress. But it will create a new business environment that has its priorities straight: prosperity, gained with meaning, morals and a little help from Spirit.

The Time Is Now

This book chronicles the shifts that will propel Spirit in business from trend to megatrend. But I've left something out—or postponed it until now. And that's the issue of timing and the business cycle.

Once a company cuts costs and shrinks the payroll, where will improvements come from? What is going to drive shareholder value? The answer is obvious: people and performance.

What will differentiate one competitor from another?

The capacity to create a culture where people outperform their peers. How do you do that? With leadership that manages to be passionate and creative, yet keeps its eye on the ball about generating results.

Companies want to know how to create an environment that's conducive to passion and creativity. "It's a huge issue for our clients," says McKinsey's Michael Rennie. "Developing strategy is not that hard. The real challenge is how to get the people aligned so it can be implemented effectively."

"You actually have to create a performance ethic first," says Rennie. (That is to say, a productive enterprise in terms of traditional business metrics, where, among other things, high performers are rewarded.) "When you have a performance ethic, then you can create a more supportive work environment. . . . Companies that try to go straight to a wonderful loving environment without having the performance ethic in place die on the vine and create bad names for people trying to go to empowerment cultures."

When you have a high performance ethic, when people deliver, Rennie says, *then* you can "push very strongly down the track of making work more of a soul journey."

The message of this chapter is that spirituality won't just nurture people—although that's already great in and of itself—but, once other best practices are in place, Spirit will drive performance and shareholder value.

7

The Socially Responsible Investment Boom

There is today on Wall Street a sizable, potent—and growing—force for Conscious Capitalism. Quarter after quarter, it wins converts and racks up impressive net inflows. Most of all, it beats the financial establishment at its own game—outstanding financial performance.

What I'm talking about, of course, is Socially Responsible Investing (SRI). In this chapter, I'll tell you why SRI is a major trend that's destined to become a megatrend. But first let's define terms.

Socially responsible investing is how Conscious Capitalists "put their money where their heart is," that is, by buying into corporations[4] whose environmental and social standards reflect their own values. How? SRI investors can select from many financial instruments and approaches—including screened mutual funds, single stock picks, SRI bond or money market portfolios and community investing—a fulfilling strategy described later in this chapter. Put simply, SRI fans pursue financial gain—without compromising their beliefs or morals.

As capitalism recovers from the worst crisis since the Depression, SRI is coming of age. Look at this one "killer" stat: In 1984, SRI was a healthy $40 billion market. By 2003, it had morphed into $2.16 trillion industry—*a 5,000 percent increase in less than two decades*. And it's still growing.

---

[4]SRI bond funds also invest in governments or government agencies.

Best of all, SRI matches and often outperforms mainstream investing, so the stock portfolios of Conscious Capitalists are green in more ways than one.

The purpose of this chapter is to chronicle the emerging megatrend of socially responsible investing, then investigate how to capitalize on it. Where should you invest your conscious capital? We'll explore several ways to navigate the wide array of SRI choices.

But first let's address a common question about socially responsible investing.

What Are SRI Screens?

Socially responsible mutual funds subject stocks to "screens"—a set of criteria that measure a company's actions and policies on social, environmental, ethical and governance matters. In reality, *all* mutual funds, not just SRI funds, "screen" stocks. Screens are simply guidelines for determining which securities to include in—or exclude from—a portfolio. If you're a small cap fund, for example, you screen out large cap stocks. If you're a value fund, you typically exclude growth companies.

There are two kinds of SRI screens: negative and positive. The questions listed below illustrate how each type of screen might be structured. Does a company:

- pollute the environment? (negative)
- reward senior managers for great environmental performance? (positive)
- display integrity in advertising? (positive)
- promote offensive stereotypes? (negative)
- violate fair labor practices, OSHA regulations, equal opportunity standards? (negative)
- hire and promote minorities and women? (positive)

Some SRI funds utilize both types of screens to conduct a complete analysis.

The SRI Universe

More than 200 U.S. funds are screened for environmental and social factors. Two of the best-known SRI companies are the $13 billion Calvert Group and the $2 billion Domini Social Investments, each of which offers

DOMINI SCREENS

Domini Social Investments, described later in this chapter, is one of the SRI industry's leaders. Domini's analysis of 100 indicators nets a company's "social and environmental profile." Domini screens in these six areas. I've rephrased their criteria here for brevity and simplicity to give you a few more examples of how screens work.

- Corporate citizenship: Does the firm promote social justice?
- Diversity: Are women and minorities on the board, in management?
- Employees: Are they involved in decision-making? Stock options?
- Environment: Are there pollution prevention or recycling programs?
- Non-U.S. operations: Are human rights honored? Are fair wages paid?
- Products: Does the company make quality products? Lead in R&D?

These are all examples of positive screens.

several funds. The PAX World Balanced Fund has $2.1 billion under management. The Ariel Fund, which specializes in small cap value stocks, counts $4.3 billion in assets, while the Ariel Appreciation Fund, a mid-cap value portfolio, has $2.7 billion in total assets. (All these figures are as of December 31, 2006.)

In recent years, as the following example illustrates, investors have been flocking to SRI funds.

In the 1990s, socially responsible investing grew nicely, but after Enron, WorldCom and Tyco, the SRI trend headed right off the charts. From 2000 through 2002, in the wake of boom, bust and scandals, the traditional investment universe contracted, while SRI funds flourished. In 2002, SRI mutual funds saw net inflows of $1.5 billion while mainstream stock funds registered $10.5 billion in outflows, says funds tracker Lipper.

"Corporate irresponsibility did for social investing what Watergate did for politics," my friend Cliff Feigenbaum told *Barron's*.

In 2005, when the Social Investment Forum (SIF) published its biennial (and most recent) report on social investing trends, the results reflected continued growth. SIF identified $2.29 trillion in professionally managed SRI assets, up 258 percent since 1995. The overall fund universe, by contrast, had increased less than 249 percent. SRI funds represented one out of every 10 dollars invested in professionally managed funds, or 9.4 percent of the total $24.4 trillion in professionally managed U.S. funds.

Is the SRI trend becoming a megatrend? It sure looks that way.

For the past decade, SRI has averaged 26 percent in annual growth, exceeding the growth of total managed assets.

No wonder mainstream finance is getting in on the act. Traditional firms like Gabelli, Smith Barney and Vanguard now offer screened funds. Consider also innovations like the Dow Jones Sustainability Indexes and the FTSE4GOOD Index. If imitation is the sincerest form of flattery, pioneers like Domini, PAX World and the rest should feel wonderful.

What does all of this mean?

Peter Kinder, president of KLD Research & Analytics, a research firm that profiles a company's SRI quotient, says that traditional analysis now tracks the issues social investors have measured for 30 years. Kinder should know. Back in the early 1980s, he co-created the Domini 400 Social Index, described later.

SRI is becoming a megatrend for two reasons, one "top-down," the other "bottom-up." At the grassroots level, people insist on "investing with their values," as Cliff Feigenbaum and the Brills would put it. At the macro level, after Enron et al., even Wall Street's institutional investors got the message: Corporate ethics—or, rather, their lack—could nuke your portfolio.

Result?

Skepticism and mistrust toward business as usual are sending investors straight into the arms of socially responsible funds.

The new "conventional wisdom," says Calvert CEO Barbara Krumsiek, is "It doesn't just matter how a company's stock price moves, but it matters, too, how it conducts its business." That shift in thinking describes exactly how capitalism is growing conscious of itself.

Along the way, SRI will blossom from trend to megatrend. Why?

Because although SRI is going great guns, it has barely started.

Today it is a lot *easier* to invest in an SRI fund than it used to be. In the early 1990s, just one in 10 401K plans offered "at least one screened fund," wrote Krumsiek in *Green Money Journal.*

By 2002, it was *nine out of 10.*

In 2012, the percentage of U.S. mutual fund assets invested in socially responsible funds may hit 10 percent (a different metric from the 9.4 percent figure cited on page 142), predicts Krumsiek—up from two percent in 2002—as more investors will grow conscious and turn to SRI.

I wonder if that 10 percent prediction is actually a little low. In the next few years, as the cost of "unconscious capitalism" grows increasingly apparent, more mainstream funds will adopt SRI criteria. Then, SRI will hit critical mass. After that, SRI will accelerate even more rapidly. By 2015 SRI will represent a healthy chunk of the investment universe.

Meanwhile, SRI is the advance team of Conscious Capitalism. Thirty years ago, it established a beachhead on Wall Street. Twenty years ago, SRI won over pioneering investors. Three years ago, it seduced more institutional investors. Today Conscious Capitalists are embracing SRI in droves. Soon the SRI trend will be recognized as, quite simply, the best game on Wall Street.

SRI's Success Secret

The most obvious benefit of SRI is the way that SRI screens red-flag a rat's nest of expensive surprises: asbestos liabilities, governance melt-downs, costly environmental clean-ups or tobacco suits. When Tyco failed a Calvert social screen, Calvert Social Equity managing partner Dan Boone sold his position over several months at an average price of $56. (As I recall, I sold Tyco at around $17. Ouch.) Boone avoided Global Crossing, WorldCom and Adelphia.

Oops!

But SRI types readily admit they dropped the ball on one very big one— Enron. Enron passed the SRI screens, says Professor Sandra Waddock of Boston College's Carroll School of Management in an unpublished but widely quoted paper entitled "Fluff Is Not Enough." Enron issued a Triple Bottom Line Report, won six environmental awards and earned a spot on *Fortune*'s "100 Best Companies to Work For" list for three years.

Was everyone fooled? Not everyone.

Joan Bavaria, president of Trillium Asset Management, the Boston-based SRI investment firm with over one billion dollars under management, recalls how Enron cautioned fund managers "not to ask too many questions" about Tyco's overseas operations.

Click!

Ethical considerations can save you money, but only if you act on the courage of your convictions. Bavaria did. She sold Enron at the first whisper of possible indictments—saving clients plenty.

In the end, Enron showed investors how the preposterous expectations (Grow! Grow! Grow!) and relentless financial pressure (profit at *any* cost) of old-fashioned capitalism can crush human integrity and seduce companies down the primrose path to self-destruction.

The silver lining? Enron sure as heck illustrated the need for better corporate governance screens, which are now in place.

A Short History of SRI

Socially responsible investing dates back to the seventeenth-century Quakers who refused to invest in armaments. But today's movement began in the early 1970s, when the first spiritual investors—church groups—protested the Vietnam war by divesting their holdings of Dow Chemical and creating the PAX World Fund. During apartheid, pioneering SRI funds pulled their money out of firms doing business in South Africa.

At first, SRI funds shunned tobacco, alcohol, gambling and weaponry. Later, new screens tracked social and environmental issues. Today's SRI screens also measure human rights, diversity and corporate governance.

Back to Basics

All well and good, you say, but let's get back to that part about how SRI often exceeds mainstream results. Okay, here's another example.

A well-known Calvert SRI fund beat the S&P 500, while espousing the following heresy: Corporations are responsible, not just to investors but to employees, customers, suppliers, communities and, ultimately, society.

But surely no fund on Earth can make money saddled with *those* socialist burdens?

Well, the Calvert Social Investment Equity Fund, which owned market leaders like Intel and Dell, outperformed the S&P 500 from 2000 to 2002. In those three years (good, bad and awful), the S&P fell 14 percent while the Calvert Social Equity Fund dropped by just 3.6 percent.

It's one thing when a fund thrives in boom times, quite another when it beats the bear. The years 2001 and 2002 were about as grim as it gets, but the Calvert fund in question clobbered the S&P. Bull? Bear? Who knows what lies ahead? So doesn't it make sense to ask yourself whether a fund holds its own in good times—and bad?

Kicking the Habit

Did that get your attention? Good. Did it rouse the desire to wean yourself off "investing as usual" and climb on the SRI band wagon?

Many would-be SRI investors passionately vow to break with status quo investing, only to get overwhelmed by: (1) the complexity of finance, (2) the abundance of unfamiliar choices and (3) the fear of making a mistake. Result: We never take action. Our returns stagnate and we suffer the dissonance that comes when our money does not reflect our values.

In this chapter, I want to begin to help you sort through some options—emphasis on the word "begin." Socially responsible investing is a huge topic. New funds and portfolio managers join the movement regularly. Entire books—and plenty of them—are devoted to SRI. I can't possibly hope to do the subject justice. As a trend tracker, however, what I *can* offer is an overview that might start you on the road to exploring SRI.

But first you ought to ask yourself one fundamental question:

Why should I take Patricia Aburdene's investment advice?

You shouldn't! Nor will I offer any. Instead I will outline a framework for your SRI research. That way, you'll be sufficiently familiar with some general investment possibilities to be ready to *ask the right questions*, the ones that will help you sort through the mounds of information that will come your way.

I know what it's like to talk to a financial advisor who, as far as I'm concerned, could be speaking Urdu—and a mile a minute. I may never speak Urdu. But I'd better know enough to say, "Does any one around here speak English?"

Armed with some basics, you can better evaluate your choices. I hope the rest of this chapter supplies those concepts. That way, if you decide to become an SRI investor, you (and your advisor) can decide what's right for you.

Covering the Bases

So here is a warning—and a modest promise. What I describe here about socially responsible investing is just the tip of the iceberg. I will fail to mention some fabulous funds and lucrative options. That is just the nature of the beast. But if you want to conduct more in-depth research—and I strongly suggest you do so—here are two simple suggestions:

1. A Book: *Investing with Your Values* (see page 31).
2. This book's appendix, which lists many of the SRI movement's top resources and their websites.

If you study both, you'll cover the bases. That said, here we go.

What Do I Want? Sample Investment Styles

How will you invest? That's something *you* will have to figure out, but if you've avoided financial decisions ("My husband handles that stuff" or "My broker's in charge of that department"), you may not even *recognize* a possible approach, let alone identify which ones suit you.

So I will propose a few sample ways to go. I do not advocate any of them, but I do want to trigger your ideas. You might say, "No way, you can have that approach, I'd rather do such and such." If so, great.

Besides, by writing this section as an options list, I can organize a lot of information under user-friendly headings. If you never invest a dime, you'll still get an SRI overview.

Give Me the *Whole* Market—Minus the Bad Guys

It is the early 1980s; Amy Domini, a young stockbroker in Harvard Square, gets a call from an elderly female client whose father has left her a nice stock portfolio. The woman, an avid birdwatcher, has just found out that one of her stocks, a paper company, produces a chemical that's poisoning the birds. Now Amy and her investor-client have an ethical dilemma on their hands: The stock portfolio definitely helps the woman make ends meet, but she cannot abide the harm that results. In time, Amy eases her client into a new portfolio of companies that, as Amy's client puts it, "demonstrate a higher regard for the interests of all God's creatures, not just shareholders." What Domini may not realize yet is that in this crisis, her destiny is born.

In 1984, Domini and Peter Kinder, now president of KLD Research & Analytics, write *Ethical Investing*, the first guide to social investing. Later, the two devise an index of socially responsible stocks by applying a series of "screens" to the S&P 500. About half of the S&P stocks make the grade. Domini and Kinder keep these "good guys," then analyze the next largest companies (the ones that are not quite large enough to make the S&P 500), until they find 100 more screen-worthy firms. Finally, they add 50 more companies whose social performance is exemplary. That totals 400 firms.

In 1990 the Domini 400 Social Index, a socially responsible alternative to the S&P 500 Index, is born. But you can't invest in an *index*, be it the S&P 500 or Domini 400, only in a *fund* based on it. So today, many investment firms sell mutual funds comprised of the stocks in the S&P 500. Similarly, Domini offered the Domini Social Equity Fund, which mirrored the Domini 400, provoking *Investing with Your Values* to suggest, "Don't be Standard and Poor—Dominate with Domini."

Today Domini Social Investments manages nearly $2 billion in no-load stock, bond and cash funds. Still, it was best known for the $1.5 billion Domini Social Equity Fund—the first socially responsible index fund.

The Domini Social Equity Fund blended growth and value stocks. The top holdings of the fund, which was heavily weighted toward tech and finance, include Microsoft, Procter & Gamble, Johnson & Johnson and Intel. In December 2006, the Domini Social Equity Fund switched to an "active management strategy," partnering with submanager Wellington Management Company LLP. (See www.Domini.com for more details.)

How much does it take to get started? $1,500 for an IRA; $2,500 for an individual account.

Get Me a Pro to Pick the Best of the Good Guys

Back in 1982, Calvert was the first mutual fund to oppose apartheid in South Africa. In 1994, after Nelson Mandela's victory, Calvert was one of the first mutual funds to reinvest in South Africa. With more than 30 years in business, Calvert manages $13 billion in assets in 25 screened and unscreened portfolios for more than 400,000 customers. Calvert's philosophy is simple: "Today's social issues . . . have a way of becoming tomorrow's economic problems." So, investing in firms with "an expanded view" of social responsibility, says Calvert, "makes good business sense."

With Calvert you can go large-cap, small-cap or mid-cap. Pick a growth, value or blended fund. Invest in stocks, bonds, cash or all three. In the same fund.

If Domini was best known for its SRI index fund, Calvert certainly gets a lot of notice in the mainstream press for its Social Investment Equity Fund. Since 1998, the fund's holdings have been managed by Atlantic Capital Management's Dan Boone. (Jim Awad of Awad Asset Management, a regular guest host on CNBC's 7 to 10 A.M. *Squawk Box* show, is another Calvert outside manager.)

For the Calvert Social Equity Fund, Boone likes stocks that serve up "high

---

MORE CALVERT FUNDS

Equities? Bonds? Cash? Can't make up your mind? Consider Calvert's Social Investment Fund Balanced Portfolio, which offers exposure to all major financial markets: stocks, bonds and money market.

Calvert Social Index Fund seeks to match the Calvert Social Index, a broad-based benchmark for large and mid cap U.S. socially responsible funds.

Calvert Social Investment Fund Enhanced Equity Portfolio is "the first socially screened fund to track Russell 1000."

---

quality growth at a reasonable price," says the *Financial Times*. His picks, which are first subjected to strenuous financial analysis, must have been in business for at least 10 years and also demonstrate:

• above average earnings and dividend growth,
• a strong balance sheet and
• a two- to five-year outlook for strong returns.

Boone and other portfolio managers next submit their choices to Calvert's 18-person, in-house research team, where they're screened for "governance, ethics, environment, employees, communities." If the companies don't measure up to Calvert's social and environmental standards, they're out.

Boone won a 2004 Standard & Poor's/*BusinessWeek* Excellence in Fund Management Award and his fund ranked in the top quartile of large-cap blended funds for three of the past five years, says Standard & Poor's. In addition to traditional metrics like P/E ratios, Boone studies economic and demographic trends.

Make It Green—and a High Flyer

Suppose you've just socked away most of your money in one or more sensible, balanced SRI funds. But part of you just wants *more*. You yearn to be out there on the cutting edge. What really floats your boat is the vision of *green* technology transforming our world. Let's say you're also willing to subject five or 10 percent of your portfolio to a bit more risk.

Winslow Green Growth, an "aggressive" no-load equity fund, might be exactly what you research next. Launched by Winslow Management founder Jack Robinson, the Winslow Green Growth Fund sports a *10-year* track record investing in small to mid cap U.S. companies that are both innovative and environmental. For the 10 years ending November 30, 2006, in good, bad and horrific years for investing, Winslow Green Growth delivered 18.02 percent in average annual total returns versus 5.11 percent for the Russell 2000 Growth Index.

In the banner year of 2003, Green Growth soared 91.7 percent.

Sure, 2003 was a great year for stocks. Even so, the S&P 500, by comparison, rose 28.2 percent. And that's not the only thing Winslow Green Growth trampled that year.

TheStreet.com, a well-known financial website, compared Winslow Green Growth's 2003 results with those of the Vice Fund (yes, folks, there is such a thing) which invests in gaming, alcohol, tobacco and defense stocks. Verdict? Vice paid, in 2003—to the tune of 34.3 percent. Not bad at all, but not nearly as well as what *virtue* delivered via Winslow Green Growth Fund's 90-percent-plus performance.

Winslow Green Growth buys high quality, eco-friendly companies. One top holding is Fuel-Tech Inc., an air pollution control company whose retro-fittable technology—for boilers, incinerators and other combustion sources—cuts nitrogen oxide emissions 30 to 80 percent. Another top fund pick is SurModics, whose "surface modification" technology allows the stents used in, say, heart surgery, to be coated with drugs. Until 2006, Green Growth clearly benefited from natural grocer Whole Foods, which traded at around $80 in January 2006 then fell below $50 in late 2006.

Just remember, Green Growth is a "high flyer." In the 12 months ending January 5, 2005, the fund grew a modest 2.9 percent, says Lipper (compared to 2.7 percent for its peer group). Interested? There's a $5,000 minimum for regular accounts; $2,500 for IRAs.

When oil was holding at around $50 a barrel, Robinson told CNBC it was a good bet that the alternative energy firms favored by Winslow Green Growth would look increasingly attractive to investors. They did—and oil hit $60 in June 2005. In late 2006, oil traded at $61 a barrel. In 2006, Winslow Green Growth and the S&P 500 finished the year neck and neck, each up about 13 percent.

What's the secret of the fund's success? Earth-friendly companies, says Robinson, beat their peers through "cost reductions, quality improvements, increased profitability and access to new and growing markets." Green companies "have less risk of environmental liability, which could have a major impact on future stock prices."

Remember the ChevronTexaco mess described in chapter two?

Walk the Talk

Walk the talk; that's your mantra. You may want to check out a fund whose governance practices are simply exemplary. Bridgeway Funds:

- contributes 50 percent of profits to charity;
- keeps fees low (how does 0.15 percent for the Bridgeway Blue Chip 35 Index Fund sound?);
- closes funds before they get too large;
- lists *worst*, as well as best, performing stocks;
- caps the pay of founder John Montgomery to seven times that of the lowest-paid employee.

Sounds good, right? But get this: The Bridgeway Aggressive Investors 2 Fund charges "performance-based" fees, ranging from 0.2 to 1.6 percent, *depending on how well Bridgeway performs* versus the S&P 500. "It's a tremendous incentive for us to beat the market and to not screw up," says founder John Montgomery.

Fine, you say, but how well does a do-gooder outfit like that perform? The funds Bridgeway manages averaged 54.3 percent growth in 2003. The S&P 500, remember, rose 28.69 percent. Bridgeway's Ultra-Small Company Fund racked up a phenomenal *88.2 percent* growth rate in 2003.

No Stocks, Please—Just Bonds

Calvert's Social Investment Bond Portfolio, composed of fixed-income securities from corporations, governments and agencies that meet Calvert's SRI criteria, won a 2004 Lipper Fund Award for "achieving the highest consistent returns" in its Lipper category. Unlike Calvert's mutual funds, the company's fixed income funds are managed in-house.

Domini Social Bond Fund is an intermediate term, investment grade, socially screened portfolio of fixed-income securities. The fund also invests in community economic development.

Make Mine Money Market

Both Domini and Calvert offer green-screened money market funds.

Calvert's Social Investment Money Market Fund is invested in short-term securities, commercial paper, CDs and government agency issues. Minimum is $1,000.

Domini's FDIC-insured Money Market Account puts your money with ShoreBank, the nation's oldest and largest community development bank. The minimum is $2,500.

The beauty of this approach is that your money is put to work in communities—where it is needed most. Will your interest rate suffer as a result? *Au contraire.* Both funds offer competitive rates. But more on this soon—under the heading "Community Investing."

Do It Yourself

Some of us are very independent. We *enjoy* doing our own investment research; we already have strong opinions on who the corporate good (and bad) guys are and insist on coming up with our own stocks. We think it's fun to track our stock picks and, as a Conscious Capitalist, to attend the annual meetings of companies we believe in.

But how on earth do we wade through the SRI universe and cobble together a customized portfolio? Here are a few simple ideas to get you started. (By the way, even if you *don't* do it yourself, the ideas on these pages will make you a better fund investor. You weren't going to hand your money over to a portfolio manager—even a SRI manager—without *some* notion of how to evaluate the stocks he or she picks, were you? I didn't think so.)

1. Your broker vs. the "100 Best." If you have a broker, compare its Recommend List against the 100 firms on the *Business Ethics* "100 Best Corporate Citizens" list. It will be interesting—and illustrative—to see if your broker likes companies (Wal-Mart? ExxonMobil?) that fail to make the Best Citizens list. Try the same tack with the *Fortune* "100 Best Companies to Work For" list. I did that once and was relieved to see how many of my broker's picks were great places to work. Any company that shows up on the Biz Ethics 100, *Fortune's* Best Places to Work list *and* your broker's top picks is definitely worth another look.

2. Raid the experts' picks. Dan Boone, for example, manager of the Calvert Social Investment Fund (CSIF) Equity Portfolio, holds a nice little gem in his mostly large cap fund: EOG Resources Inc., a natural gas and crude oil producer. Even though the size of its market cap makes it a smallish pick for Boone's fund, the stock has performed well over time.

EOG soared 58 percent for the year ending September 30, 2004. Then, like many stocks in the energy sector, it just kept going. EOG began 2005 at around $33. In late 2006, it traded near $70 and expects strong production growth in 2007. But get this: The company is a former Enron subsidiary! All the more reason Calvert's research team would subject EOG to rigorous environmental and governance criteria. Fortunately for investors, the company passed—with flying colors.

On the environmental front, natural gas—about 85 percent of EOG's total production—is much cleaner than petroleum, and that means less air pollution and greenhouse gas. While EOG's record is not "blemish free," admits Calvert, the company won awards for safety and land reclamation, and conducts its operations in an "environmentally friendly" way.

3. Hit the "Sustainable Business 20." Every year, *The Progressive Investor,* Rona Fried's dynamic online newsletter, surveys top SRI advisors, folks like Winslow Management's Jack Robinson or Portfolio 21's Carsten Henningsen. Together these SRI brains ask a simple question: Which companies stand out as the world's leaders both in terms of sustainability and financial strength? The result is *Progressive Investor's* annual list of the top 20 sustainable businesses, the "SB20."

And that's really saying something.

Why? Because Fried's website, SustainableBusiness.com, already follows more than 100 sustainable stocks. The SB20 are the cream of a universe of stocks from 16 Earth-friendly industries: Bioproducts, Components, Financial, Flywheels, Fuel Cells, Geothermal, Healthcare, Materials, Microturbines, Natural Foods, Natural Products, Solar, Superconductors, Transportation, Water and Wind.

The 2006 SB20 (see sidebar) features two names that just thrilled me: Wainwright Bank and my grocer, Whole Foods. You may also recognize Green Mountain Coffee Roasters, green carpet maker Interface and Philips Electronics. Global giant GE received an "honorable mention."

Fried's longer list of sustainable favorites is a lot less familiar, which only goes to show how much opportunity lies here. (Quick, name a flywheel company!) I, an admitted CNBC junkie, had heard of fewer than 10.

The SB20, cautions Fried, is not "a diversified portfolio based on industry, market cap or country allocations." On the other hand, the SB20 excludes companies that are not financially stable. You might decide to follow these stocks for six months or so to get a feel for how they perform. Study their P/Es, Beta ratings, analysts rankings and all the rest. Pay particular attention to companies that make the grade year after year.

Research who else owns them? Calvert? Domini?

Winslow Green Growth?

The SB20 might alert you to the next Microsoft.

That said, the SB20 raises and explores some interesting conflicts, such

THE 2006 SUSTAINABLE BUSINESS (SB) 20

Abengoa	Novartis AG
Acciona	Omat Technologies
Best Water Technology	Philips Electronics NV
Conergy	Precious Woods
Energy Conversion Devices	Renewable Woods
Gamesa Corporation Technologica	Sharp Corp.
Green Mountain Coffee Roasters	SunPower
Interface	United Natural
JM Inc.	Wainwright Bank
Maxwell Technologies	Whole Foods Market

as how do you define a sustainable company? Fuel Cell Energy, whose fuel cells will be employed in buildings and power plants, and Ballard Power Systems, which makes fuel cells for the transportation industry—and depends on the commercialization of hydrogen technology—made the 2003 list because their products and technologies "are so important to a sustainable society." Nevertheless the judges questioned both firms for a lack of interest in a sustainable business culture. Neither made the cut in 2004.

Progressive Investor, insists Fried, is not just about small environmental companies, but about global giants playing a key role in the new green economy including BP, Honda and Chiquita.

Rona Fried's SustainableBusiness.com and the SB20 are your blueprint to a green corporate future.

The Tail That Wags the Dog

Back in chapter two, we investigated the trend of corporate social responsibility (CSR), the bedrock, or so I thought, of Conscious Capitalism. I asked everyone I talked to, "What is the relationship between SRI and CSR?"

"CSR is to a large extent a *response* to SRI," said Co-op America's Alisa Gravitz. One activist after another told me the same story. Socially responsible investing, they argued, *drives* corporate social responsibility. It is the "tail that wags the dog." And how does the humble tail achieve such a magnificent feat? The answer lies in SRI's "shareholder advocacy" function. Remember Shelley Alpern from chapter two, who clued ChevronTexaco (now Chevron) shareholders in on those highly toxic oil operations in Equador? Alpern is a "shareholder advocate."

Calvert and Domini, which together manage $15 billion in assets, engage in shareholder advocacy, too. Like Alpern, they often lobby companies (this is the quiet side of advocacy) before introducing shareholder resolutions.

Calvert, for example, convinced Dell to switch from cathode ray tube monitors to liquid crystal displays, which contain less lead. Domini persuaded Avon to review the use of "parabens" chemicals in cosmetics—which may be linked to breast cancer.

The SRI industry jointly manages $150 billion in screened funds. That conveys the kind of clout dedicated activists can only dream about. The Amy Dominis of the world can—and *do*—dump the stock of companies that violate social and environmental standards.

Does the offending company's stock then tank? Not now. SRI isn't *that* huge a financial force. (Yet.) But when an SRI fund divests, the company in question will endure bad publicity. As we discovered in chapter five, that hurts the brand's reputation and repels Conscious Consumers at the cash register. The wise corporation avoids both, reaps the benefits of a good name and attracts more conscious investors.

Community Investing

I've *had* it with my bank. It has merged, acquired, been acquired and otherwise transubstantiated more times than I care to recall. Friendly Harvard Trust here in Cambridge, Massachusetts, where I started out in 1990, sold out to so-so BayBank, which later morphed into sleek impersonal Fleet Bank. Did I miss an incarnation or two? Probably.

But at least the service gets better, right? Are you kidding? The neighborhood feel of my original bank is a distant memory and so are the friendly tellers and warm, high-touch service. The day my enthusiastic "Welcome to Bank Behemoth!" letter arrived was the day I got serious about a new bank. But how would I find a good one? Fortunately for me, my bank crisis erupted when I was right in the middle of researching this chapter, so my story has a happy ending. I'll share it later, because it's part of the uplifting SRI trend we'll consider next.

The Soul of Grassroots Finance

SRI, it is often said, is a three-legged stool (it's a peculiar image, I know, but SRI types seem to swear by it). The first two legs are stock screening and shareholder advocacy. The third is community investing. For investors like you and me, it is both spiritually enriching and financially rewarding.

"Community investing," says *Investing with Your Values,* "is a powerful local form of putting your money to work in the service of your values."

But what exactly is it?

When a bank or credit union loans capital to valuable local projects that otherwise might not qualify for funding, that's community investing. It is SRI's frontline initiative to fight poverty, create jobs, fund AIDS projects and bankroll visionary entrepreneurs.

David Royster, 42, rehabbed a block of abandoned, deteriorating buildings one by one, with help from Chicago's pioneering South Shore Bank. Good-bye drugs and gangs. Hello good jobs and a safe, attractive neighborhood.

Durham, North Carolina's Self-Help Credit Union helps minorities and low-income people launch Earth-friendly businesses—like R24 Lumber, which transforms discarded wood into functional wall studs.

The Northeast Organic Farming Association had trouble with traditional lenders, who charged high rates and didn't understand small (let alone organic) farmers or how "seasonality" made regular payments difficult. Vermont National Bank's Socially Responsible Banking Fund came to the rescue, with a $90,000 low-interest loan to set up a revolving fund.

With success stories like these, no wonder the nonprofit Woodstock Institute concluded back in 1992 that community investment institutions like these were, as Jean Pogge, executive vice president of South Shore Bank, put it, having "an impact far bigger than their asset size."

There are more than 100 community development banks and more than 212 credit unions, according to the Opportunity Finance Network. Places like Portland's Albina Community Bank, Ohio's NCB Savings Bank, Louisville's Louisville Community Development Bank and New Mexico's Permaculture Credit Union. They're known as Community Development Financial Institutions, or CDFIs.

Making a Difference—and Pay Back

There are more than 700 certified CDFIs, says Opportunity Finance Network. CDFIs back affordable housing, homeless shelters, AIDS projects, food banks, minority- and women-owned business—and make money, too. CDFIs have loaned and invested more than $8.3 billion to individuals and worthwhile projects.

Typically, they loan small sums of money to people and organizations that are anything but rich. Yet their repayment rate is 96 to 99 percent!

How come?

- Loan candidates are highly screened.
- They're *motivated*, says *Investing with Your Values*. This is their big chance and they work hard to succeed.
- CDFIs often provide technical assistance to beef up the client's weak areas.

Amping Things Up

"The biggest problem with community investing," write Marjorie Kelly and Marshall Glickman in *E: The Environmental Magazine*, "is that not enough people do it." Less than *one* percent of SRI's $2.3 trillion in funds is in community investing.

But that's in the process of changing. Between 2001 and 2003 alone, community investment funds, the mainstay of community investing, grew 84 percent, from $7.6 billion to $14 billion, thanks in large part to the Social Investment Forum/Co-op America One Percent project, which encourages SRI funds to invest one percent of their assets in community development financial institutions. The 2007 community investment goal is $20 billion.

Socially responsible investors should consider allocating 10 percent of their portfolio to community investing, advise the Brills and Cliff Feigenbaum. Community investing often involves a bank, so your funds will probably be FDIC insured, they remark. No community bank nearby? Bank at a distance!

Profiles in Commitment: Wainwright Bank

Well, it sounded great to me. I was sold on the financial and moral superiority of SRI. Why not go all the way and find a community bank?

Turns out, I didn't have to find one at all. On my way to Behemoth Bank in Kendall Square, which I am now divorcing, I walk right past one of the finest community banks ever, the Wainwright Bank, with 10 branches in the Boston area.

More than 50 percent of Wainwright's commercial loan portfolio—a total of $570 million in loan commitments—supports a Who's Who of Boston-area nonprofits: the Pine Street Inn, New England's largest homeless shelter; the Greater Boston Food Bank, which feeds 320,000 people per year; Rosie's Place, the first drop-in and emergency shelter for women in the United States.

I knew none of this.

I've peeked into Wainwright dozens of times and never thought it had a thing to do with socially responsible investing or that Wainwright has won tons of SRI awards. Wainwright is, for example, one of:

- SustainableBusiness.com's top 20 sustainable businesses—in the *world*, not just the United States,
- Social Investment Forum's (SIF) "Top 10 Green Banking Firms,"
- SIF's "Top 11 Best Lenders to Women."

Why don't they plaster these kudos on the window?

Once I got the picture, I happily gave them my business. I was a bit surprised that Wainwright's interest rates beat my old bank's.

But my psychic returns are even higher.

- The 12th largest bank in the state, Wainwright financed more than $11 million in AIDS housing, *half of the area's total*, to places like Wish House, a Dorchester, Massachusetts, home for formerly homeless women and children living with AIDS.
- Wainwright bankrolled $75 million worth of affordable housing, including a $500,000 loan to rehab Victory House, a transitional housing program for 25 homeless and low income men with substance abuse problems.
- Wainwright loaned $1.8 million to the Family Center, a mental health facility whose clients are struggling with poverty, racism and violence. Each year the Center helps more than 2,000 families; 54 percent of clients earn less than $20,000 and 44 percent are people of color.

Wainwright's DNA is so deeply encoded with the commitment to social justice, you almost forget it's a bank, with more than $842 million in assets, that offers commercial loans, home mortgages, lines of credit and private banking. It might also slip your mind that Wainwright makes money, a lot of money and at an impressive rate: Net income in 2005 hit $6.8 million, up from $4.7 million in 2003. Earnings per share rose from 55 cents in 2001 to 90 cents in 2005.

And guess what? Community investing is the best-performing sector of Wainwright's lending portfolio. The default rate? About zero percent.

Socially Responsible Investing: What Now?

We'll conclude this chapter by checking in with two of Conscious Capitalism's most brilliant thinkers for their take on where SRI is today and where it's headed.

Holy Grail—Found

Marjorie Kelly, visionary founder of *Business Ethics: Corporate Social Responsibility Report* and author of *The Divine Right of Capital* (Berrett Koehler, 2001), is a 17-year observer of the SRI trend. In the Winter 2004 issue of *Business Ethics*, she writes, "There is absolute, definitive proof that CSR pays off." She draws that conclusion after the 2004 release of two SRI "meta-studies," that is, "studies of studies," which validate years and years of SRI research, so that the results, says Kelly, speak with "an outsized authority."

The first report—from Marc Orlitzky of the University of Sydney (Australia) and Frank Schmidt and Sara Rynes-Weller from the University of Iowa, entitled "Corporate Social and Financial Performance"—took on 52 studies conducted over a 30-year period. The researchers show that the link between corporate social and financial performance ranges from "highly positive" to "modestly positive."

The second meta-study, "Corporate Environmental Governance," released by the U.K. Environment Agency, was conducted by Innovest Strategic Value Advisors. It reviewed 60 research studies from the past six years and confirmed that 51 (85 percent) demonstrated "a positive correlation between environmental management and financial performance."

Some may doubt the proof these studies proffer, admits Kelly, but she is not about to pay them any mind. "Thirty years and 112 studies later," says Kelly, "the Holy Grail has been found."

A Portfolio for the 21st Century

Hal Brill, president of Natural Investment Services and co-author of *Investing with Your Values*, is an SRI veteran and one of the field's wise young men. In *Green Money Journal*, he writes: "SRI Rocks! Now What?" then offers a critique and a strategy for the future.

For Brill's taste, SRI is too heavily focused on the secondary market of stocks and bonds. It's time, he says, "to take some of the spotlight off Wall Street"—and "mobilize capital" directly into the people, projects and small businesses working for an "ecologically sound, equitable world." Here is his three-part plan.

Step One: *A Lot* **More Community Investing.** The SRI movement should advocate more noncorporate investment opportunities. So what if we beat the Street, he asks, and "witness the mass extinction of species and rapid global warming?"

Nearly 99 percent of the $2+ trillion in SRI funds is in corporate stock or corporate/government bonds. Community investing, complains Brill, is a "blip on the screen," even though it attacks "a major cause of poverty: lack of access to capital." Micro-credit—both U.S. and global—is the first step on the ladder out of poverty. And (remember those fantastic repayment rates?) it's also safe investment.

Step Two: More Green Investments. Today's "carbon-intensive, resource-extracting" economy and an energy system "dominated by fossil fuels" is the end result of "investment choices made by the last generation," says Brill. We can—and must—change that with what he calls "Regenerative Investing" in "clean energy, sustainable agriculture/forestry, recycling and green real estate."

Will returns suffer? Everything in this chapter—especially Winslow Green Growth's 90 percent surge in 2003—suggests just the opposite.

Step Three: Reclaim, Embrace and Use Our Power. We won't get the world we want, argues Hal Brill, if we keep letting large companies call the shots. Don't give up on corporations, he advises, *change* them—with time-honored SRI tools of shareholder advocacy and screening. Together, these three strategies are the foundation of what Brill calls his New Portfolios for the 21st Century.

Halfway through the first decade of the twenty-first century, SRI is robustly alive. Thanks to the failure of unconscious capitalism, SRI funds have enjoyed sizable growth. Thanks to the strength and power of Conscious Capitalism, SRI's performance, especially in some of the sectors described in this chapter, is impressive indeed. You might say that SRI advocates have earned the right to celebrate their success. But Hal Brill and Marjorie Kelly do no such thing. In fact they voice a call that goes more like:

Let's get over ourselves and move on.

SRI has spent decades justifying itself to Wall Street. Now the tide has turned and Wall Street must justify itself to growing numbers of investors who embrace SRI. Together what Hal and Marjorie are saying is, "Look, we've made the point about superb financial returns. It's time to get back to business." The business, that is, of transforming the world.

Conclusion

The Spiritual Transformation of Capitalism

Capitalism, we are frequently reminded, is the most successful economic system ever created. "Capitalism has come to dominate the world's economies, since no other system has been able to generate long-term economic growth in the 200 years since the onset of the industrial revolution," says one economic guru you'll soon meet.

No argument there. He's right. But he's left something out.

Capitalism works when it epitomizes the value of Justice.

Capitalism is, or at least should be, synonymous with economic democracy, because free enterprise, when it works well, disperses economic opportunity to everyone! The spiritual virtue of Justice and the spiritual flow of Abundance are the red-hot ingredients in the secret sauce of free enterprise.

Mainstream business, however, often forgets the sacred side of its heritage.

Meet the Guru

About a mile from my place on the Cambridge side of the Charles River is the Massachusetts Institute of Technology (MIT). That's where Lester Thurow, a professor of management and economics and former dean of the Sloan

School of Management, teaches. Professor Thurow is the author of that quote on capitalism just cited. Look at what else he has to say about free enterprise.

"Every economic system comes with its own genetic characteristics," Thurow wrote in the *Boston Globe*. "Capitalism's bad genes cannot be separated from its good genes since both flow from the fact that capitalism taps into the *greed* [emphasis added] that seems to be built into human beings."

Professor Thurow is voicing the sentiment—echoed often in the business establishment—that free enterprise is grounded in vice. The implication of this curious assertion is, of course, that capitalism and Spirit are incompatible—to say the least. Is it any wonder then that free enterprise, having vanquished Marxism, socialism and Communism, sometimes feels compelled to slam the door in the gentle face of "spirituality in business"?

The Greed Factor

Now, I don't know whether greed ever did fuel capitalism. Maybe so, once upon a time. I only know it no longer has the power to do so today. Human consciousness—a critical mass of it, anyhow—has evolved too far and too successfully for that particular kind of gasoline to work anymore. We need a new energy source. Fortunately, there's a great one available that just happens to be free and limitless.

But to tap into the power of Spirit, we must first deal with the insane idea that greed is the fountain of wealth. This wacky, self-imposed limitation is exactly what is holding humanity back from the financial abundance we have the potential to create.

It's time to heal the greed issue.

Capitalism today is clothed in a belief system that's a lot like a dress-for-success business suit cut two sizes small. Tight, pinching and much too tiny to hold the prosperity on the way to us through the many technological and spiritual advances coming in the next few decades.

Financial abundance cannot and will not flow into an economic container that's too restrictive to hold our magnificence.

What Is Greed?

Professor Thurow goes on to define greed. "The desire to have 'more,' *however much one already has* [emphasis added], is the human desire that makes capitalism work."

However much one already has? Well, that's greed all right. Perhaps the good professor has never heard of Abraham Maslow's "hierarchy of needs," which reflects humanity's capacity to satisfy basic needs like food and shelter and then move on to higher motives such as self-esteem, love and self-actualization. Heck, absent that, didn't his grandma tell him, "Enough is enough"?

Sure, I realize some individuals get stuck in greed, but that's no reason to invoke it as the foundation of capitalism, especially considering modern psychology shows us that healthy people move on to other more satisfying pursuits.

But let me concede that Lester Thurow has brilliantly capsulized the mundane grid of business thinking, what Paul Ray, co-author of *The Cultural Creatives*, calls "the Modernist Ideology." That said, is greed *really* the bedrock of capitalism?

The simple textbook definition of capitalism, cited in the *World Book Encyclopedia*, is "an economic system that calls for the control of the economy by individual households and privately owned businesses." Nothing about greed there.

If you argue that the goal of capitalism is to invest capital to create *more* capital, fine; that doesn't require greed. Self-preservation perhaps. Self-interest, certainly, but not greed. Self-interest and greed are *not* the same thing, although smart people who know better seem to ignore the distinction—especially when the talk turns to capitalism. Self-interest is concern for one's advantage or well-being, says my *Merriam Webster's Collegiate Dictionary*. Greed is "excessive or reprehensible" acquisitiveness. Big difference.

Not that I mean to imply that they are unrelated. Greed is self-interest run amok. When greed takes over, we are out of Balance. We sacrifice the other and the whole to our selfishness. And as a result, our own self-interest, rather than thriving, suffers—if not immediately, then in time.

Some of the most successful capitalists grow rich because they're suspicious of both greed and spectacular profits.

Like the folks who sold out long before the tech bubble burst.

Or Warren Buffet, who wouldn't touch the "hot stocks" with a 10-foot pole.

No one puts it better than CNBC host and long-time Wall Street veteran Jim Cramer, "Bulls make money. Bears make money. Pigs get slaughtered."

Even if you insist that greed *does* spur capitalists—at least in part—you've got to admit that there are plenty of other motivations as well, most of which are a lot more interesting—and inspiring. Like achievement, success, satisfaction, security—and creating a better life for your family.

Professor Thurow entertains *none* of these humanistic motives in describing the essence of free enterprise, but he has a few things to say about what he considers the opposite of greed, none of them good.

What Is Altruism?

"The alternatives to capitalism," writes Professor Thurow, "all tried to tap into altruism. It is more important to help one's neighbor or the society in general than it is to help one's self. This is a much nicer ethical principle than the greed that underlies capitalism, but it unfortunately does not seem to be congruent with the way human beings are constructed."

So it's either greed, capitalism and success *or* altruism, socialism (or Communism) and failure. That's it. Two big fat either/or choices for economic man, because, as Thurow puts it, that's how "humans are constructed."

Well, guess what?

"Somebody" tapped into the blueprint, changed the DNA, altered the construction and flooded us with consciousness. "They" *must* have. Because we've outgrown the allure of profit-by-any-means-necessary capitalism and now long to play a new, more enlightened economic ball game.

I am not trying to give Professor Thurow a hard time here. I briefly met him once. John Naisbitt and I shared a speaking platform with him. Thurow is an engaging fellow and a moderate. I enjoy much of what he writes. Plenty of economists make the same point about greed and capitalism, because all sorts of smart people are plugged into the mundane grid of business consciousness.

But Professor Thurow thinks greed and altruism are mutually exclusive and that altruism has not inspired a successful economic system (at least so far). But as I see it, that is not really the point. If you understand that capitalism is based on self-interest and not greed, there is a moral, spiritual and intellectual bridge that spans the distance to altruism. It is the concept of enlightened self-interest, the practical core of Conscious Capitalism.

Conscious Capitalism and Enlightened Self-Interest

History shows us that enlightened self-interest, in the hands of skilled policymakers, generates as much prosperity as greed ever did. Arguably more. Look at the GI Bill, the Marshall Plan and the reforms of the New Deal.

The liberal benefits of the GI Bill, which provided funds for veterans to go to school, forged a skilled workforce, critical to the demands of the industrial economy.

The post-World War II Marshall Plan (1948–1952), which invested $13 billion in goods and aid into the devastated European continent, produced prosperous trading and investment partners—and new markets—all of which were a boon to capitalism.

The New Deal, in fostering the creation of labor unions through the National Labor Relations Administration, built a well-to-do middle class to whom big business could sell its wares. Similarly, the Securities Exchange Commission, created in 1934, may have seemed particularly unfriendly to business, but succeeded in stabilizing markets.

Each of these policies contributed a fundamental building block to the success of twentieth-century capitalism and not one displayed an ounce of greed. Nor were they altruistic—not exactly. These brilliant initiatives explored instead the moral high ground of enlightened self-interest. To the benefit of society—and capitalism.

Greed is the *ruin* of capitalism. Here is another voice, a kindred soul to many of us, who clarifies—better than anyone I've heard so far—exactly why.

Transforming Capitalism

John Byrne, executive editor at *BusinessWeek* and vocal advocate of human values in business, recalls conducting research on one of the most "reviled" executives ever, former Sunbeam CEO Al "Chainsaw" Dunlap, whose name even now is synonymous with vicious cost cutting and massive layoffs. The result was Byrne's *Chainsaw* (HarperBusiness, 1999).

So proudly did Dunlap personify a sort of fundamentalist capitalism—which says that shareholder return is the only reason for business to exist—that he became a sort of cartoon character, who, reports Byrne, once said, "I never met a nickel I didn't like as much as a brother."

The scariest part, says Byrne, is how many people believed him!—and actually subscribed to the idea that the meaning of life is to gather as much money as you can no matter how much you harm others.

Eventually the SEC went after Sunbeam for cooking the books. Dunlap and company were forced to restate earnings, pay a fine and suffer the consequences of a tarnished reputation and an enduring, derogatory epithet.

The moral of Byrne's story is this: When corporations endorse rewards that are exclusively monetary in nature, they attract exactly what they deserve: self-serving leaders, who design corporate cultures where despicable behavior and greed are encouraged and honored. That is the path of corporate self-destruction, and shareholders had better beware.

As we saw in recent years, "Chainsaw Al" had plenty of immoral descendants—CEOs who sought personal aggrandizement rather than the chance to build a great and valuable company. And the result was the worst economic crisis since the Great Depression. Behind the economic story, I believe, was a spiritual crisis that went right to the heart of capitalism—and an even greater healing that continues today. Here's my take on both.

The Crisis of Capitalism

Just months into the new millennium, NASDAQ hit the record 5,000 level, then began a dizzying downward spiral. But NASDAQ's free fall was only the beginning. One blow after another knocked us to our knees: September 11, recession, rising unemployment, corporate scandals and two wars. The Dow and the S&P followed NASDAQ's terrible example and the major indexes wiped many of the gains won in the booming late 1990s.

Reeling from financial turmoil or—for Enron employees, whose retirement accounts were full of worthless company stock—outright disaster, many people asked: How could this happen? Is there something about the philosophy of capitalism that contributed to this crisis?

We'll begin this inquiry into the "crisis of capitalism" on what I suspect even traditional capitalists will consider an upbeat note.

The "Triumph of Capitalism"

It is the late 1990s. The cold war is over and capitalism won. Russia, China and the Eastern block are scrambling to perfect free market institutions. In the U.S., 50 percent of the population—teachers, workers, retirees, high-tech whiz-kids—own shares in American business.

At the dawn of the new millennium, a critical mass of individuals all over the planet had bought into free enterprise. But the triumph of capitalism also contained the seeds of crisis and transformation, as I'll soon explain.

Meanwhile, human consciousness is expanding by leaps and bounds. The spirituality megatrend, illustrated by all those numbers from chapter one, is taking off. Millions are reordering their lives to place Spirit at the center. *But spiritual consciousness requires us to see the Truth.*

In the collective, then, we had signed up for capitalism, Spirit and Truth. What happened next?

Out popped the shadow side of capitalism—every aspect of free enterprise that was out of alignment with Truth—the shady, secret, corrupt elements—was forced out in the open.

Why? It was the first step in spiritual healing. When spiritual energy grows, human consciousness is lifted to a higher frequency. Then, everything that's inconsistent with the new level of consciousness is revealed.

Spirit and our own higher selves determined that 2001–2002 was the perfect time to begin to shine the Light on all the greed, fraud, speculation, conflict of interest and abuse of power on Wall Street. It was as if Spirit said: "Now that you're all on the same page here about capitalism, are you sure you really want it—warts and all?"

Perhaps, from a spiritual point of view, when enough people "buy in" to an economic system, its adherents must reexamine the theories behind it—because the welfare of so many is at stake. Result: capitalism in crisis.

The "Triumph of Capitalism" Provokes a Healing Crisis

Capitalism is enduring what in spiritual terms might be called "a healing crisis," a time when pockets of negativity are propelled outward to be healed.

This is a pattern familiar to many on the spiritual path. You enjoy a great surge of spiritual growth and it's just great. "I've got faith now," you say triumphantly. You're humming along just fine. When, next thing you know, you're down in the dumps. Faith? What's that? More like total despair? You doubt yourself and even God.

What the heck is going on?

Simply this: Once you reach a new level of consciousness, everything—every stubborn old bit of fear or ego—that's *inconsistent* with your great, new, enlightened state rises up to the surface. Like a big, fat zit.

It's not pretty, but it does lead to healing—if you let it.

What happens next? If you're committed to the path, you work through the issues, one by one. Surrender this piece of ego or that attachment, until you reach a new state of well-being that's *clearer*, higher yet more grounded than where you were before the roof caved in.

So, how does this explain the healing crisis of capitalism?

In the booming 1990s we sailed along beautifully. Prosperity, high-tech advances, even breakthroughs in democratic management. But there were unconscious elements of business, capitalism—and ourselves—that we were not yet ready or willing to examine. As a result, the You Know What hit the fan. Investors watched $8 trillion vanish and suffered the worst crisis of confidence since the Depression.

At the spiritual level, the boom, bust and scandals revealed the dark corners of capitalism that must grow conscious and get *healed* before we can move on to what's next: greater spiritual (inner) and technological (external) progress—on a much firmer moral and economic footing.

The triumph of capitalism catalyzed a healing crisis. But capitalism was not and is not just for the wealthy anymore. We all felt the pain. We had to. The good news is that a system in pain becomes conscious of itself, as together we ask: Why did this happen?

Here is the Wall Street sage who I think explains it best.

Bogle Speaks

John Bogle, 77, who launched the now $1 trillion Vanguard Group and the first index fund, says, "If there was a single dominant failing of the recent bubble, it was the market's overbearing focus on the price of a stock rather than on the value of a corporation."

Exactly. Furthermore, as the bull market hit the frenzied pace of Dutch tulip mania, we renounced the spiritual value of Balance. Truth gave way to deception and fraud. Investment became speculation.

Let's return now to the question I've raised again and again:

What is the philosophy of modern capitalism? Is it to:

1. Show earnings by fair means or foul—in order to boost the price of a company's stock?
2. Build a valuable enterprise long-term where profit is the *natural* outcome of a healthy organism?

If capitalism is to survive and thrive, the answer is obviously number two. Still, you have to wonder if investors finally get that simple truth. If not, we will be tested again. Meanwhile we'd better get clear on the perfidious process that leads business *way* off track—both spiritually and economically.

To remind us how good companies go bad, I've again called upon the venerable Mr. Bogle, rephrasing here from a few of his most brilliant speeches the step-by-step process down the road to self-destruction.

If a CEO is charged with and rewarded only for increasing share price, rather than building a company long-term, an insidious sequence—that begins innocently enough—starts to unfold. You, the CEO and your top executives:

1. Achieve strong, steady earnings growth and tell Wall Street about it.
2. Set guidance targets publicly and meet them consistently.
3. First, do it the old-fashioned way: cut costs, raise productivity, schedule layoffs. But that gets harder to do. You've cut fat. Now there's a diminishing return. . . .
4. When you can't meet targets, try creative accounting! Push the numbers.
5. Do a merger, not for business reasons, but to boost those all-important short-term earnings.
6. And when that isn't enough, *cheat!*

Now the shadowy vices of profit-at-any-cost capitalism are visible for all to see. Yet, at the same time, so is the alternative—Conscious Capitalism.

As the SRI and CSR trends gain momentum, exemplary companies show us the *right* way to run a business. In the following section, we'll go to the heart of the matter and discover why Conscious Capitalism is the antidote to the vile workings Bogle describes.

The Consciousness in Conscious Capitalism

What exactly *is* the consciousness in Conscious Capitalism? Where did it come from? How did it get there? I think the greatest companies, the ones that top the CSR and SRI lists, infuse their operations with a priceless element that enhances the quest for profit.

That special factor is the consciousness inherent in transcendent human values. Now, after years of searching, I've found a fascinating study that illustrates my point.

"Intangibles" Drive Performance

A new report entitled "Clear Advantage: Building Shareholder Value," from the Global Environmental Management Initiative (GEMI), offers what it calls "compelling evidence" that invisibles like environmental performance (as well as health and safety) add shareholder value, turning "intangibles into tangibles."

The intangibles they are talking about are human values and consciousness. But who is "GEMI"—some crunchy activist coalition?

Try a confederation of senior executives from Motorola, Procter & Gamble, Duke Energy, Dell, Occidental Petroleum, DuPont, Bristol-Myers Squibb—all told, representatives from some 40 global corporate giants.

"Clear Advantage" shows how Earth-friendly policies that do not show up on the balance sheet (what I call higher consciousness) cut costs and boost profits through product innovation, market development and better techniques.

When 3M and Bristol-Myers Squibb added lifestyle review to product development, time-to-market sped up and compliance burdens shrank.

As GEMI puts it, intangibles became tangible. As I see it, consciousness becomes profit.

Let's define terms.

What Is an "Intangible"?

The International Accounting Standards Board defines an intangible as "an identifiable, non-monetary asset without physical substance held for use in the production of goods or services."

Without physical substance? That's right.

The most potent business intangibles, says Clear Advantage, include brand, leadership and strategy, environmental and social reputation, human capital, transparency, technology and innovation.

Since 1997, investment in intangibles like brand, R&D and training has exceeded investment in tangibles like property, plant and equipment, says the Organization for Economic Cooperation and Development.

Business intangibles are aspects of human consciousness that may take many different forms but are generally grounded in or profoundly influenced by people.

But how do you calculate their financial value?

Intangibles Rule

Free enterprise has long tried to monetize intangibles. Merger and acquisition history is rife with efforts to appraise the worth of "goodwill." Some firms attach a figure to it, but few CPAs would stake their license on its accuracy.

Goodwill and a great brand deliver enormous strategic and economic value, as you saw in chapter five. But consider the following: 50 to 90 percent of a firm's market value can be attributed to intangibles, concludes the GEMI report.[5]

Intangibles, then—and the consciousness that animates them—actually *rule* the material world of business.

Intangibles Are Poorly Measured—Yet They Drive Business

"A majority of executives in every industry" believe the factors that are *most* critical to success are not being measured or reported, says the GEMI study. But the report continues, Wall Street acts on these intangibles every day.

---

[5]Citing *Invisible Advantage*, by Jonathan Low and Pamela Cohen Kalafut (Perseus, 2002).

For example, 35 percent of allocation decisions by institutional investors are based on non-financial performance, says a Cap Gemini/Ernst & Young study. And 86 percent of oil and gas analysts say intangibles—such as regulatory compliance, health, safety, the environment and lawsuits—all impact a stock's value. So markets value environment, health and safety performance every day, the GEMI report concludes, whether consciously or unconsciously.

Conscious Capitalism Honors—and Measures—Intangibles

Conscious Capitalism, of course, aims to transform the valuation process from unconscious to conscious—by honoring the *financial* power of intangibles like moral leadership, vision, transparency, ethics, and all the rest.

These intangibles are the stuff of human consciousness.

Similarly, the GEMI report advises companies to "measure, manage and disclose" the impact of intangibles like the environment on shareholder value.

Exactly. And there is a mechanism already in place to do precisely that. That mechanism is the SRI screens described in chapter seven. With the help of screens, Conscious Capitalism asks questions that raise human, as well as financial, issues. These questions also gauge the input of human consciousness in a business.

What is a firm's environmental footprint?
How well does it pay employees?
Does it reflect the ethical principles of its customers?

Screens measure the extent to which human consciousness penetrates a business culture.

And as you know from the studies in chapter two and "meta-studies" cited in chapter seven of this book, the companies with the best SRI records—that is, the highest levels of human consciousness—outperform their peers.

The Success Formula of Conscious Capitalism

So, *how* do Conscious Capitalists beat the Street?

Corporate social responsibility is a proxy for good management and good management is the best predictor of financial performance.

That is absolutely correct—yet incomplete. Another, more spiritual, formula better reflects the truth behind that good-as-far-as-it-goes proposition. Here it is: The investment of consciousness and values—i.e., positive "business intangibles"—into an enterprise's people, systems and structures, in conjunction with sound business principles, generates material gain and social well-being.

Or as the GEMI report puts it: "Intangibles such as R&D, proprietary know-how, intellectual property and workforce skills, world-class supply networks and brands are now the key drivers of wealth production, while physical and financial assets are increasingly regarded as commodities."

Every one of these intangibles is composed of human consciousness.

The alchemy of Conscious Capitalism transmutes the input of human consciousness into the desirable outcomes of social and material gain.

A New Role for Business

At a Business for Social Responsibility (BSR) conference in November 2003, then-CEO Carly Fiorina offered a simple reason why Hewlett-Packard stands foursquare in favor of good corporate citizenship. In a world where:

• half the population lives on $2 a day,
• a billion people cannot read or write,
• one and a half billion never get a clean glass of water,
• corporate social responsibility is just "the right thing to do."

Agreed. But there's a practical dimension as well. Given these appalling statistics, how sustainable—or stable—is the global economy going to be?

If you answered, "not very," we are on the same page here.

If free enterprise is to thrive, it needs growing markets. The developed world's mature economies offer only modest growth potential. That means it is in the *economic* interest of the world's wealthy nations to foster prosperity in the Third World. That's where capitalism's new wealth and next lucrative markets reside.

But who is going to jump-start that growth? Governments? Government-to-government assistance has a dismal record, mired in corruption and bureaucracy. On the other hand, small-scale free market solutions like micro-lending have amassed consistent and stunning success. Throughout *Megatrends 2010,* I've shown you how people, as investors, managers and consumers, have the power to heal capitalism. Let me focus now on the second part of that equation: Capitalism has the power to change the world.

Corporations can in fact play an enormous role in global economic development. For one thing, 52 of the largest economies in the world are corporations. HP alone boasts *one billion* customers in 176 countries. Wherever HP operates, often in developing countries, it can exert enormous positive influence. Multiply that by the companies in the *Fortune* 1000—not to mention the many small to mid-size firms that do business all over the world—and you begin to see capitalism's potential for global transformation.

HP's example begins to tell the story.

Suppliers and Sustainability

In 2003, when Fiorina spoke at BSR, HP had 10,000 vendors—the largest supply chain in technology, ringing up about $46 billion a year. Today HP holds many of them to a Supplier Code of Conduct for "employment, environment, health and labor policies." That means, to win contracts, HP vendors must meet HP standards. Once one company raises the bar, argues HP, local governments and multinationals may be more inclined to measure up.

How has this CSR initiative fared so far? It has not been easy.

When HP ran the proposal past its top suppliers, a few were annoyed; others balked outright. But HP held the course and made its case: We're not being hard to get along with, the company argued, we need to look customers in the eye and say, "We're sure that the product you're buying is consistent with our standards."

By the end of FY2003, HP had won over its top 45 suppliers, representing 80 percent of what HP spends on product materials.

There's also a *practical* incentive to get on board the CSR bandwagon. The global movement to enforce higher labor, environmental and economic standards is not going away. So smart companies are getting involved now rather than wait. Better corporate initiative than government regulation. Clearly that is what HP has chosen.

There's just one problem. Government regulation notwithstanding, old-line, profit-at-any-cost capitalism still holds a big fat ace in this card game: Its tenets are woven into the legal code of the United States of America.

Decriminalizing Consciousness

Public companies, as lawful entities under state code, are required to conduct business so as to *maximize* shareholder profits.

That rule is the legal platform for a lot of antisocial behavior on the part of business, say many activists, including Michael Sauvante, chairman of

SEER (Social, Economic, Environmental Responsibility) Inc. and a Silicon Valley entrepreneur. Sauvante is also a social responsibility advocate who wants to change things.

I'll soon tell you how, but first, what exactly does that peculiar mandate *mean*? Specifically, anything a public firm can legally do to push costs "off the books"—known in business as the "externalization of costs"—legally swells corporate profit at the cost of the "external entity."

Who might that be? The way the law is written, the cost of cleaning up toxins hurts a company's bottom line—whereas to foist the problem off on society strengthens profits. So who pays? Right. Taxpayers and Mother Earth (unless there's a law against the activity in question).

The ramifications for top corporate insiders are truly disconcerting. Directors, officers and senior executives are, it would appear, legally bound to behave in ways many of us find ethically objectionable.

Lots of activists berate auto firms for making gas-guzzling SUVs. But *not* selling them to a market that's hungry for the monsters (or was until quite recently) is a breach of the car company's—and its officers'—fiduciary responsibility to shareholders.

As shareholders in XYZ corporation, you or I could theoretically take the firm to court for any of the following:

• using an expensive process to clean up the air,
• paying employees better than market wages,
• refusing to hire a cheap supplier who traffics in "sweatshop" labor.

Public companies, it seems, are legally obliged to engage in a destructive form of capitalism.

And as one observer put it, "The modern corporation has the ability to do more damage to the public interest (legally) in one afternoon than the average individual can do in a lifetime."

Whatever activists might do to persuade corporate bad guys to change their evil ways, it is "a perpetual uphill battle," says Sauvante.

What's a CSR type to do? Get the law changed!

In January 2004, one Robert Hinkley, a corporate lawyer, social responsibility activist and partner at the international law firm Jones Day, tried to do exactly that. He put a bill before the Judiciary Committee of the California State Senate that would require California corporations to be more socially and environmentally responsible. Both Hinkley and Michael Sauvante testified in its favor.

The measure was opposed by business interests and rejected. But several committee members thought California should take the lead and be a model for other states and urged advocates to submit a revised bill. Sauvante then rewrote the law so as to avoid provoking what he calls the "antibody" reaction from "pro-business" folks who heed the "profit first, last and always" dogma.

Sauvante's solution? Make the whole law "optional" (now there's an oxymoron). That is to say, create a new, *voluntary* class of corporation, a CSR corporation, for firms that want to pursue a more socially responsible and/or environmentally friendly brand of capitalism. Such a move, he says, would:

- Protect good corporate citizens from greedy shareholders—and attract shareholders who demand both profit and responsibility.
- Diffuse objections from the business lobby—since it's voluntary.
- Create a legal mandate for the Triple Bottom Line (TBL) movement and give its advocates time to prove TBL will boost, not shrink, profits.

Unfortunately the Code failed to pass in California (or in Maine or Minnesota where it was also introduced). Robert Hinkley now believes it will take grassroots support (say via the movement toward Conscious Capitalism?) to enact the Code into law. Nevertheless, Hinkley continues his crusade to introduce the Code for Corporate Citizenship into state law with the addition of these simple words:

"The duty of directors henceforth shall be to make money for shareholders but not at the expense of the environment, human rights, public health and safety, dignity of employees and the welfare of the communities in which the company operates."

From Greed to Enlightened Self-Interest

Let's recap this chapter's key point:

The doctrine of Conscious Capitalism holds that business bears moral and ethical responsibilities beyond short-term profit and maximum shareholder return. Equally important, it lifts the frequency of free enterprise from self-interest to the higher octave of enlightened self-interest.

Enlightened self-interest is not altruism. It is self-interest with a wider view. It asks: If I act in my own self-interest and keep doing so, what are the ramifications of my choices? Which acts—that may look fine right now—will come around and injure me and others one year from now? Ten years? Twenty-five years?

The spiritual transformation of capitalism is the shift:

- from greed to enlightened self-interest,
- from elitism to economic democracy,
- from the fundamentalist doctrine of "profit at any cost" to the conscious ideology that espouses both money *and* morals.

The metamorphosis of capitalism won't come about through the efforts of well-meaning regulators. It is being forged *right now* in the hearts of investors, consumers, executives—and of course "ordinary" managers. And it is to you that I address the final words of *Megatrends 2010*.

The Power Is in Our Hands

I have organized the chapters of *Megatrends 2010* to set forth the case, by introducing one theme after another, that the future of capitalism lies not in the hands of Big Business, but in our own.

We have the power to transform capitalism.

Who again are *we*?

We are "ordinary" managers, visionary entrepreneurs, socially responsible investors, spiritual CEOs, shareholder activists, corporate meditation teachers, executive coaches, transformation-based consultants, corporate activists, Cultural Creatives, Conscious Consumers, business chaplains, yoga instructors, inspiring team leaders, conscious executives, fire-walking saleswomen, forgiveness-trained brokers, heart-full HR honchos . . .

I could go on and on. But my point is this: There are an awful lot of us. Many more than we, in isolation, can recognize or count.

Seventy million of us (go ahead and review the math at the end of chapter two) are transforming capitalism, one conscious action at a time.

John Byrne believes we the people can, as he puts it, "enforce a market discipline" in favor of human values. "So many people today seek purpose and meaning in business that we potentially have the power to make values *more* important than—or at least *as important* as—shareholder value," he adds.

As consumers, he says, we can buy products only from companies and retailers whose values reflect our own. As employees, we can work only for companies that value their people and customers as much as their shareholders.

As shareholders, I would add, we can invest only in companies that we deem socially responsible. Byrne's words, which I heard at the Wisdom Business Network's online conference in February 2004 (which Byrne and I keynoted), inspired me to create a litany of the ways we can transform business. The list that follows also recaps the main ideas of *Megatrends 2010*.

How to Transform Capitalism

Melt the firewall between personal and organizational Spirit. Like Greg Merten, Ann Mincey and Marc Benioff, practice your values in business and observe how your actions influence others.

Invest in socially responsible companies—and reap a healthy, heart-centered return, while at the same time withholding your money from corporate bad guys.

Lobby your company pension fund to add or expand the SRI choices.

Take your values shopping. Boycott sweatshop labor and buy fair trade coffee—even if it costs more. Get your grocer to stock the fair trade beans. Ditto for fair trade chocolate. Order Co-op America's new *National Green Pages*.

Become a shareholder activist. Vote your proxies. Get your mutual fund to disclose its proxy votes. Lobby fund managers to take more thoughtful positions.

Get informed about the issues and support the consumer campaign that excites you most. Log on to the Co-op America website listed in this book's appendix.

Lead your colleagues with what Ron Heifetz calls "Informal Authority."

Embody your values as a manager like a "Tempered Radical."

Read Barbara Waugh's *The Soul in the Computer* and *create a brown bag book club* to discuss Barb's principles and adventures and figure out which of them might work in your organization.

Convene Sacred Space within company walls at a yoga class or brown bag meditation. Get an empty office declared the official "quiet room." Host Sacred Space *outside* the office, at a private home, café or business organization like the local chamber of commerce.

Find your soul mates at the nearest chapter of the Association for Spirit at Work. None close enough? Create your own. That's what I did in Boston.

Import the tools, techniques and teachings of Spirit into your company. Don't know where to start? Begin each meeting with a moment of silence. Move up to a five-minute morning meditation. Don't forget to monitor the improvements in productivity.

Honor coworkers with a meaningful ritual.

Identify the values of your company, division or department. Speak up and ask, "Are we living these or not?"

Tell other capitalists you stand for enlightened self-interest, not greed.

Throughout the pages of *Megatrends 2010*, I've addressed your head as well as your heart and soul. Now here we are at the end of the story and I find I want to touch your heart most of all. The message I leave you with is an old and venerable one: "Be the change you want to happen." To this wisdom, I would add one more thought: "Allow yourself to hope."

But that triggers another voice, the cry of doubt.

Business hasn't changed before. Why would it now?

It seems that I am back talking to *all* of you, heart, soul—and mind. So here goes.

We are all suffering the same collective heartbreak over the failure of institutional transformation. Personal change—okay. Organizational? Never. Acknowledge the feelings of hopelessness and the pattern of inertia.

But open yourself to take in the truth: Times are changing. The "game" of business is over. What Spirit allowed in the name of free will—the greed and fraud on the shady side of capitalism—is out in the open now. We've seen it, endured the consequences and made our collective choice. We don't want it because the cost is too high. It is not who we are.

Even so, doubt lingers.

Why should I believe it this time?

Okay, so *don't* believe it. Just Do It.

Why? Because you've lived the dream of transformation for so long that it won't let you go. Give in to hope. Choose to co-create with a Higher Power the spiritual blueprint of business. You *will* make a difference. Spirit guarantees it. The only question is whether you'll *perceive* that difference. So much goes unseen.

So do it anyway.

What is at stake?

Your job? Not if you're a quiet leader or a tempered radical.

Your belief systems about corporate inertia? Definitely.

Prosperity? The future of capitalism? Yes and yes.

If you're tempted to say, it's been a while since my last tête-à-tête with the CEO, I take your point. But remember, distance from mundane power is not the same as the lack of power.

Yours is a different kind of power. Spiritual power.

Your job is to flood the system with the medicine of spiritual values and fresh, clear consciousness. And that is *completely* within your power.

It is said, in spiritual circles, if you want to change the world, you must first change yourself. Well, most of you already *have!* You've learned to listen to the silence, hear the inner voice, speak from your heart, trust something greater than yourself.

You've walked the path for years, a decade or even longer.

Maybe you're not the CEO, but you've got a track record and a platform and you mean to use it. What marks you as a grassroots leader is the commitment that ignites the potent mixture of inner power and action. Stand in your truth and act on your values right here, right now, and touch the people around you.

What will you do? That's up to you. Tempered radicals, says author Debra Meyerson, draw on a five-part spectrum of possibilities ranging from "quietly resisting" to "collective action."

How will you do it? With passion, courage, modesty, fear, trepidation, commitment, the fellowship of colleagues—and perhaps even joy!

How successful will you be? That depends a lot on your persistence. You may fail at first. Or achieve real results that your mind dismisses as meaningless. But in time you will see the fruits of your commitment, if you're willing to look.

Why will you do it? Because you're already transformed and it's time to give it away. Because you were born to be the Light and pass the torch. Because your mission is bigger than your job.

Because this is the only game in town.

Because the transformation of capitalism depends on you—though not entirely. Give Spirit a chance and let the magic begin.

Appendix

Resources

Socially Responsible Investing

Social Investment Forum (SIF)
(212) 872-5319
www.socialinvest.org

Wainwright Bank
(888) 428-BANK
Steve Young
SVP Retail Banking
(617) 478-4000
www.wainwrightbank.com

Bridgeway Funds
(800) 661-3550
www.bridgewayfund.com

Calvert Group
(800) 368-2748
www.calvert.com

Domini Social Investments
(800) 762-6814
www.domini.com

Winslow Green Growth Fund
(888) 314-9049
www.winslowgreen.com

Trillium Asset Management
(800) 548-5684
www.trilliuminvest.com

Green Money Journal
(505) 988-7423
www.greenmoneyjournal.com

Business Ethics
(212) 875-9381
www.business-ethics.com

Progressive Investor/The SB20, the World's Top Sustainable Stocks
(631) 423-3277
www.sustainablebusiness.com

Spirituality in Business

Centers/Groups

Association for Spirit at Work
(203) 467-9084
www.spiritatwork.org

Spirit in Business
www.spiritinbusiness.org

Center for Visionary Leadership
West Coast: (415) 472-2540
East Coast: (202) 237-2800
www.visionarylead.org

Heartland Circle (formerly Institute)
(952) 925-5995
www.heartlandcircle.com

International Spirit at Work Award
www.spiritatwork.org
ISAW 2005 Awards
A full list of winners is also at
www.spiritinbusiness.org

John Renesch
(877) 2RENESCH or (415) 437-6974
www.renesch.com

San Francisco Chamber of Commerce
"Spirit in Business Conversation" brown
bag lunch.
Second Thursday of the month.
Chamber of Commerce
235 Montgomery St., 12th Floor,
between Bush and Pine Streets
from 12 noon to 1 P.M.
debra@temptime.com
Sarah Hargrave (650) 756-6175

Wisdom Business Network
www.businessnetwork.meetup.com

Practitioners

Balance Integration Corp.
Tevis Trower
(212) 414-9393
tevis@balanceintegration.com

Conscious Pursuits
Cindy Wigglesworth
(713) 667-9824
www.consciouspursuits.com

Corporate Transformation Tools
Richard Barrett and Associates
(828) 452-5050
www.valuescenter.com

Clarity Seminars
David and Karen Gamow
(650) 917-1186 or (888) 917-1186
www.clarityseminars.com

Forgiveness Project
Fred Luskin
learningtoforgive@comcast.net
www.learningtoforgive.com

HeartMath
(800) 450-9111
www.heartmath.com

Maio and Company
Elsie Maio
(212) 505-0404
www.soulbranding.com

Marketplace Chaplains USA
(972) 385-7657
www.marketchaplains.com

New Dimensions Radio Network
www.newdimensions.org

WorkLife Seminars
Eric and Paula Biskamp
(972) 380-7996
www.worklifeseminars.com

Richard Whiteley
(617) 723-8889
www.corpshaman.com

Conscious Consumption

Co-op America
(800) 584-7336
www.coopamerica.org

LOHAS Journal
(303) 222-8283
www.lohasjournal.com

E: The Environmental Magazine
(203) 854-5559
www.emagazine.com

Hybrid Cars: American Council for an
Energy Efficient Economy
(202) 429-8873
www.GreenerCars.com

U.S. Green Building Council
(202) 828-7422
www.usgbc.org

Endnotes

Preface and Introduction

xiii   Gordon Gekko from "Greed Is Good" speech, American Rhetoric online speech bank. "Address to the Teldar Paper Stockholders," from "Wall Street," www.americanrhetoric.com.

xiv   Alan Greenspan quotes from Federal Reserve Board's semi-annual Monetary Policy Report to the Congress. Testimony before the Committee on Banking, Housing and Urban Affairs, U.S. Senate, July 16, 2002.

xv   For Medtronic data, see endnote for page 47.

xxiii   Hill & Knowlton/Harris poll study cited on Business for Social Responsibility website, "BSR Issues Briefs: Overview of Corporate Responsibility," www.bsr.org.

xxv   Michael Rennie quote from his speech at the Global Scenarios Workshop, Macquarie Graduate School of Management (Australia), reprinted as "Getting Economics to Serve the Spirit," *Manzine*, an online collection of articles. See endnote for page 139.

Chapter 1: The Power of Spirituality—From Personal to Organizational

1–2   Greg Merten story from author interview and Greg Merten keynote at the Spirit in Business Conference in San Francisco, June 10, 2003.

5   Gallup survey data from "God and Business" cover, *Fortune*, June 26, 2001, *Workforce Management*, "A New Approach to Faith at Work," October 2004, pp. 76–77 and in *BusinessWeek* story cited below.

Sixty percent figure cited in "Religion in the Workplace," *BusinessWeek*, November 1, 1999.

Time/CNN/Harris Poll cited in "We Gather Together," *Time* cover story, November 19, 2001. [Note from author: Unfortunately this poll data, which appears in a sidebar on page 38, does not show up in electronic versions.]

Yoga figures cited in "Transforming an Ancient Exercise," ABC (online) news report, March 28, 2005.

5–6   Numbers who meditate, where they do so, Shambhala and Catskills examples from "Just Say Om," *Time* "Meditation" cover story, August 4, 2003.

6   Book sales from *Fortune*, "God and Business," June 26, 2001.

     Lynn Garrett from "The Missing Link," *The Los Angeles Times*, April 6, 1998.

     Susan Petersen Kennedy quoted in "Publishing: Mainstream Houses Tap the Power of Christian Fiction," *The Wall Street Journal*, January 20, 1998.

8–9   Alternative health cost and numbers who use it from "The Science of Alternative Medicine," *Newsweek*, December 2, 2002.

9–10   Gladwell quotes from "What Is the Tipping Point?" Author Q&A, www.Gladwell.com.

10   Paul Ray quote from *Alternatives: Resources for Cultural Creativity* (online), interview with Ray by Peter Moore, Summer 2001 (Issue 18).

11   Social Investment Forum SRI figures quoted in "Working Capital," *E: The Environmental Magazine*, March/April 2004.

11–12   Bill George interviewed by author and correspondence.

12–13   Marc Benioff and Salesforce.com data and quotes from "Who Says CEOs Can't Find Inner Peace?" *BusinessWeek*, September 1, 2003, and "The Big Benioff," *Fortune*, December 13, 2004, and company sources.

14   Jay Sidhu from "Post Enron, Spirituality Grows," *Christian Science Monitor*, April 29, 2002, and Opinion, *Boston Business Journal*, March 14, 2003.

     S. Truett Cathy from CNBC On Assignment: "God and Money," March 14, 2003.

     Jeff Swartz and Kris Kalra from "Religion in the Workplace," *BusinessWeek*, November 1, 1999.

     Bill Pollard quote from "God and Business," *Fortune*, June 26, 2001.

14–20   Ann Mincey from various interviews and correspondence with author and Mincey's keynote at the Spirit in Business Conference in San Francisco, June 10, 2003.

20–21   Cultural Creatives material from the book, cited in full in text and from "Discovering the Cultural Creatives," *LOHAS Journal*, March/April 2000, "The Cultural Creatives: We Are Everywhere," *Alternatives*, Summer 2001.

Chapter 2: The Dawn of Conscious Capitalism

22–24   Timberland info from Jeff Swartz address to Boston Chamber "Future Leaders," October 21, 2003, and from interviews, correspondence and company materials from Timberland's Robin Giampa.

24   Sabbatical quote from *Fortune*, "The 100 Best Companies to Work For" list, January 24, 2005. Timberland is number 18.

     CEO quote from Carly Fiorina speech to BSR Annual Conference, November 12, 2003.

26   BSR description and figures from www.bsr.org, "BSR Issue Briefs: Overview of Corporate Social Responsibility," October 23, 2003, and from interviews with BSR representatives.

26   CERES description and principles from www.ceres.org.

27   Global Reporting Initiative from www.globalreporting.org.

            Conference Board Study cited in "Working Capital," *E: The Environmental Magazine*, March/April 2004.

            3M figure from "3M Environmental Excellence Award," *Business Ethics*, Winter 2003.

            General Mills example from "100 Best Corporate Citizens," *Business Ethics*, Spring 2003.

            P&G example and quote and Motorola example from "100 Best Corporate Citizens," *Business Ethics*, Spring 2004.

27–28   Cummins, Wild Oats and Intel figures from "100 Best Corporate Citizens," *Business Ethics*, Spring 2003. Added Intel data from Dave Stangis.

28–29   Starbucks section info drawn from numerous sources including interviews and correspondence with company representatives; *Business Ethics* special sponsorship page, "Starbucks Coffee Co.: A Model Global Citizen," Winter 2003; BSR Issue Briefs, "Overview of Corporate Responsibility. Leadership Examples: Starbucks Coffee Co."; "Conservation Coffee Program," www.starbucks.com; and Starbucks brochure, "Living Our Values," widely available at Starbucks outlets.

29   "Good hearted saps" quote from "Working Capital," *E: The Environmental Magazine*, March/April 2004.

            Governance Metrics cited in Calvert Investments presentation at the Spirit in Business Conference, June 2003, and "Tree Huggers, Soy Lovers and Profits," *Fortune*, June 9, 2003.

            Morningstar ratings from "Working Capital," *E: The Environmental Magazine*, March/April 2004.

30   DePaul study from BSR Issue Briefs, "Overview of Corporate Social Responsibility," www.bsr.net and in online press release "Business Ethics 100 Best Citizens Outperform S&P 500," April 29, 2002, www.SocialFunds.com.

            Towers Perrin study cited in Joe O'Keefe's presentation at the Spirit in Business Conference, San Francisco, June 10, 2003, and described in detail in "Ongoing Conversations with Disbelievers: Persuading Business to Address Social Challenges," The Center for Corporate Citizenship at Boston College, 2000, www.conversations-with-disbelievers.net.

            Watson Wyatt study cited by O'Keefe at SIB conference in above note. See www.watsonwyatt.com Research Reports: "Human Capital as a Lead Indicator of Shareholder Value."

            Boone quoted in "Good Vibes: Socially Responsible Investing Is Gaining Fans and Clout," *Barron's*, July 7, 2003.

            2005 study of *Fortune's* 100 Best from press release "Stocks of 'Best Companies to Work For' Beat Market," Great Places to Work Institute (online pressroom), March 15, 2005.

31   Cliff Feigenbaum from author interview and correspondence.

32   Cone Corporate Citizenship Study cited in online press release, "Multi-year study finds 21 percent increase in Americans who say corporate support of social issues is important," December 8, 2004, www.coneinc.com.

            Hill & Knowlton/Harris Poll and CSR Monitor survey from BSR "Overview of Corporate Social Responsibility," www.bsr.org.

32–35   Alisa Gravitz material from author interview and correspondence.

35   3M sidebar quotes and material from "3M Environmental Excellence Award," *Business Ethics,* Winter 2003.

36   "Untamed beast" quote from "Working Capital," *E: The Environmental Magazine,* March/April 2004.

            SRI fund that owns Altria stock from Cliff Feigenbaum.

            Sierra Club activism and bullets about shareholder activist successes with Pepsico, GE, Ford, etc. are cited in "Working Capital," *E: The Environmental Magazine,* March/ April 2004.

            Whole Foods resolution on GE food from author interview with Shelley Alpern, shareholder activist at Trillium Investment Management.

37   Shareholder resolutions filed, 2001–2003 from "Good Vibes: Socially Responsible Investing Is Gaining Fans and Clout," *Barron's,* July 7, 2003.

            Intel shareholder votes from "Intel Shareholders Approve Plan to Expense Stock Options," *Associated Press,* May 19, 2004.

            Avon vote and Lippman quote from "Good Vibes," *Barron's,* July 7, 2003.

            2005 shareholder resolutions from Social Investment Forum and Investor Responsibility Research Center press release, "Social Shareholder Resolutions Close to 2004 Record," April 7, 2005.

            "Old-growth" campaign against Home Depot and Shelley Alpern quote from "Working Capital," *E: The Environmental Magazine,* March/April 2004.

37–41   Shelley Alpern and ChevronTexaco (now Chevron) story from author interviews and correspondence.

41   Chiquita sidebar from *Winslow Environmental News,* January 2004 and BSR Issue Briefs, "Overview of Corporate Responsibility. Leadership Examples: Chiquita," wwwbsr.org, and company sources.

            Alisa Gravitz quote from "Working Capital," *E: The Environmental Magazine,* March/April 2004.

42   Cliff Feigenbaum observations from author interview.

43   *Fast Company* circulation and mission from "Letter from the Editor," *Fast Company,* August 2003.

43–44   Cultural Creatives material from book cited in text, and from "The Cultural Creatives: We Are Everywhere," *Alternatives,* Summer 2001. Videoconference audio provided by Wisdom Business Network.

44   Sherry Anderson from "A Conversation with Sherry Anderson," *The Monthly Aspectarian,* December 2000.

44   Paul Hawken and Amory & Hunter Lovins material from books cited in
            text and from websites, www.paulhawken.com and www.natcap.org.

Chapter 3: Leading from the Middle

46   *Fortune* on Lou Gerstner from *Fast Company*, "Memo to CEOs," June 2002.

            Katzenbach info from *Fortune*, "Wanted: Company Change Agents,"
            December 11, 1995, and from www.jonkatzenbach.com.

47   Bill George quote from interview with author and elsewhere. Medtronic
            profit history from "Pacing the Field," *Forbes*, January 8, 2001, and
            "Medtronic: Good Vital Signs," *Kiplinger's Personal Finance*, May 20, 2005.

49–50   Ron Heifitz quotes from *Leadership without Easy Answers* (Belknap/Harvard
            University Press, 1994). In particular: small groups, p. 56; blind spots, p. 183;
            King, Sanger, Gandhi, p. 183; benefits of informal leadership, pp.
            187–189; Creative Deviance: latitude for, p. 188; single issue focus, pp.
            188–189; and proximity to the front line, pp. 189–194.

50   Waugh quoted in "Diary of a Change Agent," *Strategy + Business*, Issue 28,
            Third Quarter 2002.

51   "Only 47 percent rate leaders . . ." from 1999 National Business Ethics
            Study, www.walkerinfo.com and "Memo to CEOs," *Fast Company*, June 2002.

            Pew Forum survey data from press release Pew Research Center for the
            People & the Press, "Honesty Up in Washington, Down in Boardrooms,"
            March 20, 2002, and *Fortune*, "System Failure," June 9, 2002.

            Collins quoted in "CEOs Are Going, Going, Gone," *USA Today*, June 10, 2002.

            Khurana quote from *Fortune*, "Star CEOs: Should You Bet on the CEO?"
            November 5, 2002.

51–52   Breen information from Associated Press report, "CEO Breen Is Tyco's
            New Sheriff in Town," March 21, 2004 (reprinted on MSNBC.com), and
            from "Exorcism at Tyco," *Fortune*, April 28, 2003.

52   Scarth and both Olstein quotes as well as Wiersema and Helfat studies
            cited in "Star CEOs: Should You Bet on the CEO?" *Fortune*, November 5,
            2002.

52–53   Both merger studies (of 21 and 302 firms) cited in "Why Most Big Deals
            Don't Pay Off," *BusinessWeek*, October 14, 2002.

53   *BusinessWeek's* explanation of merger mania from "Why Most Big Deals
            Don't Pay Off," *BusinessWeek*, October 14, 2002.

            Description of Gaughan's new book from his publisher at www.wiley.com.

54   Numbers of CEO departures (Challenger, Gray and Christmas) from
            "CEOs Are Going, Going, Gone," *USA Today*, June 10, 2002.

            January 2005 CEO firings from "Why Carly's Out," *Time*, February 21,
            2005.

            Booz Allen Hamilton study on CEO succession cited in "Why CEOs Fail,"
            Strategy + Business, Issue 28, Third Quarter 2002.

54   Drake Beam Morin study from "CEOs Are Going, Going, Gone," *USA Today,* June 10, 2002.

          Growth in CEO pay in 1990s compared to profits and employee pay from "Memo to CEOs," *Fast Company,* June 2002.

          Kozlowski, Skillings cash-out from "System Failure," *Fortune,* June 9, 2002.

          Greenspan quote from Federal Reserve Board's semi-annual Monetary Policy Report to the Congress. Testimony before the Committee on Banking, Housing and Urban Affairs, U.S. Senate, July 16, 2002.

          Bogle on independent chairman from his speech, "After the Fall: What Lies Ahead for Capitalism and the Financial Markets" at the University of Missouri, October 22, 2002.

55   Elliott and Schroth quoted from Introduction, *How Companies Lie,* cited in text, www.howcompanieslie.com.

56–57   Bossidy quotes from "Larry Bossidy: The Thought Leader Interview," *Strategy + Business,* Issue 28, Third Quarter 2002.

57–59   Debra Meyerson quotes from *Tempered Radicals* (Harvard Business School Press, 2002). On Wiley, pp. 3–4. Additional quotes cited below by page number only.

58–59   Badaracco quotes from *Leading Quietly* (Harvard Business School Press, 2001). On Olson, pp. 12–13. Additional quotes cited below by page number only.

          Meyerson on Ziwak, p. 10.

          Badaracco on Cortez, p. 36.

          Badaracco quote "swift" vs. "careful," p. 9.

          Badaracco case studies used, p. 186.

          Badaracco quote "Would be leaders . . . direct them," pp. 34–35.

          Badaracco quote "cavalry" vs. "guerilla warfare," p. 177.

          Meyerson on tempered radicals, p. 4 and p. 7.

          Meyerson on Peter Grant, p. 37.

          Meyerson on identity and difference, p. 5 and pp. 23–28.

          Meyerson quote "when something is tempered . . .," p. 7.

60   Waugh quote from her book *Soul in the Computer* (Inner Ocean, 2001), p. 9.

60–62   Additional Waugh material from author interviews and Waugh's book cited above.

Chapter 4: Spirituality in Business

66–67   San Francisco Chamber of Commerce brown bag from author interviews with Sarah Hargrave and Debra Mugnani Monroe and correspondence.

67   Headlines from (in order): *Fort Worth Star Telegram,* December 28, 2004; *Los Angeles Times,* May 15, 2005; *Charlotte Observer,* January 9, 2005.

          Boston and Minneapolis spiritual gatherings cited in "Religion in the Workplace," *BusinessWeek,* November 1, 1999.

67   Faith@Work from "Spirituality, God and Business," *Fortune,* June 26, 2001.

67–68   BEEJ description from *The National Catholic Register,* November 21, 2001. Figures updated by researcher interview.

68   Yacullo comment from "Spirituality," *Newsweek Japan,* September 9, 2001. English translation. Article reprinted on www.avodahinstitute.com.

            Gallup poll finding half speak of faith at work from "Spirituality, God and Business," *Fortune,* June 26, 2001.

            High Tor Alliance findings from "Spirit Matters: Using Contemplative Disciplines in Work and Organizational Life" by Christopher Schaefer and Jeri Darling, High Tor Alliance, November 1996.

            Times (of London) quote from "The Workplace Gets Spiritual," *Times* (online), July 24, 2003.

            Terry Mollner story from author interview and correspondence.

            Wong quoted on website of International Network on Personal Meaning, "President's Letter," September 2003, www.meaning.ca.

            Miller's count of spiritual nonprofits from author interview and website www.yale.edu/faith.

68–69   Gonzalez quote from "In Focus: Center for Faith and Culture," *Yale Bulletin & Calendar,* December 5, 2003.

69   Sounds True, Saint Francis Health Center and SREI International Financial Limited descriptions from Spirit at Work Awards materials including press release and program guide, Awards, June 9, 2003. See Association of Spirit at Work website, www.spiritatwork.org. Click "2006 International Spirit at Work Awards."

            Ford, American Airlines and Intel examples from "A New Approach to Faith at Work," *Workforce Management,* October 2004.

            Billy Graham training, Coca-Cola Bottling Co. and HomeBanc Mortgage examples from "Visibility of Religious Beliefs Grows in the Workplace," *Charlotte Observer,* January 9, 2005.

            Gregory Pierce on piety from "Spiritual Beliefs Blend into Work," *Chicago Tribune,* January 3, 2005.

            Pierce quote "not going to pray" from "Visibility of Religious Beliefs Grows in Workplace," *Charlotte Observer,* January 9, 2005.

70   Pierce quote from "Spirituality, God and Business," *Fortune,* June 26, 2001.

            Harvard Business School example from "Leadership, Values and Spirituality Forum," April 4, 2003, www.lvconference.org/mobius_vision.htm.

71   Spiritual MBA courses at Columbia, Stanford and Notre Dame from "MBAs Get Lessons in Spirituality, Too," *The Wall Street Journal,* January 11, 2005, as is Pauchant quote.

            Mitroff study cited in "God and Business," *Fortune,* June 26, 2001, and elsewhere. Interviewed in brief by researcher Jill Reurs.

71   Tom Sullivan quoted in "A New Approach to Faith at Work," *Workforce Management*, October 2004.

72   Ford Interfaith Network, plus American Airlines and Intel Christian groups, from "A New Approach to Faith at Work," *Workforce Management*, October 2004, as are comments from Intel's Dunnigan and American's Holley.

            Marketplace Chaplains USA description and quotes from interviews and from "Dallas-based International Organization Offers Spiritual Aid in Workplace," *Fort Worth Star Telegram*, December 28, 2004.

73   Workplace violence figures from Bureau of Labor and Statistics and from "How to Prevent Violence at Work," *Fortune*, February 21, 2005.

73–74   David Miller quote from "Spirituality," *Newsweek Japan*, September 9, 2001 (translated into English), and reprinted on www.avodahinstitute.com.

74–76   All TELUS Mobility information from "Nomination for the 2002 International Spirit at Work Award," January 31, 2002, generously shared by TELUS Mobility's Linda Lewis, National Wellness Manager, and Karen Goodfellow, Regional Wellness Coordinator and former corporate change consultant.

76–77   Judi Neal and ASAW from author interview and ASAW website www.spirit atwork.org.

77   2005 ISAW winners from "Spirituality in Organizations: International Spirit at Work Awards Honors Ten Companies Leading Emerging Trend," press release issued by Cindy Wigglesworth, Chair, ISAW Selection Committee, August 5, 2004. A complete list of ISAW Award winners and a description of their programs, websites and contact people appears on ASAW website, www.spiritatwork.org under Awards heading.

            ISAW award nomination information at website cited above. See Item 3: How to apply for the Award and download Word application, and Item 4: Criteria for Selection.

77–79   Sections entitled "Explicitly Spiritual" and "Sound Familiar" and other Wigglesworth quotes from author interview and correspondence.

79–80   Richard Whiteley's website is www.corpshaman.com.

80–81   For more information on Center for Visionary Leadership, John Renesch and Heartland Circle, see this book's appendix, Spirituality in Business, Centers/Groups.

81–82   Joyce Orecchia story from author interview and correspondence.

82   Mitroff quote from "Post-Enron Spirituality Gains," *The Christian Science Monitor*, April 29, 2002.

82–84   "Dangers of Spirit in Business or Human Resources to the Rescue" from author interview with Wigglesworth.

83   2004 complaints from "Religious Discrimination," EEOC website, www.eeoc.gov/types/religion.html.

83–84   Discrimination cases cited in "A New Approach to Faith at Work," *Workforce Management*, October 2004.

84–87   Table 1. All descriptions from ASAW website (www.spiritatwork.org) under ISAW Award Winners except Medtronic ceremony from author interview, Memorial Hermann ritual and leadership training from 2003 Willis Harman Spirit at Work Award Nomination.

87–89   San Francisco brown bag information from author interviews.

89   Pierce quote from "Spiritual Beliefs Blend into Work," *Chicago Tribune*, January 3, 2005.

Chapter 5: The Values-Driven Consumer

90–91   Christiane Perrin interviewed by author.

91   One million hybrids estimate from "Hybrids Headed for Boom or Bust?" MSNBC.com, January 17, 2005.

         Bill Evans quote, Schmidt & King story and hybrid headquarters data from "Seattle's Hot Affair with Hybrid Cars," *Seattle-Post Intelligencer*, June 2, 2004.

92   Cliff Feigenbaum from author interview.

93   Numbers of Conscious Consumers, percentage of population and size of values-driven commerce market, as well as natural products figure, from "They Care about the World (and They Shop, Too)," *The New York Times*, July 2, 2003. Updated from 2006 LOHAS customer trends study.

         LOHAS market sectors from *LOHAS Journal* online, "About LOHAS," www.lohasjournal.com.

         Ninety percent of LOHAS customers cited in "They Care about the World (and They Shop, Too)," *The New York Times*, July 2, 2003.

         Ray on values predict consumer behavior from "Discovering the Cultural Creatives," *LOHAS Journal*, March/April 2000.

94–95   Sheri Shapiro and Roper ASW from *New York Times* story cited above.

         LOHAS 2004 from LOHAS website cited above.

         Three types of consumers. See endnotes for page 32.

95–96   *National Green Pages*, Co-Op America's 2004 Edition, www.coopamerica.org, (800) 58-GREEN.

97   Judy Cunningham quoted from "Straw House Defies Winter," *Associated Press*, March 6, 2003.

         David and Jean Wallace home described in "More Power to Them: House Produces Energy," *Billingsgazette.com*, May 9, 2004.

         Northeast Iowa home information from "Northeast Iowa Residents Blend Old and New into Energy Efficient House," *The Waukon Standard*, February 13, 2003.

         Mark Wilhelm quoted from "Green Building Is Taking Root in America," *The Arizona Republic*, February 7, 2005.

97   "Most talked about topic" quote from "Greener and Higher," *Wall Street Journal*, January 31, 2005.

Green Building headlines from: *The Arizona Republic*, February 7, 2005, *The Daily Texan*, July 21, 2003, *Chicago Tribune*, July 21, 2003.

98   USGBC membership growth figures from USGBC website, www.usgbc.org.

USGBC's LEED certification program described in "Environmentally Conscious Development," *New York Times*, August 25, 2004, which is also the source for Krasa & Watson quotes.

Department of Energy building energy use figure from "Greener and Higher," *Wall Street Journal*, January 31, 2005. Other energy bullets from USGBC, www.usgbc.com.

99   Numbers of LEED-certified buildings from researcher interview with USGBC representatives.

LEED levels (standard, silver, gold, platinum) and "Chinese menu" from "Environmentally Conscious Development," *New York Times*, August 25, 2004.

Giant Eagle food market building information from *Green Building News* (a service of Oikos Green Building Source), http://oikos.com/news/ "Ohio Store Becomes First LEED Supermarket," January 12, 2005.

Reed Park Zoo story from "Green Building Is Taking Root in America," *The Arizona Republic*, February 7, 2005.

One Bryant Park skyscraper construction design from "Environmentally Conscious Development," *New York Times*, August 25, 2004.

100   Godrej Green Building Center from "Environmentally Conscious Development," *New York Times*, August 25, 2004, and "President of India Inaugurates LEED Building," USGBC press release, July 13, 2004.

Fedrizzi on cost savings from "Environmentally Conscious Development," *New York Times*, August 25, 2004, and researcher interview with USGBC.

Mark Wilhelm on green construction savings cited in "Green Building Is Taking Root in America," *The Arizona Republic*, February 7, 2005.

Standard LEED buildings "cost about the same" from "Environmentally Conscious Development," *New York Times*, August 25, 2004.

2004 California State LEED building study, as well as Gregory Kats comment from "Environmentally Conscious Development," *New York Times*, August 25, 2004.

100–101   NAHB Research Center study from "Survey Shows Buyers Want Green Materials," *Green Building News*, November 2004. (See Oikos above.)

101   Department of Energy's "Zero Energy Home" designation and 2004 Home Builders Show from "Zero Energy Home Produces Electricity," U.S. Department of Energy press release, undated, www.usgovinfo.com/cs/consumer/a/zeroenergy.htm.

Vista Montana "built green" community described in "Green Homes Grow:

Solar Powered Complex Shines in Watsonville," *Santa Cruz Sentinel*, August 29, 2003, and "Clarum Opens California's Largest Zero Energy Home Community" press release from Clarum Homes, Palo Alto, California, August 28, 2003.

Build Green program in Washington state from "Building Green Market Is Ripe for Green homes," *Seattle Daily Journal of Commerce* (online), March 11, 2004.

Fort Collins, Colorado, Zero energy workshops from Colorado Energy Science Center "CESC" workshop announcement, March 18, 2005.

102   Mary McLeod quote from "Green Building Will Save Homeowners, Businesses Money," *The Daily Texan*, July 21, 2003.

Green Communities $550 million pledge and Dr. Sandel quote from "Groups Join Forces to Build 8,500 Affordable Homes," *Green Building News*, January 12, 2005. See Oikos in endnote p. 99.

Wall Street Journal quote from "Greener and Higher," *Wall Street Journal*, January 31, 2005.

103   Whole Foods financial data from "The Anarchist's Cookbook," *Fast Company*, July 2004, and Whole Foods website, www.wholefoodsmarket.com.

Grocery profit margins and 2010 projections from "Whole Foods: No Preservatives, No Union, Lots of Dough," *Fortune*, September 3, 2003.

103–104   Data on OCA and OTA from their websites, (respectively) www.organicconsumers.org and www.ota.com.

104   Size and growth rate of organic food market from many sources including "Organic Farming Interest Grows," *Journal Star* (Peoria, Illinois) via *Knight Ridder/Tribune Business News*, February 1, 2005.

Whole Foods survey from "Organic Foods Continue to Grow in Popularity," press release from Whole Foods Market, October 21, 2004.

Earth Day survey and 17-member coalition from "Nearly Six in Ten Americans Concerned about Pesticides," press release from Go Organic for Earth Day Campaign, April 2005, www.organicearthday.org.

104–105   GE soybeans and corn, how GE weakens natural pesticides, and most Americans want GE food labeled from "Food Fight: Genetic Engineering vs. Organics," *E: The Environmental Magazine*, July/August 2003.

105   Lauren Ornelas and Mackey exchange from "The Anarchist's Cookbook," *Fast Company*, July 2004.

Leadership and economic democracy bullets from "The Anarchist's Cookbook," *Fast Company*, July 2004.

Detroit Auto Show from "Hybrids Headed for Boom or Bust?" MSNBC.com, January 17, 2005.

2003 hybrid registration figure from "U.S. Sales of Hybrid Cars Rise," *Associated Press*, May 9, 2004.

Percentage increase since 2002 from "Study: Hybrids to Peak at 3% of Market," *Associated Press*, February 4, 2005.

106   100,000 figure calculated from 2003 hybrid registrations (43,435) plus
          hybrids sold in 2000 (9,350), 2001 (20,287), 2002 (35,000), cited on
          www.hybridcars.com.

107   2004 hybrid sales and 2005 projections from "Hybrids Headed for Boom
          or Bust?" MSNBC.com, January 17, 2005.

          2005 Toyota shipments to United States from various sources including
          "New Hybrid Cars Driving U.S. Wild," *Miami Herald*, November 4, 2004.

          Mercury Mariner hybrid SUV debut from "Ford Unveils Its Second Hybrid
          SUV," MSNBC.com, February 9, 2005.

          Ford Escape data from "U.S. Sales of Hybrid Cars Rise," *Associated Press*, May
          9, 2004.

          "Mild" hybrids from "Hybrids Headed for Boom or Bust?" MSNBC.com,
          January 17, 2005.

          Wired comment from "Rise of the Green Machine," *Wired*, April 2005.

          Advance interest/orders for Lexus Hybrid SUV and Toyota Highlander
          from "Hybrids Headed for Boom or Bust?" MSNBC.com, January 17,
          2005.

108   Toyota research: half of consumers think hybrids need plug from "A
          Hybrid in Every Garage," *BusinessWeek*, October 11, 2004.

          Signs about the plug from "Hybrids Headed for Boom or Bust?"
          MSNBC.com, January 17, 2005.

          130 mph Prius from "Hybrids Headed for Boom or Bust?" MSNBC.com,
          January 17, 2005.

          Perrin quote from author interview.

          Minnesota state tax breaks for hybrids, "U.S. Sales of Hybrid Cars Rise,"
          Associated Press, May 9, 2004.

          Virginia tax breaks from "Seattle's Hot Affair with Hybrid Cars," *Seattle
          Post-Intelligencer*, June 2, 2004.

          Florida solo driver hybrid HOV article from "New Hybrid Cars Driving
          U.S. Wild," *Miami Herald*, November 4, 2004.

          A complete list of state incentives can be found at Hybridcenter.org, a
          project of the Union of Concerned Scientists, at www.ucsusa.org/hybrid
          center/incentives.cfm.

          Bill Ford assertion from "U.S. Sales of Hybrid Cars Rise," *Associated Press*,
          May 9, 2004.

          US bill for hybrid tax credit from "Bill Would Expand Hybrid Tax Credits,"
          MSNBC.com, February 10, 2000.

          Thad Malesh 2010 projection from "Hybrids Headed for Boom or Bust?"
          MSNBC.com, January 17, 2005.

          J. D. Powers estimate and Pratt comments from "Study: Hybrids to Peak at
          3% of Market," *Associated Press*, February 4, 2005.

109	Reinert figure from "Hybrids Headed for Boom or Bust?" MSNBC.com, January 17, 2005.

109   Reinert figure from "Hybrids Headed for Boom or Bust?" MSNBC.com, January 17, 2005.

GM-DaimlerChrysler partnership widely cited, including, "Hybrids Headed for Boom or Bust," MSNBC.com January 17, 2005.

Carlos Ghosn of Nissan quoted from "Study: Hybrids to Peak at 3% of Market," *Associated Press*, February 4, 2005.

Fuel cell vehicles and Takeo Fukui quote from "Hybrids Headed for Boom or Bust?" MSNBC.com, January 17, 2005.

Hydrogen car in a decade or two from numerous sources including "Study: Hybrids to Peak at 3% of Market," *Associated Press*, February 4, 2005.

110   Data on yoga, meditation and book sales cited in endnotes for pages 5–6 of chapter one.

Billboard figure from "CNBC on Assignment, God & Money," March 14, 2005.

110–113   Elsie Maio and SoulBranding from author interviews and correspondence.

110–111   Financial brand data from "The 100 Top Brands," *BusinessWeek*, August 2, 2004.

113   "Detroit snickered . . ." from "Toyota Full Speed Ahead," *Fortune*, January 24, 2005.

GM earnings shortfall from "GM Hits the Skids," *Fortune*, May 30, 2005.

114   River Rouge car plant described in "Mr. Natural," *Fortune*, October 28, 2002, and in "Beyond the Triple Bottom Line: A New Standard for 21st Century Commerce," *Green Money Journal*, Winter 2004.

McDonough and Ford quotes from "Mr. Natural," *Fortune*, October 28, 2002.

Bill Ford meditates from "Just Say Om," *Time* ("Meditation" cover story), August 14, 2003.

Chapter 6: The Wave of Conscious Solutions

115–116   Joel Smernoff interviewed by author.

116   Yoga at your chair article at www.yogajournal.com/practice/949_1.cfm.

117   Sources for bullet points cited in full in pertinent sections ahead.

118–121   Michael Rennie story told in "Lunch with Maxine McKew: Michael Rennie, McKinsey Partner," *The Bulletin* (Australia), March 7, 2001.

120–121   ANZ Bank initiative, results and Stojanovic quote from "Will Big Business Save the World?" *What Is Enlightenment?*, March–May 2005.

121   Meditation experiment from "Meditation Changes Temperatures: Mind Controls Body in Extreme Experiments," *Harvard University Gazette*, April 18, 2002.

122   Cost of stress plus examples of AOL, Apple, Google, Yahoo!, McKinsey, Hughes Aircraft, AstraZeneca all cited in "Zen and the Art of Corporate Productivity," *BusinessWeek,* July 28, 2003.

           Clarity data and clients from Clarity Seminars website, "Breaking the Cycle of Stress," www.clarityseminars.com.

           Biskamp info from "Zen and the Art of Corporate Productivity," *BusinessWeek,* July 28, 2003, and from author interview.

           BusinessWeek quote from "Zen and the Art of Corporate Productivity," *BusinessWeek,* July 28, 2003.

123   500 studies, journals and an H. A. Montgomery story from "Meditating on the Bottom Line," *The Washington Post,* October 1, 1996.

           Results from *Fortune* 100 company cited in Roth's *TM: Transcendental Meditation* (Plume, 1994), chapter five.

124–125   American Express Forgiveness Project described in "The Effect of Training Emotional Competence in Financial Service Advisors," November 2002, www.learningtoforgive.com and update about subsequent cohorts from memo provided by Fred Luskin, Ph.D., to author.

125–126   HeartMath clients and results from "Stress—It's Just Not What It Used to Be," and "HeartMath Decodes Stress," HeartMath press releases, both undated and from "Business Solutions," Case Studies, from HeartMath website.

126   Fire walking described in "Firms Spend Millions to Fire Up Employees," *USA Today,* May 10, 2001; "Bosses Will Do Almost Anything to Light Fires under Salespeople," *The Wall Street Journal,* April 27, 1993; and in an untitled story from *Mass High Tech,* May 3–9, 1999, on Insight Development website, www.insightdevelopment.com.

           "New way to challenge them" from *Mass High Tech* story cited above.

           "Go over the head of" quote from *USA Today* story cited above.

127–129   The Methodist Hospital story from presentation by Cindy Wigglesworth at the Spirit in Business Conference in San Francisco, June 10, 2003, "Corporate Transformation Tools" brochure and from "True Believers at Methodist Hospital," *Workforce Management,* February 2005.

127   Daugherty quote and turnover/vacancy bullets from *Workforce Management* cited above.

128   Wigglesworth quotes and "33 of 35 values," from Wigglesworth presentation cited above.

129   Nurse vacancy rates and patient satisfaction from Wigglesworth presentation cited above.

           Values match "90% of the time" from *Workforce Management* article cited above.

129–130   Vision Quest described in "Religion in the Workplace," *BusinessWeek,* November 1, 1999, and in "Reports from the U.S. on how to make office life good for the soul," *The Evening Standard,* February 28, 2001.

129   Elter quote plus Ford, Nike, Harley-Davidson from *BusinessWeek* cited above.

           DeJong and Berretta quotes from *The Evening Standard* cited above.

130   Xerox comeback stats from "The Un-Carley," *Red Herring*, May 9, 2005.
           Mulcahy named a "Best Manager of the Year," *BusinessWeek*, January 10, 2005.

130–133   Tevis Trower information from author interview.

134   All Therapeutic Touch info from *Therapeutic Touch: A Practical Guide*
           (Knopf, 1996) by Janet Macrae. Specifically: laying on of hands, p. 3; his-
           tory of experiment and milestone, p. 6; healings, p. 11.

134–135   Percentages who pray, believe prayer heals and and sites of prayer research
           from "Why Prayer Could Be Good Medicine," *Parade*, March 23, 2003.

135   Dartmouth study, Dr. Matthews and Annals of Internal Medicine study as
           well as illnesses prayer has helped heal from *Parade* cited above.

           "We cannot explain" quote from *Parade* cited above.

135–136   Krucoff's pre-op prayer, description of MANTRA pilot results and of those
           who pray from "Can Prayer Heal?" *Hippocrates*, August 2000, Volume 14,
           No. 8.

136   Sister Patricia quote from "Geisinger Profiled on TV Special," The Daily
           Item, www.dailyitem.com, October 30, 2003.

137   Dr. Targ's AIDS study and her quote from "Can Prayer Heal?" *Hippocrates*,
           August 2000, Volume 14, No. 8.

           Bill George quote from author interview.

138   Medtronic grant reported in "Health. Faith. Mind-Body-Spirit Research
           Grant," *Inside DUMC* (Duke University Medical Center), August 28, 2000.

139   Rennie quotes: "huge issue" and "strategy is not that hard" from "Bal-
           anced Corporate Culture Will Give Firms the Edge," *Newsline: Biweekly Up-
           date from GSB*, a publication of The University of Capetown (South Africa)
           Graduate School of Business, October 15, 2003.

           Michael Rennie quotes about "performance ethic first" and "create bad
           names" from the edited version of his speech at the Macquarie Graduate
           School of Management posted on Manzine (Australia): a collection of
           online articles on the website Manhood Online, under the title, "Getting
           Economics to Save the Spirit," undated. [Note from the author: the web-
           site, www.talk.gelworks.com/manhood, is problematic, however. To find
           this excellent reference I suggest you "Google" Michael Rennie McKinsey
           Australia and select the speech title.]

Chapter 7: The Socially Responsible Investment Boom

140   Figure on socially responsible investing from *2003 Report on Socially
           Responsible Investing Trends in the United States*, Social Investment Forum,
           2003 (the next report will be in 2005).

           Increase since 1984 from "Working Capital," *E: The Environmental
           Magazine*, March/April 2004.

141   Two hundred socially responsible mutual funds from "Working Capitol,"
       E: The Environmental Magazine, March/April 2004.

141–142 The values of funds like Ariel or Domini change with the market but are
         available on many financial websites.

142   Domini screens data from website Domini Social Investments, "Social and
       Environmental Screening," www.domini.com.

       Lipper figure and Feigenbaum quote from "Good Vibes: Socially Respon-
       sible Investing Is Gaining Fans and Clout," *Barron's*, July 17, 2003.

142–143 SRI funds and fund growth data from *2003 Report on Socially Responsible
         Investing Trends in the United States*, Social Investment Forum, 2003 (the
         next report will be in 2005).

143   Traditional firms and new indexes as well as Kinder information from
       "Good Vibes: Socially Responsible Investing Is Gaining Fans and Clout,"
       Barron's, July 17, 2003.

       Krumsiek quote from "Good Vibes: Socially Responsible Investing Is
       Gaining Fans and Clout," *Barron's*, July 17, 2003.

143–144 Barbara Krumsiek investment predictions for 2012 from "The Difference a
         Decade Can Make," *Green Money Journal*, Winter 2004 (reprint of a 2002 article).

144   Calvert's Boone selling Tyco from "Good Vibes: Socially Responsible
       Investing Is Gaining Fans and Clout," *Barron's*, July 17, 2003.

       Enron information and Sandra Waddock, Boston College Carroll School of
       Management cited in "Working Capital," *E: The Environmental Magazine*,
       March/April 2004.

       Joan Bavaria and Tyco from "Good Vibes: Socially Responsible Investing Is
       Gaining Fans and Clout," *Barron's*, July 17, 2003.

145   SRI history including shunned industries from various sources including
       "Working Capital," *E: The Environmental Magazine*, March/April 2004, and
       "Good Vibes: Socially Responsible Investing Is Gaining Fans and Clout,"
       Barron's, July 17, 2003.

       Calvert Social Investment Equity Fund figures and background from
       "Ethical Stance Pays Off for Calvert," *Financial Times*, March 12, 2003.

147   Amy Domini as young stockbroker from *Investing with Your Values*, by Hal
       Brill, Jack Brill, Cliff Feigenbaum (Bloomberg, 1999), p. xvi–xvii. This
       source is cited in brief below as Brill et al.

       Ethical Investing (now out of print) cited in Brill et al., pp. 52–54.

148   Birth of Domini 400 Social Index from Brill et al., p. 54.

       Domini slogan from Brill et al., p. 54.

       Description of Domini Social Index Fund from "Portfolio Overview,"
       www.domini.com.

       Calvert history, philosophy, numbers of funds and customers as well as
       Fund descriptions from Calvert website, www.calvertgroup.com.

149   Calvert sidebar data from Calvert online, "Socially Responsible Funds," www.calvertgroup.com.

Dan Boone stock criteria from "Ethical Stance Pays Off for Calvert," *Financial Times*, March 12, 2003.

Screening process for fund managers described in "Social Investing for the Long Haul," *Observer: Global Investor*, September 2004.

Excellence in Fund Management Award information "CSIF Equity Portfolio's High Quality Strategy," from Calvert *InVision* newsletter, Summer 2004.

150   Winslow performance from Winslow Green Growth Fund, "Fund Facts," December 31, 2004, www.winslowgreen.com.

2003 Winslow Green Growth performance cited in various sources including "Working Capital," *E: The Environmental Magazine*, March/April 2004, and TheStreet.com cited below.

Winslow Green Growth vs. the Vice Fund from "Profiting from Morality Plays," TheStreet.com online article, August 9, 2004.

Fuel Tech N.V. holding from "Portfolio Update," *Winslow Environmental News*, October 2004, and from website www.fuel-tech.com.

SurModics technology from *Green Growth Fund Facts*, December 31, 2004, and "Clean Green Machines," *CBS Marketwatch*, January 7, 2005, which is also the source for Lipper growth figure.

Jack Robinson quote on the fund's success factors "Latest Winslow Management Study Shows Enviromental Responsibility Can Be Profitable," from *Winslow Environmental News*, April 2004.

151   Bridgeway data from: various sources, specifically:

Low fees from "6 Funds You Can Trust," *Fortune*, December 22, 2003.

Charity contributions and lists worst stocks from "Greening the Money Machines: Socially Responsible Investing Is a Growth Industry,"*Barron's*, July 26, 2004.

Bridgeway closes funds from "Funds You Can Trust," *Wall Street Journal*, November 19, 2003.

Salary cap from "Runners Up for Managers of the Year 2003," *Morningstar*, January 6, 2004.

Bridgeway "performance-based" fees and John Montgomery quote from "Bridgeway Bases Fees on Performance," *Investors Business Daily*, October 21, 2003.

Bridgeway 2003 performance from "Greening the Money Machines: Socially Responsible Investing Is a Growth Industry," *Barron's*, July 26, 2004.

Calvert Bond Portfolio Lipper Award from *Calvert Invision* newsletter, Summer 2004.

151–152   Calvert and Domini Bond and Money Market Fund options from their websites, www.domini.com and www.calvertgroup.com.

152–153   EOG Resources Inc., from "CSIF Top Equity Holding," *Calvert InVision* newsletter, Winter 2004, and from Calvert Social Investment Equity Fund: First Quarter 2005 Performance Update.

153–154   "Hit the Sustainable Business 20'" section based on "Sustainable Investing: Introducing the 2003 SB 20," *Green Money Journal*, Summer 2004. Information on "The Progressive Investor" and the 2004 SB20 from the Sustainable Business website, www.sustainablebusiness.com.

153   "Not a diversified portfolio" comment from *Green Money Journal* cited above.

154   Alisa Gravitz quote from author interview.

155   Calvert/Dell information from "Social Investing for the Long Term," *Observer Global Investor*, September 4, 2004.

Domini/Avon information "2003 Highlights: Shareholder Advocacy," Domini Social Investments website, www.domini.com.

$150 billion figure from "Working Capital," *E: The Environmental Magazine*, March/April 2004.

156   Community investing quote from Brill et al., p. 120.

Royster story and Self Help Credit Union from "Working Capital," *E: The Environmental Magazine*, March/April 2004.

Northeast Organic Farming Association from Brill et al., p. 125.

Pogge quote from "Community Investing Moves to the Next Level," *Green Money Journal*, Winter 2004.

Numbers of community development banks and credit unions from National Community Capital Association (NCCA) website, "Industry Statistics," www.communitycapital.org.

All CDFI numbers from NCCA website cited above.

157   Repayment rate and success factors from Brill et al., p. 122.

Marjorie Kelly and Marshall Glickman quote on community investing from "Working Capital," *E: The Environmental Magazine*, March/April 2004.

Surge in community investment from *2003 Report on Socially Responsible Investing Trends in the United States*, Social Investment Forum, updated December 2003 (next report out in 2005), p. ii.

Ten percent to community investing and FDIC-insured from Brill et al., p. 123.

Wainwright 50-percent figure and Wainwright awards from Wainwright Bank's "CreativeEconomy," Edition 9, undated and from Wainwright 2005 Annual Report. Total loan figure updated by Wainwright.

157–158   Wainwright clients and projects from website, www.wainwrightbank.com.

158   Wainwright financial data from 2005 Annual Report.

Wainwright default rate on community investing from Brill et al., p. 126.

159   Marjorie Kelly on proof SRI pays from "Holy Grail Found," *Business Ethics*, Winter 2004.

159–160   Hal Brill quotes and three part strategy from "SRI: Where Do We Go from Here?" *Green Money Journal*, Spring 2004.

Conclusion: The Spiritual Transformation of Capitalism

161   Capitalism quote from "Market Crash Born of Greed," *Boston Globe*, April 17, 2001.

162   Thurow quote on "genetic characteristics" and "bad genes" from "Market Crash Born of Greed," *Boston Globe*, April 17, 2001.

           Thurow on greed, from *Boston Globe* story cited above.

163   Definition of capitalism from "Capitalism," *World Book Multimedia Encyclopedia* (online), 2001.

164   Thurow on altruism from "Market Crash Born of Greed," *Boston Globe*, April 17, 2001.

165   Marshall Plan info from "Marshall Plan," *World Book Multimedia Encyclopedia* (online), 2001.

           New Deal data from "Great Depression," *World Book Multimedia Encyclopedia* (online), 2001.

           John Byrne from "Profit and Meaning: A New Competitive Imperative," his presentation to IONS Wisdom Business Network's "Profit with Meaning" online conference, February 23–24, 2004.

168–169   John Bogle quote and his analysis of the corporate path to self-destruction from his speech "After the Fall: What Lies Ahead for Capitalism and the Financial Markets," University of Missouri, October 22, 2002. See also "Rebuilding Faith," Bogle's speech to the Changing of the Game Thought Leadership Forum, New York, New York, June 12, 2002.

169–172   "Clear Advantage: Building Shareholder Value," *Global Environmental Management Initiative* (GEMI), February 2004.

           Specifically:

169   "Compelling evidence" and "intangibles into tangibles," Section 1, p. I.

           List of corporate members, Section 1, p. II.

170   Lifestyle review example, Section 2, p. 4.

           Intangibles, definition, Section 2, p. 2.

           Intangibles list, Section 2, p. 9.

           Intangibles, investment in, Section 2, pp. 2–3.

           50–90 percent of value from intangibles, Section 1, p. 1.

           "A majority of executives," Section 2, p. 3.

171   35 percent base allocation decisions, Section 2, p. 7.

           86 percent of oil and gas analysts, Section 2, p. 7.

           "Measure, manage and disclose" Section 1, p.1.

172   Intangibles quote, Section 2, p. 2.

172–173   Carly Fiorina quote and descriptions of HP global footprint and supplier code from her speech at Business for Social Responsibility Annual Conference, November 12, 2003, Los Angeles, California.

173–175   Michael Sauvante from "Creating a Triple Bottom Line," his presentation to IONS Wisdom Business Network's "Profit with Meaning" online conference, February 23–24, 2004.

175   Robert Hinkley and the Code for Corporate Citizenship from "Robert Hinkley's Plan to Tame Corporate Leadership," *The Sun*, September 2004, and "People v. Profits: A False Dicotomy," *Business Law Journal*, University of California, Davis, School of Law (online), January 10, 2005.

176–177   John Byrne from "Profit and Meaning: A New Competitive Imperative," his presentation to IONS Wisdom Business Network's "Profit with Meaning" online conference, February 23–24, 2004.

Index

Hampton Roads Publishing Company

. . . for the evolving human spirit

HAMPTON ROADS PUBLISHING COMPANY publishes books on a variety of subjects, including metaphysics, spirituality, health, visionary fiction, and other related topics.

For a copy of our latest trade catalog, call toll-free, 800-766-8009, or send your name and address to:

HAMPTON ROADS PUBLISHING COMPANY, INC.
1125 STONEY RIDGE ROAD • CHARLOTTESVILLE, VA 22902
e-mail: hrpc@hrpub.com • www.hrpub.com